Keep Dec 2017 (1)
Keep March

C2081198

KT-554-659

Grief and Loss

Understanding the Journey

THE LIBRARY

ALEXANDRA HOUSE,
CHELTENHAM GENERAL HOSPITAL
SANDFORD ROAD
CHELTENHAM
GL53 7AN

Grief and Loss

Understanding the Journey

STEPHEN J. FREEMAN
California State University
Sacramento, California

THOMSON

BROOKS/COLE

Australia • Canada • Mexico • Singapore • Spain
United Kingdom • United States

THOMSON

BROOKS/COLE

Executive Editor: *Lisa Gebo*
Editor: *Marquita Flemming*
Assistant Editor: *Shelley Gesicki*
Editorial Assistant: *Amy Lam*
Technology Project Manager: *Barry Connolly*
Marketing Manager: *Caroline Concilla*
Marketing Assistant: *Mary Ho*
Advertising Project Manager: *Tami Strang*
Art Director: *Vernon Boes*

Print/Media Buyer: *Lisa Claudeanos*
Permissions Editor: *Kiely Sexton*
Production Service: *Judy Ludowitz, Shepherd, Inc.*
Copy Editor: *Cheryl Ferguson*
Cover Designer: *Lisa Henry*
Cover Image: *J. A. Kraulis/Masterfile*
Text/Cover Printer: *Webcom*
Compositor: *Shepherd, Inc.*

COPYRIGHT © 2005 Brooks/Cole, a division of Thomson Learning, Inc. Thomson Learning™ is a trademark used herein under license.

ALL RIGHTS RESERVED. No part of this work covered by the copyright hereon may be reproduced or used in any form or by any means—graphic, electronic, or mechanical, including but not limited to photocopying, recording, taping, Web distribution, information networks, or information storage and retrieval systems—without the written permission of the publisher.

Printed in Canada
1 2 3 4 5 6 7 08 07 06 05 04

For more information
about our products, contact us at:
Thomson Learning Academic Resource Center
1-800-423-0563
For permission to use material from this text or product, submit a request online at
http://www.thomsonrights.com.
Any additional questions about permissions can be submitted by email to
thomsonrights@thomson.com.

Library of Congress Control Number: 2003116788

ISBN 0-534-59391-7

Thomson Brooks/Cole
10 Davis Drive
Belmont, CA 94002
USA

Asia
Thomson Learning
5 Shenton Way #01-01
UIC Building
Singapore 068808

Australia/New Zealand
Thomson Learning
102 Dodds Street
Southbank, Victoria 3006
Australia

Canada
Nelson
1120 Birchmount Road
Toronto, Ontario M1K 5G4
Canada

Europe/Middle East/Africa
Thomson Learning
High Holborn House
50/51 Bedford Row
London WC1R 4LR
United Kingdom

Latin America
Thomson Learning
Seneca, 53
Colonia Polanco
11560 Mexico D.F.
Mexico

Spain/Portugal
Paraninfo
Calle Magallanes, 25
28015 Madrid, Spain

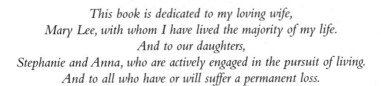

This book is dedicated to my loving wife,
Mary Lee, with whom I have lived the majority of my life.
And to our daughters,
Stephanie and Anna, who are actively engaged in the pursuit of living.
And to all who have or will suffer a permanent loss.

It can be frightening to love what
death can touch. A. J. Porteus

Contents

Preface

dward Rynearson, in his foreword to the June 1990(b) issue of *Psychiatric Annals*, tells of a client any counseling professional might encounter. This client was a woman with small children who was still dealing with the death of her husband a year earlier. She was referred to Rynearson by her physician because of a "pathologic grief reaction." When she came to therapy, she was feeling guilty because she had been told she was not grieving properly. Upon further investigation, he learned that her energies were spent doing everything possible to help the children cope with this tragedy. When Rynearson explained what she might expect in the future and gave her encouragement that she was doing well under difficult circumstances, she began to cry and grieve the death of her husband for herself, not just for her children.

Each day approximately 250,000 to 300,000 people die. Some die by accident; others are murdered; still others commit suicide. Some die by overeating; others by starvation. Some die while still in the womb; others in old age. People die as they must, and they leave behind the task of grief for the survivors (Levine, 1984).

Lewis Thomas (1974) wrote in *The Lives of a Cell: Notes of a Biology Watcher:*

> The obituary pages tell us of the news that we are dying away, while the birth announcements in finer print, off at the side of the page, inform us of our replacements, but we get no grasp from this of the enormity of the scale. There are 3 billion of us on the earth and all 3 billion must be dead,

on a schedule, within this lifetime. The vast majority, involving something over 50 million of us each year, takes place in relative secrecy. (p. 98)

More updated figures would note that there are approximately 6 billion of us, and the annual morality rate is approximately 100 million. Not one of us can escape the certainty that grief will reside within our hearts at some time during our lives.

Students in the counseling professions often have as their guiding light, and rightly so, the idea that counseling and therapy should instill hope. They pronounce that the aim of their work is to help individuals grow and learn to live. In light of these views, they are sometimes hesitant to venture into the perceived hope-defeating realm of death and bereavement. So why study such topics? Because death is a natural part of life, and bereavement is an inescapable concomitant part of that life and of our natural inclination to relate and bond with others.

In the absence of, or in addition to, perceived social support, some bereaved will turn to counseling professionals to guide them through the most painful moments of their lives (Lenhardt, 1997; Ruskay, 1996; Worden, 1991). Training in grief counseling is not typically part of a counseling professional's education, yet the odds of a counselor seeing people in various stages of grief are great. Zisook and Devaul (1985) discovered that 17 percent of patients entering an outpatient psychiatric facility in California had unresolved grief, according to their own reports. John Bowlby (1980) had earlier suggested such a phenomenon:

> Clinical experience and a reading of the evidence leaves little doubt of the truth of the main proposition—that much psychiatric illness is an expression of pathological mourning—or that such illnesses includes many cases of anxiety state, depressive illness, and hysteria, and more than one kind of character disorder. (p. 23)

Bowlby (1980) additionally suggests that clinicians might sometimes have unrealistic expectations about the progress that people should be making during bereavement. In the final analysis, the truth is probably that there are no absolute or universally correct expectations, nor is there one right way to effectively work with the bereaved; however, there are some assertions that are worthy of mention. This book attempts to identify some of these assertions and to provide those who work with the bereaved the basic theories and techniques. Readers are, however, cautioned to critically examine the information presented and its applicability, acknowledging the words of Gordon Allport that each man (or woman) is like all other men, each man is like some other men, and it is also true that each man is like no other man. With this in mind, shall we begin?

1

⁂

Introduction

What is this experience we call death? This question is more complex than it appears. Kastenbaum (2001) exposed this complexity, noting that death can be an event, something that happens at a specific time under specific conditions, or death can be a state that follows the event. Life has ceased, so what happens now? The answer to the latter question is not empirically accessible, so our focus will be on the former. What is this empirical event we call death?

Ideas about what defines death as an event vary from culture to culture and in different epochs. In Western civilization, the soul has historically been viewed as the source of life in all things. Naturally, then, one idea or concept of death has traditionally been the departure of the soul from the body. However, the soul has no corporeal manifestations, and its departure cannot be seen or otherwise determined. Therefore, the cessation of breathing has typically been designated as the sign that death has occurred.

Moving forward in history, contemporary society [medicine] has linked death with the cessation of vital functions, meaning respiration and cardiac function. However, advances in modern medical technology have made it possible to sustain an individual's vital functions almost indefinitely. These advances have required yet another redefining of the concept or event called death. More recently, the concept of death has been associated with the lack of brain function or brain death. Brain death is defined as the irreversible loss of brain function. Even this concept of death has its limitations. Challenges to this concept have arisen, resulting from the fact that an individual can lose all capacity for higher-level brain functioning while centers in the old brain controlling vital functions continue to function. The heart continues to beat, the lungs continue to function, and reflex responses may still be elicited. Despite all this, the essence of the individual person is not there. Under such circumstances, there might be hesitation to declare the individual dead. A committee of Harvard Medical School faculty (Ad Hoc Committee, 1968) seeing a need for criteria for the determination of brain death, offered an opinion that has since become known as the *Harvard criteria*. The five criteria are as follows:

1. *Unreceptive and unresponsive.* No awareness is shown for external stimuli or inner need. The unresponsiveness is complete even when ordinarily painful stimuli are applied.

2. *No movements and no breathing.* There is complete absence of spontaneous respiration and all other spontaneous muscular movements.

3. *No reflexes.* The usual reflexes that can be elicited in a neuropsychological examination are absent (e.g., when a light is shined in the eye, the pupil does not constrict).

4. *A flat EEG.* Electrodes attached to the scalp elicit a printout of electrical activity from the living brain. These are popularly known as brain waves. The respirator brain does not provide the usual patterns of peaks and valleys. Instead, the moving stylus records a flat line. This is taken to demonstrate lack of electrophysiological activity.

5. *No circulation to or within the brain.* Without the oxygen and nutrition provided through blood circulation, brain activity will soon terminate.

Despite the Harvard criteria, controversy continues to exist about what constitutes brain death. The controversy involves concepts such as *whole-brain death,* the irreversible destruction of all neural structures within the intracranial cavity; *cerebral death,* the irreversible destruction of both hemispheres, excluding the lower centers in the cerebellum and brainstem; and *neocortical death,* the irreversible destruction of neural tissue in the cerebral cortex. These controversies have prompted some authorities to argue that the concept of brain death should be defined by the loss of capacity for conscious social interaction or relationships.

The conception of what constitutes death is of more than academic interest. Meteoric advances in medical technology have given rise to serious ethical/legal questions and posed a plethora of new problems, both for those who are dying and for their survivors. A definition of death is necessary and must be as inclusive as possible given our current knowledge base. Therefore, this book will operationally define death as the irreversible cessation of life involving a complete change in the status of a living person—the loss of his or her essential characteristics. It should also be noted that living and dying are two phases of the same human process, one that begins at our birth and ends at our cessation. The question, however, still remains: What human form(s) does death take?

TYPES OF DEATH

Sudnow, in his book *Passing On: The Social Organization of Dying,* posited four types or forms of death: social death, psychological death, biological death, and physiological death. Each type or face of death has implications both for the dying and for those left to grieve the loss.

Social Death

Social death, according to Sudnow, represents the symbolic death of the individual in the world he or she has known. The concept of social death might have implications for the individual dying as well as for the survivors. In either case, socially and interpersonally, the world as it was known begins to shrink. This constriction might be the result of a change of lifestyle (e.g., involuntary retirement, sudden or abrupt relocation from familiar surroundings) and/or brought on by physical or mental illness or degeneration (e.g., cancer, dementia, Alzheimer's, or other cerebral impairment).

No matter what the cause, the result is the removal of the individual from familiar environments (e.g., work, home, friends, or community) and/or lessening the potential for related social contacts. The dying may experience social death as a result of anticipatory grief by friends and/or family. *Anticipatory grief* is a form of normal grief that occurs in anticipation of a future loss and can include premature detachment, possibly not desiring to prolong the inevitable. Calls and visits become less and less frequent until they finally cease. Separation of the dying individual from others might result in magnification and preoccupation with the malady and grieving for the losses to come. Exclusionary practices may also ostracize or alienate individuals with illnesses such as AIDS. The potential devastation of exclusionary practices involving individuals who are still very much alive and capable of meaningful interaction is echoed by William James (1890):

> We are not only gregarious animals liking to be in sight of our fellows but have an innate propensity to get ourselves noticed favorably, by our own kind. No more fiendish punishment could be devised were such a thing physically possible, than that one should be turned loose in society and remain unnoticed by all the members thereof. (p. 293)

In the case of the bereaved survivor, especially a spouse or partner, the losses associated with social death may begin with decreased contact with friends or organizations as they care for the dying person. Following the death, activities that were enjoyed jointly may be shunned for a multitude of reasons. Due to depression, social anxiety, or other reasons, bereaved individuals might no longer feel that they fit in with couples, or they might have lost the mechanism of attachment to groups of friends.

Psychological Death

Psychological death, according to Sudnow, refers to the death of aspects of the dying individual's personality. In debilitating injury or terminal illnesses, this is often part of the dying process. Regression and dependency often occur as the degree of independence and autonomy of the individual diminishes. The dying, as well as the survivors, must deal with these losses, as well as others—control, productivity, security, the sense of self as they were but are not now, and future existence, to mention only a few. How dying individuals move through the grieving process and deal with their losses may bring about changes in the individual's personality. Changes might also occur as a result of the disease process and/or medications. Toward the end of life, dying individuals might withdraw into themselves as if to prepare for the task ahead. These changes may represent to the survivors rejection; or, at best, the loss of those that they knew and loved. The personality that made individuals who they were no longer exists.

Psychological death may also occur in acute situations involving traumatic brain injury or stroke that leave an individual permanently psychologically altered or in a vegetative state. The individual, though alive, is not the person the bereaved has known and loved. Although physically the same, the individual's personality might be altered such that the loved one is now a stranger. Psychological death may precede biological and physiological death and be one of many death losses the bereaved suffers.

Biological Death

Biological death, according to Sudnow, refers to death in which the organism, as a human entity, no longer exists. As an example, biological death may be seen when an individual suffers a heart attack severe enough to damage the heart beyond repair, causing it to cease functioning. Brain death may occur as a result of a head injury sustained in an accident. In both cases, other vital organs might be unharmed. Although the person is biologically dead, advances in medical science allow organs to be kept alive and functioning by means of artificial life support even though the human traits of conscious awareness and capacity for relationships are forever gone. This may have significant implications for the bereaved and others.

Biological death, though a true death event, might not represent the final stage of death. Organ donation can be a gift of incalculable value to both the recipient and the donor's bereaved family, epitomizing the interdependency of well being that each of us has on the other. To the recipient it might bring a reprieve from death, and to the bereaved family it extends the life for the deceased through others.

Physiological Death

Physiological death, according to Sudnow, occurs when there is a cessation of the operation or function of all the vital organs. Physiological death (organ failure) might occur even when artificial life support has been implemented. In such cases when biological death precedes physiological death, especially when the interval is significant, critical questions (both legal and moral/ethical) arise, such as organ donation and/or cessation of life support or pulling the plug.

Types of Death: An Example

For the survivors of the death event, answers to the question, "What happens now?" are accessible. The following case provides an example of all four types of death and what happened to one bereaved survivor.

Mr. X was 70 and Mrs. X 67 years old. They had been married for 48 years and their relationship had been good, though Mrs. X was highly dependent on Mr. X, both financially and socially. She had been a traditional homemaker and mother and had never worked outside the home since their marriage. Mr. X was a large, physically robust man who had recently retired after working 40+ years with his company and was now working part-time at the local golf course. This was more an avocation that allowed Mr. X to pursue his passion for golf for free. Mr. X was returning home after working at the golf course when his car was struck head on by another vehicle traveling in the wrong lane. Paramedics attended to him at the scene, and he was taken by ambulance to a local hospital with serious injuries, which included massive head injuries. At the hospital, he was taken to surgery and an emergency craniotomy was performed. After the operation, he was taken in coma to the surgical intensive care unit (SICU), where he was on artificial life support. Following the accident, Mrs. X's first encounter with her husband was in the SICU. Trauma from the accident and swelling following the surgery had disfigured Mr. X's head and body to the point that she was not able to recognize him. He was comatose and unable to respond to stimuli. The following day, doctors informed Mrs. X that her husband was brain dead. After deliberation, Mrs. X made the decision to donate his organs. However, while on life support, but before Mr. X's organs could be harvested, his organs began to fail, making donation impossible. Following this encounter, Mr. X, with his wife's consent, was removed from life support and died. A total of three days had elapsed since Mr. X had been brought to the hospital following the accident.

This case demonstrates the four faces of death as experienced by the bereaved. The first is psychological death. To Mrs. X, her husband was a large, robust man whom she perceived as bigger than life and physically impenetrable. The broken, disfigured person Mrs. X encountered in the SICU could not respond and bore no resemblance to the robust, indestructible husband with whom she had lived for 48 years. Psychologically, to Mrs. X, this person was not her husband. Even if he had survived, given the nature and severity of his head injuries, his personality would not have been the same as the individual she had known. Mrs. X had now, regardless of further outcome, psychologically lost her husband.

Biological death was the next face of death that Mrs. X encountered. This occurred when Mr. X was pronounced brain dead. This was an acknowledgment that her husband, as a human entity, was gone. Though his vital functions could be maintained, the capacities for conscious awareness and relationship were now gone. There now existed a state of limbo, a paradox, where death was acknowledged but life remained.

Following the acknowledgment of her husband's death, Mrs. X decided to perform a final act of charity and donate her husband's organs. This benevolent act would allow for some form of continuation of the life of her husband. This, however, was not to be, as the third face of death, physiological death, was to appear next. Before a surgical team could be assembled, Mr. X's organs began to fail and he experienced physiological death. Mrs. X, in an attempt to rescue some aspect of her husband's life, was to again experience another face of death.

Following her husband's death, Mrs. X was confronted by the fourth face of death. The causes may be seen premorbidly. Mrs. X had always been a shy, introverted person and had been highly dependent on her husband. He had been the primary mechanism through which she interacted with the outside world. This social symbiosis had worked very well for 48 years. However, Mr. X's death left her without a means and with a decreased will to remain socially connected. Without her husband, her social world began to shrink, and she experienced the final face of death, social death.

For the dying, the obvious goal is to promote circumstances in which all four types of death can occur together, or as coincidentally as possible. In the case of the bereaved, care givers must be aware that death has many faces and each must be acknowledged and the associated loss grieved. In the case of Mrs. X, she experienced many losses, each one significant. Her grieving was complex and multifaceted.

This example serves to broaden our framework and discussion of loss and bereavement. Death, especially the death of a loved one, is often the most intense form of loss; however, the loss of the person is only one category of loss. There are many more, as is demonstrated in this case. Mrs. X has also lost some aspect of self. In this case, role confusion was created by the loss of her husband and involved a struggle between the *we* and the *I,* and fears associated with her new autonomy. She had also lost her full-time cook, financial advisor, and best friend. These losses and others, as we will see in future chapters, can play a major role in the process of grief and bereavement.

SOCIAL INFLUENCES
ON THE GRIEVING PROCESS

A society's temperament toward death is a function of how death fits into its teleological view of life. Our society once had a death-accepting temperament. Death was viewed as an inevitable and a natural part of life. However, today's society, with its emphasis on technology, has moved from being a death-accepting to being a death-denying society. There is a pervasive refusal to encounter or confront death. There appears to be a belief that death is incompatible with or even antithetical to life and therefore not a natural part of the human experience. Feifel (1971) suggested that in American society there is a fear of death. Euphemisms such as *passed away, passed on* or *at rest* have been created to perhaps sanitize our experience of death and help to allay our fears.

Once a natural occurrence, dying at home is now rare. Most of us will live out our final hours or days in hospitals or possibly nursing or retirement homes. Medical technology has lengthened our lives and improved our quality of life overall, but it has come at a cost. At the very moment that most of us look for the comfort of family, we are confined to a hospital room alone or with strangers, doctors, and nurses who often view death as the enemy to be fought until the bitter end.

Elizabeth Kubler-Ross, in her classic book *On Death and Dying,* recalled the "old-fashioned" customs relating to death:

I remember as a child the death of a farmer. He fell from a tree and was not expected to live. He asked simply to die at home, a wish that was granted without questioning. He called his daughters into the room and spoke to each one of them alone for a few moments. He arranged his affairs quietly, though he was in great pain, and distributed his belongings and his land, none of which was to be split until his wife should follow him in death. He also asked each of his children to share the work, duties, and tasks that he had carried on until the time of the accident. He asked his friends to visit him once more, to bid good-bye to them. Although I was a small child at the time, he did not exclude me or my siblings. We were allowed to share in the preparations of the family just as we were permitted to grieve with them until he died. When he died, he was left at home, in his beloved home which he had built, and among his friends and neighbors, who went to take a last look at him where he lay in the middle of flowers in the place he had lived in and loved so much. In that country today there is still no make-believe slumber room, no embalming, no false makeup to pretend to sleep. Only the signs of very disfiguring illnesses are covered up with bandages and only infectious cases are removed from the home prior to the funeral.

Why do I describe such "old-fashioned" customs? I think they are indications of our acceptance of a fatal outcome, and they help the dying patient as well as his family to accept the loss of a loved one. If a patient is allowed to terminate his life in the familiar and beloved environment, it requires less adjustment for him. The fact that children are allowed to stay at home where a fatality has stricken and are included in the talk, discussions, and fears gives them the feeling that they are not alone in the grief and gives them the comfort of shared responsibility and shared mourning. It prepares them gradually and helps them view death as part of life. (pp. 5–6)

In this example, Kubler-Ross paints a picture that would be foreign in today's society. However, she provides this as an example of what many would consider the *good death*. So why is the picture she paints so foreign to us?

Robert J. Lifton in his book, *Death in Life: Survivors of Hiroshima,* noted six factors that have increased our difficulty in dealing with death.

1. *Urbanization.* Individuals are increasingly removed from nature and natural settings; therefore, they rarely witness the natural cycle of life and death. Urbanization and increased mobility has led to lessening of the sense of community with others and fewer common or shared rituals to aid in the expression of feelings and guide behavior.

2. *Exclusion of the aged and dying.* These individuals are segregated away from the general population into nursing or retirement homes or hospitals. This exclusion fosters fears of aloneness or abandonment, making death an even more foreign and potentially frightening experience.

3. *Movement toward the nuclear family.* Many people experience the absence of extended family and, concomitantly, the vulnerability to devastation and loss of support following the death of a loved one. There is little opportunity to see aged relatives die and to experience death as a natural part of the life cycle.

4. *Secularization from religion.* Religion has traditionally minimized the impact of physical death by focusing on the hereafter, endowing death with a special meaning and purpose, and providing for a future immortality. Without this, death is an abyss from which many can find no solace.

5. *Advances in medical technology.* Medical technology has given individuals more of a sense of control over their lives and death. Life expectancy is increasing and technology is touting immortality through cryonics and future medical technology. As this occurs and despite bioethical quandaries, death has become more infrequent as terminal illnesses become chronic ones. All of these advances have compromised the ability to understand and accept death as a natural part of human life.

6. *Mass death.* Our sensitivity to individual death has become somewhat blunted. News reports including accounts of disasters of pandemic proportions have conditioned us to at times feel good that only fifteen people died in a terrorist bombing instead of fifty. In the not so recent past, just one death would have been horrifying.

The public's response to the Oklahoma City bombing that killed hundreds of people stands in contradiction to the idea that exposure to disasters of pandemic proportions may blunt our sensitivity to individual death. The nation's response to the events of September 11, 2001, demonstrates that in certain circumstances mass death might actually heighten our sensitivity.

OUR ATTITUDES TOWARD DEATH
AND THE GRIEVING PROCESS

Lifton also provided hope to those who struggle to cope with death. In a 1973 work, *The Sense of Immortality: On Death and the Continuity of Life,* he noted that there are cognate modes of thought on immortality that offer comfort in dealing with death:

1. *The biological mode.* We believe that we extend ourselves into the future through our children and their biological inheritance from us. Immortality is thereby achieved through procreation and something of us lives on.

2. *The social mode.* Through living a meaningful life our lives have direction and purpose. The residual of this life is, after death something worthwhile that we leave as a note to others that we were here.

3. *The religious mode.* Religion provides a clear message of an immortal hereafter. Death is not the end but rather the beginning.

4. *The natural mode.* We are a part of the natural evolution or circle of life. We live and experience and then return to nourish the next generation. The chain of which we are a part is continuous and never broken.

5. *The experiential transcendental mode.* There are, some believe, psychological states, religious or secular mysticism, that are so intense that there is a feeling of being beyond the confines of normal existence. In these states there is an extraordinary psychic unity and perceptual intensity in which there is no longer any restriction, including that of mortality.

Solace may be found for many in one or more of these modes, as well as other ways of coping with death anxiety (e.g., hedonism, belief in reincarnation, or other practices).

Human behavior can best be understood in context. That is, one's behavior is an interaction between the person and the social context in which the person lives. If one observes those bereaved individuals in our society, it appears that they frequently receive the message that their loss should be only of temporary concern, both to them and others. Generally speaking, the more temporary the better. It is standard practice to receive three days or so off work to handle a death in the family. Then it is generally expected that in a few weeks or a month you should be over your loss and back to business as usual. Individuals who mourn openly or for "extended" periods of time are often viewed as weak, engaging in self-pity, or in need of psychological or psychiatric help.

To understand the individual's experience with grief, one must understand the tremendous influence society and social rules have on the grieving process. Most of us either have been told or have heard someone else being told to be "strong." The message is that the refusal to allow tears and the disavowal, at least publicly, of our pain are admirable behaviors. The concept of being strong dates to the early stoic philosophers who encouraged others not to mourn, believing that self-control was the desired response. In general, our society seems to embrace this thinking as evidenced in its impatience with those who are grieving. Grief is viewed as something that should be overcome rather than experienced. We live in a society where the rules encourage and reward the suppression of emotions such as grief, as opposed to the expression. The result is that all too often individuals grieve in isolation or attempt to distance themselves from their grief through whatever means they possess. There exist unwritten but nonetheless socially mandated rules or edicts that require individuals not to bring up sensitive subjects such as death or loss and/or to respond by changing the subject if someone else becomes visibly upset or distressed. The bereaved, if queried following a death, observe the rules by saying, "I'm fine," in essence saying, "I'm over it, I'm OK, I'm not grieving anymore; you don't have to worry." Family and friends are relieved and refrain from upsetting him or her by further discussing the loss. This socially sanctioned behavior tends to be more often than not accepted, at least on some level, by everyone involved.

Our society prizes rationality and emotional control, which has resulted in the subtle but ubiquitous message, don't be: don't be sad, don't be depressed, don't be whatever you are in response to your loss. Given this potent message it is no surprise that Zisook found that 17 percent of patients entering an outpatient psychiatric facility had unresolved grief or that Bowlby posited that much psychiatric illness is an expression of pathological mourning.

In order to better understand how social influences affect the grieving process, you must understand your own and others' responses to death and related loss(es). Social influences are a reflection of the macrocosm that is society. Our attitudes toward death may be viewed as or represent a microcosm of the whole of society of which we are a part.

In viewing our attitudes toward death we must all acknowledge that to some degree we all share a delusion, a false belief. One might even say a vital delusion. We are all future oriented, and in the course of daily living we make considerable plans for that future. In doing so, we believe and act as if there is and always will be a future. We hold tenaciously to this delusion of perpetual existence; not to do so would be debilitating. Think what life would be like if you did not anticipate tomorrow.

Death threatens us with the negation of ourselves and all that we value. To confront this threat is to arouse anxiety even in the strongest of us. Each of us is continually subject to the threat of death, and we must find a way to cope with this intimidation. Possible responses abound, and attitudes toward death range from complete denial to some degree of existential acceptance. The attitudes we adopt exert tremendous influence on how we live our lives. One attitude might be death-denying. These individuals might avoid most or all topics related to death. Wakes or funerals will be avoided. Yearly medical exams and the making of a will are not in the repository of necessary functions. Other behaviors (e.g., focus on youth, work, sex) will be intensified and will serve as distractions. So long as nothing interferes with the distracters, the focus remains on them. Inevitability of death and its related signs or indicators are avoided.

Another attitude might be death-defying. These individuals may be extreme risk takers or thrill seekers appearing to be masters of their fate and proving their control over death. The realization, conscious or unconscious, and the related attitude we adopt toward the fact that at some point in time we will die and cease to exist has significant ramifications for how we live our lives in the present.

Our attitudes toward death vary greatly and are sometimes, oftentimes, less than positive. Robert Kavanaugh, in his book *Facing Death,* makes a unique contribution to those who study and work in the field of death and bereavement. Kavanaugh notes that our attitudes and feelings do not preclude us from working effectively with the dying and the bereaved if we are aware of them. In the following he explains that it is normal to have less than positive feelings about death.

> Most Americans have no more than a shadowy indication of their feeling toward death. Ask a friend how they feel about dying or death and you will hear how they would like to feel or how they think they ought to feel. . . . It became clear to me that an honest and humane approach to death can begin only when we allow ourselves to get in touch with our visceral feelings. Otherwise any stance we adopt toward death will be no more than another form of blocking and avoiding honest confrontation. It is not the dying or dead that we fear as much as the unknown and the untested feelings they evoke within ourselves. . . . (p. 22)
>
>   Kavanaugh goes on to provide reassurance, saying:
>
> Let me reassure you that it is okay to feel uneasy or afraid. It is okay to want to run, to send floral wreaths or Mass cards instead of self. It is okay to feel eerie or unduly tense, to hide and cry, to want to swear or scream or lash out at angry targets. It is okay to feel relieved and even happy when someone dies. It is okay to feel whatever is real. Feelings have no morality. They are neither good nor bad, always ethically neutral. (p. 39)

The Chinese pictogram for "crisis" is a combination of two symbols: danger and opportunity. There is danger [fear] involved in facing our fear emanating from our unknown and untested feelings about death. However there is also great opportunity for new-found freedom. The interdigitation of life and death is a concept that is as old as recorded history. It is one of life's most self-evident truths that our reality, our existence, is temporal and that we fear our passing, but we nonetheless must live in the presence of our fear. Montaigne, in his piercing essays on death, asks, "Why do you fear your last day? It contributes no more to your death than each of the others. The last step does not cause the fatigue, but reveals it." (p. 65)

Existentialists posit that death gives meaning to life. Paradoxically, it is true that the physicality of death destroys us; however, it is that same awareness that allows to us be free to live. But what, precisely, does that statement mean? A brief encounter with Martin Heidegger and a core concept of existential philosophy may help clarify the paradox.

Heidegger explored the question of how the idea of death may save man, and arrived at the important insight that our awareness of our own personal death acts as a stimulus to shift from one mode of existence to a higher one. He believed that there are two fundamental modes of existing in the world: (1) a state of forgetfulness of being or (2) a state of mindful being.

In a state of forgetfulness of being, one lives in the world of things and immerses oneself in the everyday diversions of life. Here one is stereotyped, unimaginative, lost in the crowd, surrendering oneself to the everyday world concerned about the way things are.

In the state of mindfulness of being, one marvels not at the way things are, but rather *that* they are. Not only is one mindful of the fragility of being, but mindful too of one's responsibility for one's being. It is only in this mode that one is in touch with one's self-creation, that is, the power to change oneself.

Heidegger believes that ordinarily, we live in the forgetfulness of being, an inauthentic mode, one in which one is unaware of one's authorship of one's life and the world. However, when one encounters the second mode, the mindfulness of being, one exists authentically and is self-aware, embracing both the possibilities and limits, absolute freedom and nothingness.

Now what does death have to do with all this? Heidegger understood that one does not simply move from a state of forgetfulness of being, inauthenticity, to a more enlightened mindfulness (authentic) state of being by simple cogitation. There are certain unalterable, irremediable conditions or experiences that shock one from the everyday inauthentic state of existence to the authentic state of being. Of these experiences, death is the nonpareil. Death is the condition that makes it possible for us to live in an authentic fashion. This point of view that death makes a positive contribution to life is not always easy to accept. However, one need only suspend judgment for a moment and imagine life without any thought of death. Here life loses something of its intensity, its flavor.

Some of our greatest literary works provide us with examples of the positive effects confrontations with death have on an individual. Tolstoy's *War and Peace* provides us such an example. Pierre, the protagonist, experiences the inauthentic and meaningless empty life of the Russian aristocracy. A lost soul searching for some purpose in life, he is captured by Napoleon's troops and sentenced to death by the firing squad. He watches the execution of the men in front of him and prepares himself to die, only at the last moment to be unexpectedly reprieved. The experience transforms Pierre, who is able to now live his life authentically, and to discover a task in life that has meaning for him and to dedicate himself to it.

Another of Tolstoy's works, *The Death of Ivan Ilyich,* contains a similar message. Ivan Ilyich, a mean-spirited bureaucrat, develops a fatal illness and suffers extraordinary pain. His relentless anguish continues until shortly before his death, when Ivan Ilyich comes upon a staggering truth: He is dying badly because he had lived badly. In the few days remaining, Ivan Ilyich undergoes a dramatic transformation and personal growth. He is able to finally live without the false pride, arrogance, and bitterness associated with his previous state of forgetfulness of being.

Senator Richard Neuberger, shortly before his death from cancer, described these changes:

> A change came over me, which I believe is irreversible. Questions of prestige, of political success, of financial status, became all at once unimportant. In those first hours when I realized I had cancer, I never thought of my seat in the Senate, of my bank account, or the destiny of the free world. . . . My wife and I have not had a quarrel since my illness was diagnosed. I used to scold her about squeezing the toothpaste from the top instead of the bottom, about not catering sufficiently to my fussy appetite, about making the guest list without consulting me, about spending too much on clothes. Now I am either unaware of such matters or they seem irrelevant. . . .
>
> In their stead has come a new appreciation of things I once took for granted—eating lunch with a friend, scratching Muffet's ears and listening for his purrs, the company of my wife, reading a book or magazine in the quiet cone of my bed lamp at night, raiding the refrigerator for a glass of orange juice or slice of coffee cake. For the first time I think I actually am savoring life. I realize that I am not immortal. I shudder when I remember all the occasions that I spoiled for myself—even when I was in the best of health—by false pride, synthetic values, and fancied slights.

These examples provide us a glimpse into some possible answers to a well-worn hackneyed question, "What would you do differently from what you are doing now if you knew that you had only one day left to live?" Confronting our own death and our related attitudes provides us with the mechanisms through which we can authentically experience life and similarly enter into relationships with others. Death places limits on us and our experiences and at the same time opens up infinite possibilities and experiences.

On a gravestone in a New England cemetery an epitaph provides us a unique encounter further clarifying our existential task.

> "Listen friend as you walk by,
>   as you are now so once was I
>   as I am now so you shall be,
>   prepare yourself to follow me."

QUESTIONS FOR THOUGHT
AND REFLECTION

1. Suppose that life is just as you know it with one exception: There is no death. Disease, aging, and environmental concerns have been conquered and immortality is possible. What are the consequences for you individually? What are the consequences for society? How would this change your beliefs, values, needs, and actions?

2. Describe your earliest experience with death. When did it occur? Who died? Who told you? What were you told? What was your reaction? What were the reactions of those around you? What messages about death were conveyed to you? What were your feelings, thoughts, concerns, and/or fears?

3. Are you more comfortable with euphemisms *passed on* or *at rest* than you are with the words *death* or *dead?* Share your thoughts and feelings by exploring the reasons in small group discussions.

4. Is denial of death necessary for survival? Is there a vital delusion that is necessary for us to work, play, and to plan for a future that has no guarantee or permanence?

5. What are some questions about death that you wish you had the answers to?

6. What are your thoughts/feelings about your own death?

7. Who or what will you miss most when you die?

8. What do you fear most about death?

9. Describe your deathbed scene. Where will it be? Who will be present? What will be your physical/mental condition?

10. In your deathbed scene, what happened to you after you died?

2

Death and Dying:
A Process

In the first chapter we undertook the task of defining death. Now we shall examine the transition leading up to that event, dying. Dying is, in reality, one of many transitions we experience as part of our lives. Some transitions are long awaited and eagerly anticipated (e.g., becoming a teenager, first date, driving) while other, often less desirable ones (e.g., turning 30, first gray hair), are met with ambivalence or sometimes dread. *Transition,* the passing from one state to another, is accepted as a normal aspect of life. The key here is that in these transitions we are passing from one state to another, and the process, as well as the outcome, is fairly predictable. The progression is identifiable and familiar, at least in the fact that others have been or are in the same transitional state that we are. However, the transition from life to death is different in that it represents a final transition and is one in which we cannot forecast the outcome.

WHEN DOES DYING BEGIN?

An obvious question needing to be addressed here is, "When does dying begin?" Existentialists would posit that we die from the moment we are born. This self-acknowledgment is viewed as forming the bases of an authentic personal philosophy of life. Few of us, however, are so existential, and most of us prefer to trivialize or simply ignore this fact in an effort to avoid the fear and anxiety associated with it. Dying may be said to begin with an initial awareness of impending death. This awareness, however, may not initially include the person who is actually dying. Our health care providers are generally the ones who "officially" determine that we have a terminal or life threatening illness and are dying. Dying, from the individual's perspective, begins when the person becomes aware of his or her impending death. This awareness might occur in a multitude of ways. An individual may receive a terminal prognosis from his or her physician or health care provider, or overhear statements made by the physician or other health care providers to other personnel or to family members. The communication may be nonverbal, such as changes in the behavior of the physician, health care providers, family, or friends.

How information is provided may help or hinder patients' or families' ability to process and/or accept the information, and that has implications for the grief process. Those whose responsibilities include talking directly with patients and families regarding their prognosis should be apprised that there are some good and some not so good ways to proceed. It is not good to give the bad news and all the facts and options at once. Neither is it a good idea to be sure that you "break through" the denial immediately and/or make it clear that nothing more can be done. Leaving immediately after individuals have been told their prognosis is usually not helpful. It is helpful to spend time with an individual and/or the family before and after providing information. Keep it simple, do not say anything that is not true, and provide information a little at a time, observing how it is assimilated before providing more. Encourage questions and assure the individual and the family that you will be with them for the duration.

Even when the facts are communicated, most people do not accept themselves as dying until the situation has been realized, personalized, and accepted. In some situations, the individual is aware of what has been said but does not put the information into clear focal awareness. In other situations, the dying individual might not accept his or her fate, thinking there is something more that can be done.

When impending death is realized, regardless of how the realization occurs, the result is usually a crisis. Pattison (1978) describes five aspects of crisis resulting from knowledge of impending death:

1. *This stressful event poses a problem that by definition is unsolvable in the immediate future.* In this sense, dying is the most stressful crisis because it is a crisis to which we bow but do not solve.

2. *The problem taxes one's psychological resources because it is beyond one's traditional problem-solving methods.* One is faced with a new experience with no prior experience to draw from, for although everyone has lived amidst death, that is far different from one's own death.

3. *The situation is perceived as a threat or danger to the life goals of the person.* Dying interrupts a person in the midst of life; and even in old age it abruptly confronts one with the goals one set in life.

4. *The crisis period is characterized by a tension that mounts to a peak; then falls.* As one faces the crisis of death knowledge, there is a mobilization of

either integrative or disintegrative mechanisms. The peak of anxiety usually occurs considerably before death.

5. *The crisis situation awakens unresolved key problems from both the near and distant past.* Problems of dependency, passivity, narcissism, identity, and more may be activated during the dying process. Hence, one is faced not only with the immediate dying process but also with unresolved feelings from one's own lifetime and its inevitable conflicts. (pp. 145–146)

There are many ways that individuals can react to the news that they are facing a terminal illness. They can accept or deny the reality or do both, vacillating between them. They can intellectually accept but emotionally deny the reality. Emotional acceptance may result in a person being overwhelmed and rendered unable to verbally express anything. Whatever the response, it is an effort by the individual to cope; and, by whatever method available, to meet the demands of this crisis situation.

TASKS FACED BY THE DYING

As noted earlier we all recognize that we are going to die, but the rationalizations, "So we're all dying and ain't life grand," are ways to cope with this unpleasant reality. The diagnosis of terminal illness results in a crisis, as these rationalizations are abruptly rendered useless. Pattison (1978) calls the period of time between the crisis created by the knowledge of impending death and the point of death the *living–dying interval.* Moos and Tsu (1977) identified a novel set of tasks that may present themselves during this interval period. The relative importance of each task will vary, depending on the nature of the illness, the personality of the individual, and the environmental circumstances.

The first task is one of adaptation. Most individuals in our society place a high value on control and independence. The individual in this living–dying interval will need to find ways to adjust to the dying role and deal with discomfort, incapacitation, helplessness, and related symptoms.

The second task is to manage stress resulting from the diagnosis, related treatments, and/or the possibility of being in an institutional setting. Treatment settings are usually foreign environments that place the stress of additional demands on patients and their families. Separation from family members during treatments can also be stressful.

Coping with the health care system (including managed care) while developing and maintaining relationships with caregivers is the third task. Dealing with a potentially impersonal system can be somewhat intimidating. Patients as well as family members might feel insecure about expressing their needs or obtaining necessary information.

Preserving a satisfactory self-image and maintaining a sense of competency and mastery constitute the fourth task. Any physical and/or psychological changes that occur during this transition period must be incorporated into a new and revised self-image. The limits of independence must be realized, and the virtue of being a receiver may be considered. Without receivers there would be no opportunity for others to show that they care.

Kalish (1970) identified other tasks unique to the terminally ill. Dying individuals must arrange a variety of affairs. Each one serves as a signal of the progression of the impending and unrelenting death. Examples of these unique tasks include getting the will in order, updating insurance policies, making funeral arrangements, and generally looking after the welfare of those who are left behind. However uncomfortable this task may be, it gives the dying a sense of control and allows one to take care of those left behind. Obviously, denial might cause some individuals to reject the notion of imminent death, and then such arrangements will not be made by them.

Coping with loss of loved ones as well as the loss of oneself is a major undertaking. Open and honest discussion between the dying and their family and close friends regarding their shared grief, needs, vulnerability, and future relationships may serve to draw them closer together and allow them better, more intimate use of the time available.

Simultaneously, the dying individuals must accommodate and deal with the impending loss of their entire world and everyone in it, including themselves. This may be viewed as a combination of an individual's reaction to the loss of self, the loss of others, and the empathy the person feels for those who survive and are bereaved.

Planning for the future is also a task facing the dying. Whatever time, energy, and resources exist must be allocated in light of the time remaining. In some situations the time remaining will be uncertain and planning will be made more difficult. Here it may be wise to remember that life is for the living, and as long as the individual is living, involvement in life is an option.

A related task that is increasingly present is the decision whether to attempt to slow down or to speed up the process of dying. Advances in medical technology have made possible extraordinary potentially life extending procedures. At the same time, social changes have brought about in some areas the option of euthanasia. Controversial issues in death and dying will be the focus of chapter 3.

DYING, CERTAINTY, AND TIME

Pioneering studies by Glaser and Strauss (1966, 1968) identified a variety of sequences or pathways to death and their distinctive characteristics. They called these pathways *trajectories of dying.* The trajectory is the path of the individual's dying experience and has to do with the certainty of death and the time at which death is anticipated. There are four types of death expectations: certain death at a known time; certain death at an unknown time; uncertain death but a known time when certainty will be established; and uncertain death and an unknown time when the question of certainty will be resolved. It is generally easier to cope when we are fairly certain about our expectations of death because uncertainty or ambiguity leads to anxiety and increases stress.

Certain Death at a Known Time

In the first type of death expectation, certain death at a known time, Glaser and Strauss found several types of possible trajectories. In very acute illness or following serious accidents, the focus is on imminent death that may occur quickly and follow one of several trajectories. In a pointed trajectory the individual may be exposed to a very risky medical procedure necessary to save his or her life, but the procedure also has the potential of resulting in his or her death. In this situation the individual may have the opportunity to act on personal matters or share time with family. The focus here is on the most efficient use of the time available. There are other situations with similar expectations but that involve watching and waiting (danger-period trajectory). The individual in this situation has experienced a high-risk surgical procedure, heart attack, or stroke, and survival is uncertain. In this scenario, the individual might be unconscious or only partially alert and responsive. The waiting or danger period can last from hours to days, with the family maintaining vigil. A third possibility is the crisis trajectory. Here the individual is not in acute danger at the moment; however, his or her status may suddenly change with death being imminent. The last trajectory identified is the will-probably-die. In this situation, everything possible has been done and the goal is to keep the individual as comfortable as possible until death occurs, usually within hours or days.

There are some common problems associated with situations in which death is expected within a given time. The individual is usually in an institutional setting such as a hospital, which is stressful for both the patient and the family. Families are often kept in the waiting room away from the patient, which adds to the stress and anxiety for both. Given the time urgency, communication between staff and family and staff and patient is critical. Finally, whether there is a chance to save the individual's life will, in part, depend on the perceived social value. Elderly patients may be perceived as having lived their life and being ready to die, whereas younger individuals are just beginning life and warrant an all-out rescue attempt.

Certain Death at an Unknown Time

The second type of death expectation, certain death at an unknown time, is the trajectory usually associated with chronic terminal illnesses. Death following a long terminal illness may be perceived as more acceptable because all that could be done has been done, and it is now time to end the suffering. However, actual physical death in this type of trajectory may be preceded by social death. The individual may be in a hospital or long-term care facility, and family members may give more and more care-giving functions over to the staff as time progresses. The frequency and duration of visits from friends and family might also begin to decline gradually until visits virtually cease.

In this second type of death expectation, patience of the family and/or staff may be strained when the individual fails to die as anticipated following a lingering trajectory. This reaction is not callous, as it at first glance may seem. Rather, it is often the result of stress experienced by family members caught in the lengthy uncertainty of the living—dying interval. In this situation, the family and/or staff experience anticipatory grief. Futter, Hoffman, and Sabshin (1972) conceptualized anticipatory grief as a series of five functionally related aspects:

1. *Acknowledgment.* Becoming progressively convinced that death is inevitable
2. *Grieving.* Experiencing and expressing the emotional impact of the anticipated loss
3. *Reconciliation.* Developing perspectives on the expected death and the worth of life in general
4. *Detachment.* Withdrawing emotional investment from the dying person
5. *Memorializing.* Developing a relatively fixed conscious mental representation of the dying person that will endure beyond his/her death (p. 252)

In some situations, if the death does not occur, the bereaved have already grieved in anticipation to such an extent that they have detached themselves from the dying individual and are unable to reinvest without significant emotional cost. This may lead to feelings of frustration and anger, brought on by the possibility of having to again repeat the grieving process. It should be noted that although the tasks of grief have begun well in advance of death, they are rarely completed. Significant grief work will generally remain.

This trajectory does have some potential advantages for both the dying individual and his or her family. The most obvious is the time with which to acclimate to the impending loss. The opportunity exists to work through unresolved issues or misunderstandings, and also to review one's life and relationships and plan for new and different ones.

To effectively live with dying requires one to minimize the stress of uncertainty. Said another way, one must focus on what is certain. The focus on long-term or even short-term goals and aspirations must be replaced with predictable day-to-day specific issues of daily living. This allows the dying individual and his or her family to experience some certainty and control and to make the best use of whatever time is available.

Uncertain Death with a Known Time for Establishing Certainty

The third type of death expectation, the uncertainty of death, but with a known time when certainty will be established, occurs in cases where certainty of death depends on further information (i.e., biopsy results, or an organ for transplantation). Intense emotions and stress are often aroused for those involved. The problem is how to respond to the stress and anxiety generated when the question of the certainty of death, which is the core of the problem, remains unresolved. Response strategies may include attempts at maintaining an illusion of control by continuing to work, play, and plan as if an outcome were already known. This strategy might include either the best or the worst possible outcomes and related actions.

Uncertain Death at an Unknown Time

The final type of death expectation, uncertain death and an unknown time when the question will be resolved, involves chronic illnesses such as multiple sclerosis or genetic diseases. Here the possibility of death looms but is uncertain, and it is ambiguous as to when the question of the certainty of death will be resolved. Maybe, maybe not, probably, probably not—who knows? Some individuals caught in this double bind of sorts may be prone to develop dysfunctional coping mechanisms and a hypochrondrical fixation on their physical condition. Others may see this potential double bind created by uncertainty and step out of it. In doing so, they existentially accept their limitations (if any) and the anxiety they might experience as a concomitant fact of life and an acknowledgment that, in fact, they are still alive. This final trajectory in its broadest sense is a reality that applies to all of us for we know neither the day nor the time of our death.

FACTORS INFLUENCING
THE DYING EXPERIENCE

Just as there are factors that influence the grief reaction, there are factors that influence how the phenomenon of dying is experienced. Age and interpersonal relationships are two significant factors.

Each individual changes emotionally and cognitively throughout his or her lifecycle (Inhelder & Piaget, 1952; Ginsberg & Oppers, 1987; Piaget 1960, 1973); so too do his or her concepts and attitudes about death (Nagy, 1948; Speece & Brent, 1996). For example, children under the age of three have been very busy at many of the tasks of development. Initially, tasks involve the determination of what is me and what is not me. However, as children grow they are exposed to experiences that are related to death (e.g., peek-a-boo games, bye-bye, all gone, separation from parents). At this age they are not cognitively able to grasp the concept of death. This stage of development involves early preoperational thinking (i.e., magical thinking) and the child communicates through play and make believe. What the child fears most at this age is separation from the primary caregiver. A three-year-old does not understand the permanence of death or casual relationships and may ask repeatedly when the deceased parent is returning. This may continue for weeks or months after death. The child might become frightened by prolonged, emotive expressions of mourning by adults. The child might become very angry when told that mamma or daddy has gone to heaven, and might respond by saying that he or she wants them here. The child might demand a replacement or even several (e.g., next time I get two . . . in case you lose one again).

Indications of possible complicated bereavement include severe and persistent separation anxiety when away from the surviving parent or caregiver that lasts more than six months after the reestablishment of a stable predictable home environment. Other indications are continuing or worsening of regressive behaviors (encopresis, or bed wetting) beyond six months following the death.

From the age of three to approximately age six or seven, the child's world is largely egocentric and involves fantasy, daydreams, and magical thinking. Concepts such as right and wrong, praise, and punishment are very important. Some perspective of death as permanent and universal is forming; however, it is not unusual for the child to vacillate and see death as reversible or temporary. Some rudimentary understanding of cause and effect begins; however, this is a tenuous beginning, and cause and effect is easily misunderstood. Terminal illness and death may be viewed as punishment for wrongdoing, real or imagined. Fears may exist that bad thoughts, words, or wishes will result in harm or death. Additionally, children may erroneously assume self-blame and guilt for a parent's illness and/or death. Separation from parents continues to be a critical issue because parents are the primary source of self-esteem for the child. The mourning process might include joyful reminiscences as well as tearful ones. The lost parent is thought to be located in a place (generally heaven) and is seen as having a function (e.g., guardian angel or tooth fairy).

Indications of possible complicated bereavement include continued regressive behavior with loss of emotional and behavioral control, persistent physical symptoms without identifiable cause, school or other phobias, static or exacerbated mourning for three or more months following the death, and/or persistent talk of dying (suicide) as a means of being with the deceased parent.

During the school-age years, children begin and then finally achieve an understanding of the concept of death. Concrete operational thinking improves logic and understanding of cause and effect. However, at this age children cannot draw inferences from limited information and need age-appropriate detailed explanations about illness and course of treatment. Children at this age are able to compartmentalize and use distraction to avoid strong emotions. They may need help to balance avoidance of sadness and other feelings with activities such as planned rituals for reminiscing. At this age it is not uncommon for children to report feeling a strong sense of the deceased parents presence.

Withdrawal from peers and/or family, increased moodiness, anger, or misbehavior persisting more than three to six months after the death may be signs of complicated bereavement. Decreased academic performance and/or interest in after-school activities may be further indications.

Adolescence is a time when children are deeply involved in the task of determining who they are. Adolescents have the cognitive abilities of adults and therefore an adult understanding of the concept death. However, for the younger adolescent (12–15), formal operational thinking is often inconsistent. Standing on the threshold of adult life, not yet fully emerged from the cocoon, the adolescent is ambivalent about their new found independence and the familiarity and safety of parental dependence. Egocentric and possible insensitive response to parental illness and needs, especially when it interferes with peer activities, may be understood in light of normal adolescent emotional withdrawal from parents and investment in peer group. Following death, early adolescents may express a strong sense of the deceased parent and engage in ongoing conservations with them. They might desire to wear clothing of the deceased parent. Possessions, clothing and/or other articles belonging to the deceased might take on great importance as a mechanism of attachment.

Late adolescence is a time of integrating change. Formal operational thinking is more consistent, and there is greater integration of the future with the present and the past. Ambivalence about independence is lessening as maturity increases. Mourning in this stage of development has more adult-like qualities; however, the duration is usually shorter. Conversations with the deceased parent continue, and there might be an interest expressed by adolescents in fulfilling their parents' dreams for them.

Indications of possible complicated bereavement may include development of marked mood swings, withdrawal from peer interactions or other normal group activities, and increasing high risk behaviors involving drugs, sex and/or antisocial activities.

Adults face their own unique developmental tasks, ranging from the tasks of young adulthood, which include establishing families and developing careers, to the developmental tasks of the elderly, which involve attempts at emotionally integrating and finding meaning and acceptance of the experience of one's life. Counselors would do well to remember that more often than not, terminal illness and the prospect of death are usually unexpected, even in old age. Taking into account the uniqueness of the individual, therapeutic interventions may include identifying and working through losses, reconciling what is with what might have been, expressing feelings, and helping the individual achieve an appropriate death. Where on the developmental continuum an individual is and what life experiences the person has had will significantly influence his or her experience of dying.

The importance of interpersonal relationships should not be underestimated in the end of life experience. Weisman and Worden (1975) found that among hospitalized patients, those who maintained active and mutually responsive relationships were found to survive longer than those patients with poor social relationships. The researchers also found that patients who died rapidly tended to have fewer friends, more distant relationships with their family, and more ambivalent relationships with colleagues and associates. They also noted that the patients with poor relationships often expressed a desire to die, but that this did not represent an acceptance of death but rather a frustration and disappointment with life. Weisman and Worden (1976) later found that terminally ill patients who were experiencing the most distress were also those with the most interpersonal difficulties. It was found that not only the length of survival but also the quality of life associated with survival was associated with the kind of interpersonal relationships enjoyed or suffered by the patient.

THE STAGES OF DYING

Hesitancy often results from a lack of familiarity or understanding. People often hesitate to interact with the dying for many reasons, one of them being a lack of understanding or perspective on the dying process. Theoretical models have been helpful in understanding the process or tasks of grief. Likewise, models of the dying process will help provide a perspective from which to work with the dying.

Elizabeth Kubler-Ross, in her book, *On Death and Dying* (1969), introduced five stages of dying. These stages were thought to begin when an individual becomes aware of his or her condition, or, in the case of grief, has experienced or anticipates a loss. Kubler-Ross presented these stages as a normal response to the anticipation of one's own death. The process begins with denial and progresses, if time allows, through the remaining stages of anger, bargaining, depression, and acceptance. As with all the stages and phases of reactions to loss, progress might be arrested at any stage along the continuum and there might also be regressions or slipping back and forth among various stages. Kubler-Ross conceptualized this process as universal and yet recognized the idiosyncratic nature of human beings, acknowledging individual variation in matriculation of the stages. It is evident that, when faced with the prospect of one's own death, individuals experience some if not all of the feelings Kubler-Ross describes and attempt some of the coping strategies while matriculating the stages included in her theory. However, it is not known whether everyone goes through the same stages or necessarily all the stages or under what conditions acceptance takes place. The role of theory is to provide useful observations and guidance until research is able to answer the questions definitively.

Stage 1. Denial is the initial reaction to the "bad" news. "No, not me, this cannot be happening" is the typical thought that first occurs. In this stage, what appears to be shock or numbness can be viewed as self-protection from anxiety and the approaching nihilism that death may represent. Recuperation and the wearing off of the initial shock reaction is a gradual process and allows for entry into the second stage.

Stage 2. Anger may well up and boil over after the initial shock and related denial have abated. "Why me" is characteristic of the thought process. Anger is fueled by frustration, resentment, and feelings of helplessness and hopelessness. These awesome emotions can be unleashed in all directions. Medical personnel and even God are likely recipients of the rage. The release of intense emotions may seem out of control and spur the individual on to the next stage, seeking that elusive sense of control.

Stage 3. Bargaining, the middle stage, can be seen as an attempt to exert some control in an otherwise uncontrollable situation. Possibly out of anxiety and/or the fear of dying, a deal is attempted. "I'll do . . . if I can only have two more years . . ." The negotiation may go on between the dying individual and family members, caregivers, or very often God. The obvious futility of the negotiations and other factors may influence movement to the next stage.

Stage 4. Depression usually follows as bargaining proves ineffective or the individual experiences physical or mental deterioration, weakness, and/or physical discomfort. Increasingly, symptoms become too obvious to ignore, and the individual is unable to avoid the fact that he/she is not getting better. Guilt, possibly associated with the anger displayed in the previous stage or related to other issues, may now arise together with feelings of low self-esteem and worthlessness. The individual may become less responsive and more preoccupied with the loss to come—death. Should time and circumstances allow, the final stage can be entered.

Stage 5. Acceptance (the recognition of "yes, me"), the final stage, symbolizes the end of the struggle and a letting go. Acceptance does not necessarily signify a happy or blissful time. Kubler-Ross describes it in the following way: "It is almost void of feelings. It is as if the pain has gone, the struggle is over, and there comes a time for 'the final rest, before the long journey' as one patient phrased it." (1969, p. 100)

Charles Corr (1993), attempting to address what he saw as the shortcomings of stage models, stated "An adequate model for coping with dying will need to be as agile, malleable, and dynamic as is the behavior of each individual." (p. 77) He saw the need for a model that allowed for the fact that people may try out certain coping strategies and reject them or pursue several strategies at the same time, even if they are not compatible. He believed that for the model to be practical for caregivers, it must respect individual differences as expressed in needs and associated tasks important to the individual while not ignoring universality.

In a coping model for the dying process, Corr identified four challenges that dying people encounter: the *physical,* which consists of satisfying bodily needs and reducing stress; the *psychological,* which involves maintaining a sense of security and feeling of control and the perception that one still has a life to live; the *social,* which entails maintenance of valued attachments to other individuals as well as groups and causes; and the *spiritual,* or finding or affirming meaning, having a sense of connectedness, transcendence, and hope.

COPING MECHANISMS

In the process of contending with the stress of dying, everyone, to some degree, employs coping mechanisms. Years ago these were called *defense mechanisms* and somehow, over time, they erroneously developed the negative connotation of unhealthy denial or avoidance responses associated with running away. *Coping mechanisms,* when used appropriately as adaptive mechanisms when confronted with threat or stress, are quite healthy. In fact, the lack of or inability to use appropriate coping mechanisms may be seen as an indicator of deficient emotional functioning. The following is a brief overview of some of the coping mechanisms commonly associated with the dying process.

Denial is the coping mechanism that occurs to a greater or lesser degree in all patients with terminal illnesses. Denial is a way to avoid that which the individual considers intolerable. Denial is usually temporary; however, it can vary tremendously in magnitude. For example, an individual can deny totally that anything is wrong or can accept that there is something wrong but deny the seriousness of it. In yet another scenario, the individual might accept that there is something wrong and that it results in death, but deny that he or she will die from it. Denial is not an all-or-none phenomenon, as individuals may deny and accept at the same time. An individual might accept that he or she is terminally ill, but might deny that everything has been done and request treatments that are inappropriate.

As we have seen in chapter 1, most all of us practice some form of denial by creating our own realities and planning and acting as if we were not faced with the reality that we will die. Denial is indeed a normal coping mechanism; but, like everything else, too much of a good thing is unproductive.

Regression is to a large degree characteristic of behavior associated with terminal illness. Regression involves a return to earlier forms of behavior associated with more pleasant or secure times. Some behaviors associated with regression are egocentricity, restriction of interest, increasing dependence on others, disengagement, and withdrawal from previous activities and involvement. For terminally ill individuals, these behaviors may be both necessary and therapeutic. Refusing to submit to normal regressive tendencies may be problematic and indicate psychological problems. However, emotional reactions to such normal occurrences as a decrease in or lack of independence and productivity can be severe and are not necessarily abnormal. Regression may be looked at in the dying process as a necessary balancing act. Too much one way or too little the other way could be disastrous.

Rationalization is probably one of the most common of coping mechanisms. Rationalization is a type of thought process that rejects selective casual relationships and in their place magnifies the attention focused on minor aspects of the situation. Major aspects of a situation might be minimized and perception distorted in order to achieve a desired view. The fable of the fox and the grapes is an excellent example of rationalization, and goes as follows:

> The fox spotted some luscious grapes hanging in the tree just out of reach. The fox dearly loved grapes and proceeded to try any number of methods to reach the grapes. Despite repeated attempts, the grapes remained just out of the reach of the fox. Finally after repeated frustration the fox gave up, saying, "I didn't want them anyway; they are probably sour."

In the dying process rationalization may serve to distort or to devalue a reality that is potentially overwhelming (e.g., symptoms of a heart attack may be explained away as gas pains). Aspects of the threat of death can be explained away so as to deny their existence. Care must be taken in evaluating the effectiveness and appropriateness of rationalization because in some cases the threat doesn't go away, making a potentially bad situation worse.

Intellectualization is a close cousin of rationalization. In this coping behavior feelings are disconnected from thoughts. Potentially distressing feelings are defused by intense and total focus on the intellectual or cognitive aspect of the subject or event. Terminally ill individuals may become preoccupied with their illness or associated symptoms. They may read and research their illness incessantly trying to "understand" it better or envisioning the contribution that they are making to the knowledge base on this fatal illness. Intellectualization may indeed result in an individual better understanding his or her illness, or, as in the case of cyclist and five-time Tour de France winner Lance Armstrong, a better treatment approach. His intellectual pursuit led him to an awareness of different treatment approaches and ultimately to one that saved his life.

Repression, as a coping mechanism for the terminally ill individual, may be of only limited usefulness because symptoms and/or treatments are most likely to be a constant reminder of his or her condition. Repression involves the removal of anxiety provoking or troubling thoughts of death from awareness or consciousness. Repression may be viewed as similar to forgetting. The failure of repression to function adequately and remove the threat could herald the emergence of auxiliary coping mechanisms such as denial or rationalization.

Obsessive-compulsive coping mechanisms are also not uncommon in the dying process. To obsess is to be preoccupied with thoughts or ideas. This can create a distraction or diversion and the terminally ill individual does not have to think about his or her situation and experience the collateral anxiety. Compulsions generally take the form of rituals that are repeated over and over. Obsessive-complusive behaviors are seen as the individual's attempt to order an otherwise disordered world and function to reduce anxiety. As long as neither is carried to an extreme resulting in restrictions in functioning, these behaviors may provide the individual a sense of control, order, or security.

Sublimation was once referred to as the only true defense mechanism because it allowed for catharsis. This coping mechanism involves the channeling of unacceptable thoughts and/or feelings into socially and/or personally acceptable outlets. A terminally ill individual who is angry at his or her disease or at hospital personnel or physician might go hit a bucket of golf balls or vigorously hit a tennis ball against a wall. Often terminally ill individuals, while able, expend large amounts of energy working for organizations such as the American Cancer Society.

In embracing and employing the guidance provided by any theory or model, it is important to keep in mind that the dying individual is still very much alive and is attempting to cope as resourcefully as possible. Whatever strategies the person employs are probably the result of accumulated life experience, and despite how odd or bizarre that might seem to us, the strategies might work well for that individual. Before fixing something, be sure that it is indeed broken.

QUESTIONS FOR THOUGHT
AND REFLECTION

1. When does the dying process begin?

2. Do you have a will and/or other instructions to be carried out after you die? If so, why? If not, why not?

3. List the five most significant people currently in your life. Choose one and write a farewell letter to them as if you have just been diagnosed terminally ill and have only days left to live.

4. Describe the dying process as you perceive it to be.

3

Ethics and End-of-Life
Decision Making

I swear by Apollo the physician, and Aesulapius, Hygeia, and Panacea and
all the other gods and goddesses, that, according to my ability and
judgment, I will keep this oath and this covenant. I will give no deadly
medicine to anyone if asked, nor suggest any such counsel, and in like
manner I will not give to a woman an abortive remedy. With purity and
with holiness I will pass my life and practice my Art. (The Hippocratic
Oath)

The Hippocratic Oath is thought to have originated from the writings of
a physician who practiced on the Greek island of Cos 2,500 years ago
(Edelstein, 1943). Although no longer a required recitation for all medical students, this oath and what it represents is still very much an issue today.

Advances in medicine and medical technology have resulted in an
increased life expectancy and also the possibility that death will be a long and
drawn-out process that will include a lengthy period of physical and possible
mental decline. Some individuals are able to cope with these changes that precede death and find meaning and value in the experience. Others, however,
experience only suffering and a life s/he considers not worth living. For most
individuals facing the final stages of life, the quality of that life takes on paramount importance, possibly outweighing the extending of time and life itself.
Given this scenario, how we think about death, as individuals and as a society,
is undergoing dramatic changes. Life-sustaining treatment has long been the
focus of public and professional attention. However, since the case of Karen

Ann Quinlan, no issue in bioethics has been more prominent than the debate surrounding life-sustaining treatment and the right to die. Recently the focus and subsequent debate has expanded to include euthanasia, voluntary active euthanasia, and physician-assisted suicide.

TERMS AND CONCEPTS

Before moving further into the issues and related controversy, it will be helpful to define some key terms and concepts.

Euthanasia

Euthanasia literally means happy or good death. However, the original usage of the term is more accurately understood as a death without pain or suffering. This meaning has evolved over time to include those actions performed that hasten death. Today's meaning includes both the idea of a death without pain and suffering and also the intentional shortening of a person's life in order to spare that person from future pain and/or suffering.

Active and Passive Euthanasia

The evolution of the term *euthanasia* has further bifurcated to include active and passive euthanasia. The term *active euthanasia* has been given to those actions that are intended to end the life of a person who is or will suffer greatly and has no chance of recovery. Administration of a lethal injection of morphine or other similar drug is a clear example of active euthanasia. *Passive euthanasia* refers to the withholding of treatment or other actions that may prolong life. Not treating pneumonia or other opportunistic infections and allowing the person to die is an example of passive euthanasia. Today, acts of passive euthanasia are most commonly referred to as what they are, either withholding or withdrawing treatment or life supports.

Assisted Suicide

Assisted suicide, physician-assisted suicide, and medicide are all similar to but differ from suicide in that they involve the actions of another person and not just the person desiring to die. A person who commits suicide does so based on his or her own intentions and actions. All of these assisted forms of suicide require the active participation of another individual in the desired outcome. If someone has the desire and intent to end his or her life, then the difference between suicide and assisted suicide may seem to some like semantics; however, there is an ongoing open and heated debate over how important these differences are.

In 1988 there was an unsuccessful attempt in California to bring the issue to the ballot. In 1991 voters in Washington State defeated a proposal to legalize euthanasia. In November 1994, Oregon voters passed the Oregon Death with Dignity Act by a margin of 51 percent to 49 percent. In November 1997, voters retained the act by a margin of 60 percent to 40 percent.

The Oregon Death with Dignity Act allows terminally ill Oregon residents to obtain from their physician self-administer lethal doses of prescription medication. However, the Death with Dignity Act prohibits euthanasia, where the physician or other person directly administers a medication intended to end another person's life. According to the act, when an individual self-administers a lethal dose of prescribed medication ending his or her life in accordance with the law, the action does not constitute suicide.

Rather than quell the controversy, legal decisions such as Oregon's Death with Dignity Act appear to further fuel the debate over which end-of-life decisions and related acts are ethical and moral and which are not. Those working with the terminally ill and their families will at some time become involved in the controversy. What caregivers will need is a method of approaching the controversy that provides grounding and assistance in justifying moral/ethical decisions that has room for and includes the preferences of the terminally ill and dying.

Ethical Principles

Beauchamp and Childress (1979, 1983, 1989, 1994) propose an approach to ethical decision making that directs attention to general ethical principles (respect for autonomy, beneficence, nonmaleficence, and justice) and argues that these principles represent a common morality shared by members of society. They assert that these ethical principles are rooted in common-sense morality and have as their structure a set of prima facie obligations. These ethical principles can be seen as an attempt to condense higher-level abstract ethical reasoning, the result being a simpler paradigm that may be used for making ethical judgments. The ethical principles central to the issues surrounding end-of-life decisions are beneficence (act to assist and/or benefit others) and nonmaleficence (refrain from causing harm). Respect for autonomy is frequently cited as a concomitant principle and advocates for patient preferences.

Respect for Autonomy. Individual autonomy or the right to self-determination is probably the most cherished right individuals living in a free democratic system possess. Self-determination allows each individual to live and possibly die in accordance with his or her perception of the good life. In doing so s/he assumes responsibility for the person s/he will become. The ethical principle of respect for autonomy recognizes the human capacity for self-determination and dictates that the autonomy of persons ought to be respected. However, the concept of capacity for self-determination carries with it several minimal requirements. First, to be autonomous, an individual must be free from undue influence (e.g., strong desire including fear, ignorance, or other limiting factors). As an example, when an individual's interpersonal relations are the result of threat, fear, or unrelenting coercion or manipulation by others, then the individual has little or no capacity for autonomy (Benn, 1988; Haworth, 1986). Autonomy also requires that the individual have an adequate range of options and be informed of them and any consequences associated with them. Again, coercion, manipulation, and the lack of information may limit options. Options may also be limited by the social and physical environment (Raz, 1986). Finally, autonomy also requires the capacity for rational decision making (Childress, 1990; Dworkin, 1988) which bears with it its own minimal assertions.

Beneficence. Beneficence by definition is the act of doing good; active kindness. The focus here is on promoting good for others, which is seen as a professional duty. Issues involving the principle beneficence can prove to be a slippery slope when the question to be answered is, "In whose best interest?" Good for others is often viewed by practitioners as the patient's good in a given situation, but again this view is too narrow. Value conflicts can arise when one is faced with respecting the autonomy of an individual and beneficence toward another person or group. To compound this problem, one need only refer to Burt's (1979) brilliant and equally disturbing psychoanalytic interpretation of a burn patient's adamant refusal to be treated and request to die. Burt acknowledged the validity of the principle of autonomy as well as the sincerity of the patient's request to die. He enlarged the understanding of the case by attempting to place the patient's response in an emotional context. Burt suggests that perhaps the patient's refusal was less an unambiguous thrust of freedom than a plea for recognition, acceptance, and love from those around him. Instead of being a statement, perhaps it was a question in disguise.

Clearly, the relevance of the principles of autonomy and beneficence for this case depends on whether one views the refusal as a statement or a question. Whether one agrees or disagrees with Burt's possible interpretations, the implications are clear that the search for moral justifications through the application of principles is far more complicated than it might first appear.

Nonmaleficence. Nonmaleficence means doing no evil, mischief, or harm; causing no harm. This refers to both acts of commission as well as omission. Certain actions may be appropriate for certain situations, yet not for others. The principle of nonmaleficence is a caution that beckons us to be ever vigilant and to develop an awareness and sensitivity to the individuals and situations that we encounter, ferreting out the unique requirements of each encounter. Rather than being a template to provide answers, this principle warns of the dangers of not viewing each encounter as unique and in need of unique answers.

The central question for caregivers surrounding the ethical principle of respect for autonomy is whether an individual's self-determination extends to the time and place of one's own death. Before this question can be answered, the obligations relating to the ethical principles of nonmaleficence and beneficence must be addressed. In addressing these obligations, one also lays the groundwork necessary to [partially] meet the minimal requirements necessary to sanction ethical self-determination. However, in addressing the above-noted obligations, obvious conflicts exist. For example, the act of euthanasia may be seen as producing two outcomes: one beneficial (alleviating pain and/or suffering) and the other harmful (causing death). How, then, is one to decide what is morally/ethically correct?

Obligations of beneficence and nonmaleficence are central to bioethics and end-of-life decision making. Because life does not typically provide opportunities to produce benefits or eliminate harms without creating unavoidable risk or bad consequence, a principle weighing and balancing the good of an action against the costs and possible harms is needed. End-of-life decision making needs a way to balance the preservation of life and the desire to die peacefully with dignity. Before pursuing a mechanism through which to achieve this balance, the following cases provide some concrete examples of the problem.

Case Examples of End-of-Life Controversies

It is impossible to determine what will benefit a patient without presupposing some quality of life standard and some conception of the life the patient will live after the intervention. Should medical intervention be construed as obligatory, or as optional? How should we decide, and under what circumstances? To aid in the discussion, the following cases are provided.

Following a party on the night of April 14, 1975, a 21-year-old woman named Karen Ann Quinlan entered a coma from which she would never recover. At some time during the party Karen Ann stopped breathing. A friend applied mouth-to-mouth resuscitation while another called for the police and she was transported to the hospital. The diagnosis of drug-induced coma was later made after valium and quinine were found in her blood. This diagnosis was later disputed and is still to be resolved. Regardless of the cause, Karen Ann suffered severe and irreversible brain damage as the result of oxygen deprivation. In a "chronic vegetative state," she was maintained on life support (respirator and artificial feedings). After several months in this state, her weight had dropped to 60 pounds and she had assumed a permanent fetal position.

Her parents, who were deeply religious, maintained hope for nearly six months before deciding on moral/religious grounds that extraordinary means should not be used to prolong Karen Ann's life, and sought to have her taken off the respirator. Despite the doctors' judgment that Karen Ann no longer had any cognitive function and that there was no hope for recovery, they [the doctors] refused. The doctors were not sure of the moral implications of such action and were further concerned about the possibility of malpractice charges owing to the lack of clear legal precedence in such situations at that time.

Her parents sought relief from the court, arguing that freedom of religion should ultimately allow the removal of the life support system. Initially the court ruled against the Quinlans, but on appeal the New Jersey Supreme Court agreed that the respirator could be removed and Karen Ann allowed to die. This was the first time a court ruled that life support could be discontinued. Fourteen months after lapsing into a coma, the respirator was disconnected; however, Karen Ann was able to breathe without assistance. Removal of her nasogastric tube, which allowed nutrition and hydration as well as antibiotics to

be administered, was not considered an option. Karen Ann Quinlan lay comatose in a fetal position for more than 10 years without ever regaining consciousness until she died in June of 1985 of pneumonia (In re Quinlan, 1976).

In January 1983, Nancy Cruzan was severely injured in an automobile
accident. When paramedics arrived on the scene she was not breathing and
had no heartbeat. Paramedics were able to revive both her respiratory and cardiac functions and she was taken unconscious to the hospital, where she
remained in a coma. Respiration and circulation were spontaneous and it was
not necessary to use a respirator; however, she required feeding through a sur-
gically implanted gastrostomy tube. Rehabilitation was attempted, but Nancy
failed to respond; and, after a number of years, it was clear that she, like Karen
Ann Quinlan, would not recover and would continue in a persistent vegetative state. Her parents requested that she not be kept alive by extraordinary
means and that the gastrostomy tube that kept her alive be removed. The hospital objected, and the court was asked to intervene. A state court argued that
Nancy Cruzan was not in a terminally ill condition, and that unless there was
clear and convincing evidence that she had authorized the termination of
treatment, the state could require the continued use of life-sustaining treatment, which it did. The argument reached the Supreme Court and ultimately
returned to the state court, where this time the request was not impeded. The
tube feedings were stopped and Nancy Cruzan died on December 26, 1990
(*Cruzan* v. *Director, Missouri Department of Health,* 1990).

A final case to consider is one that was reported in the *Journal of the American Medical Association,* 1988, entitled, "Its Over, Debbie." The article was
reported as personal experience; however, no author name was attributed to
it. The following is a synopsis of the brief story:

A young resident in gynecology was on duty when called in the middle of
the night to a gynecologic-oncology (cancer) unit. The patient was a 20-year-
old woman dying of ovarian cancer. An attempt had been made to sedate her
using an alcohol drip, but this had resulted in unrelenting vomiting.

What the resident observed upon entering the room was a patient who
appeared much older than her stated age, who, despite receiving nasal oxygen,
was breathing with great difficulty and experiencing severe air hunger. The
article noted that the patient had not eaten or slept in two days and had not
responded to chemotherapy. The resident viewed this situation as cruel and
unnecessary and was heard to say, "Let's get this over with."

Returning to the nurses' station, the resident decided to give the patient
rest and requested that the nurse prepare morphine sulfate for intravenous
administration, enough to do the job. Returning to the patient's room, he told
the two women there that he was going to give Debbie something that
would let her rest and to say good-bye. Immediately following the intravenous
injection, the patient's breathing slowed, her eyes closed, her distress abated,
and she slept.

The resident waited for the next inevitable effect of depression of respiratory function to occur. Within four minutes breathing slowed further and
then ceased. "It's over, Debbie."

This brief, anonymous report raised a furor among readers as well as the public as the media quickly picked it up. The response was divided, though critical reactions dominated.

As these cases demonstrate, end-of-life decisions compel us to address questions to which there are no easy or simple answers. We are required to confront the most basic of human concerns: our own mortality and that of our loved ones. The question begging an answer in end-of-life decision making is how one responds to the moral obligation to act to benefit others while also responding to the moral obligation not to inflict intentional harm. This section will explore the principle of double effect and virtue ethics as a complementary mechanism helpful in addressing these questions.

Current issues central to end-of-life decisions include, but are not limited to, euthanasia and life-sustaining treatment. In this section, euthanasia will refer to aid in dying given by another in either an active (e.g., administration of a lethal drug) or passive manner (e.g., withholding life-sustaining treatment). Life-sustaining treatment refers to any medical means, whether mechanical or artificial (including providing hydration and nutrition), to sustain, restore, or replace vital function which, when applied, would serve to prolong life and thus the process of dying. Predicated here is the belief that we can and should protect individuals against some types of harm; however, we can and should avoid causing harm to them or unnecessarily prolonging their suffering.

Recall that the principle of nonmaleficence declares that there is an obligation not to inflict harm intentionally. It is a widely accepted moral principle that it is wrong to kill the innocent. Yet this appears precisely what we seek justification to do when questions of euthanasia, administration of dangerous amounts of analgesics to the terminally ill, and other similar acts arise. Former Surgeon General of the United States C. Everett Koop condemns the practice of omitting medically administered nutrition and hydration as intentional acts of killing that amount to active euthanasia because they cause a preventable death (Koop & Grant, 1986).

The principle prohibiting acts resulting in the killing of innocent people are actually implausible because they make no allowances for accidents and/or unintended killings. As an example, is there a difference between cases in which medical personnel intend patients to die (euthanasia) and those in which they merely acknowledge the foreseen consequence of palliative treatment? Active euthanasia, as in the case of Debbie, appears to violate the principle of nonmaleficence. However, in cases like Karen Ann Quinlan and Nancy Cruzan, there is the moral obligation of beneficence that can be interpreted as intentional avoidance of interventions or life-sustaining treatments so that disease or injury causes a natural death.

The principle of beneficence refers to a moral obligation to act for the benefit of others. Beneficence can be viewed as an inclusive principle involving elements of restraining from inflicting harm and preventing or removing evil (nonmaleficence), as well as an obligation to actively promote good (Frankena, 1973). Frankena divides the principle of beneficence into four general obligations: (1) one ought not to inflict evil or harm, (2) one ought to prevent evil or harm, (3) one ought to remove evil or harm, and (4) one ought to do or promote good. He utilizes this arrangement so that in situations of moral conflict, other things being equal, the first element takes moral precedence over the second, the second over the third, and the third over the fourth. (p. 47)

Beauchamp and Childress (1994) adopted Frankena's elements but reclassified them according to two distinct principles without proposing a hierarchical structure. Nonmaleficence is seen as the obligation not to inflict harm. Beneficence is the obligation to prevent harm, to remove harm or evil, and to promote good.

PRINCIPLE OF DOUBLE EFFECT

Regardless of whether one looks at these principles as bifurcated, problems remain. In certain situations (where other things are not equal), obligations of beneficence are more stringent than obligations of nonmaleficence; however, in other situations the obligations of nonmaleficence are more stringent than the obligations of beneficence. Add to this confusing scenario the fact that a single action might bring about two effects, one good, and the other harmful. Now the two principles (beneficence and nonmaleficence) are in conflict with each other, and a right course of action might be unclear. In circumstances where an agent's action has two consequences, one beneficial and the other harmful, the principle of double effect may be utilized to specify the conditions of the principles of nonmaleficence and beneficence.

As an example, consider a terminally ill patient experiencing intense pain and suffering who asks to be euthanized. If the patient is euthanized to end his or her pain and suffering, the agent's intent is to kill the patient, a highly questionable act at best, even if it is to relieve the pain and suffering. However, a large dosage of a strong analgesic medication could be provided to alleviate the pain and subsequent suffering; but as a consequence, the patient may die prematurely because of complications associated with the administration of the medication. This action clearly has two effects: one good, the other bad. If the potent palliative medication is not administered or administered at a reduced dosage, the patient will experience harm by continuing to experience pain and suffering; however, if the medication is given in adequate dosage, the patient's death may be hastened. According to the principle of double effect, actions and/or omissions are permissible only when their gravely bad effects are allowed for a good reason. Therefore, under the principle of double effect, the potent palliative medication, if given, must be intended to alleviate the patient's pain and suffering but not be (directly) intended to hasten death. If the intent of the act is beneficent, to alleviate the patient's pain, and no intention of a lethal effect exists, then giving the medication is not prohibited by the principle of do no harm (nonmaleficence).

Consider, in the cases of Quinlan and Cruzan, a similar argument for the cessation of nutrition and hydration. In these cases, the tube feedings resulted in improved nutritional and fluid levels, but the patients did not improve, as evidenced by their continued vegetative states. The burdens associated with continued tube feedings—in this case maintenance of a persistent vegetative state—potentially outweigh their benefits. Few would argue that one should be denied the right to die; however, in these cases the question is whether it is morally right to withhold treatment and allow the patient to die.

Functions and Conditions

The principle of double effect allows for the justification of an act or omission with two effects—one right and one wrong—when four conditions are met. They address the object of activity or nature of act, the intention, material cause or the distinction between means and effects, and proportionality between the good effect and the bad effect (Boyle, 1980, 1991; McCormick, 1981). The conditions are as follows:

1. *An act (whether an active intervention or an omission) must be good or morally neutral; it cannot be intrinsically wrong.* This condition states that an act is immoral if it is of a type that is wrong regardless of the (good) outcome or desired effect.

2. *The intent of the agent is the good effect.* The bad effect, though foreseen, is tolerated or permitted but must not be intended. This condition views as pivotal the intent of the moral agent.

3. *The bad effect cannot be the means to the right effect.* The bad effect must not be pursued in order to bring about the good. In the previous example, the patient's death cannot be directly sought as a means to relieve pain and suffering. This condition specifies circumstances in which it is not plausible to deny that a bad effect is intended. A good effect cannot be brought about by intentionally using a bad effect. The end does not justify the means.

4. *The good effect must outweigh the bad effect.* The bad effect is permitted only if a proportionate reason is present that compensates for permitting the foreseen bad effect. If the bad effects of an act are much greater than the good effects, the act is illicit.

Technically, the conditions function as a sort of checklist; if the case meets all of the conditions, the action is justified under the principle of double effect. Using the example of the suffering patient, the first condition (object of activity) rules out giving a lethal injection because the result of such an act would be the direct killing of an innocent person and intrinsically wrong. Similarly, it is intrinsically wrong to prolong continued suffering in situations where death is the inevitable outcome. Here it is the object of the activity and not the activity itself that is under scrutiny. In the cases of Quinlan and Cruzan, to prolong their lives artificially in persistent vegetative states is objectively wrong.

The second condition (intention) prohibits using potent analgesics as an excuse for killing people. However, an effective dose needed to alleviate the patient's pain might endanger the person's life, and is permissible as long as death is not actively intended. In the cases of Quinlan and Cruzan, there is a conceptual difference between killing and allowing to die. One can act nonmaleficently in allowing to die, but maleficently in killing or even in not allowing to die. Unless the maintenance of biological life devoid of the essential quality of human relationships is of benefit to the patient, then one acts nonmaleficently in allowing death to occur. Often it is seen as being more satisfactory conceptually to discuss optional versus obligatory treatments; however, a change of words does not change the issue at hand. In certain situations or under certain conditions, failing to provide treatment (i.e., artificially providing nutrition and hydration) and allowing death to occur is not the same as intentionally killing.

The third condition (material cause) forbids the use of a lethal dose of medication as a means of alleviating the patient's pain. The right effect, pain relief, is not caused by the patient's death; rather it is brought about by the judicious use of analgesic medication. The right effect, benefit to the patient, is not always brought about by avoiding or prolonging death, but rather, by allowing it to occur.

The final condition (proportionate reason) allows for more and stronger dosages of the analgesic to the extent that the pain is intolerable and the hope of recovery negligible. Proportionate reason also asks, under what conditions, if any, is it permissible to forgo treatment so that the patient dies?

Boyle (1980; 1991) reduced the conditions to two (intention and proportionality). He further acknowledged that it is not always clear whether the function of the double effect is to distinguish more culpable agents from less culpable ones, or to distinguish permissible acts from impermissible acts. He added that if the latter is true, then the function of the principle of double effect is either to provide a procedure to be used in decision making or as a criterion of wrongdoing for moral judgments to be used in determining wrongful acts. Boyle notes that double effect has, at times, been employed to address both questions. Regardless of the function of the principle of double effect, an account of intentional actions and intended (not merely foreseen) effects of action that properly distinguishes them from nonintentional (foreseeable causing or allowed) actions and unintended side effects is needed (Beauchamp & Childress, 1994).

Intentional and Nonintentional Effect

An agent who knowingly and voluntarily acts to bring about an effect does so intentionally. An intended effect may, however, not be desired, and may not be the goal of the action. In the case of the patient experiencing extreme pain and suffering, the agent administers an analgesic that will both alleviate the pain but also hasten death. The desire is only to alleviate the patient's pain, but this cannot be done without also hastening death. Although the agent does not desire to hasten the patient's death, it would be conceptually mistaken to say that he or she unintentionally hastened the patient's death.

No moral agent desires a bad effect for its own sake, and no moral agent would tolerate a bad effect if avoiding it were morally preferable. As the principle of double effect implies, a bad effect might be accepted under conditions where it cannot be eliminated without also losing the good effect.

Bratman (1987) sheds some light on this controversy over intentional and nonintentional effect. According to Bratman, intentional action requires a plan or representation of the means and ends proposed for the execution of an action. An intentional action therefore requires the agent to conceive of what effect is desired and how it is to be planned and executed. Accepting Bratman's differentiation between what is an intentional and nonintentional effect, the question of proportionality remains to be addressed.

Proportionate Reason

A point of diminishing returns occurs where the immediate bad effect of a given action is overwhelmingly large by comparison with the immediate good effect, and it no longer makes sense to say that it is incidental, not directly intended, but nonetheless permitted. Examples include allowing a terminally ill patient to continue to experience intense pain for fear of hastening death as a side effect of effective medication administration, and tube feedings that result in improved nutrition and fluid levels but do not benefit the patient who remains in an irreversible vegetative state. In such circumstances, common sense repudiates the interpretation of what is happening. Merely saying that one does not intend this directly will not change the actual state of affairs. This brings up the question, "Would a moral agent in actual practice not avoid the direct intention of bad effects?" Phrased another way, is it psychologically and honestly possible to avoid the direct bad effect when an action is taken as a last resort?

Proportionate reason has as a focus the justification of the claim that the distinction between what is intended and what is incidental or nonintentional can bear the weight that the principle of double effect assigns it. This distinction questions whether there are actions and effects that are wrong in all circumstances, or whether there are actions and effects that can be intended and justified by an appeal to the needs of others.

These conditions, intention and proportionality, may be seen as necessary, but not sufficient for the adoption of a course of action as morally right. A course of action allowed under the above conditions may still be prohibited for other reasons (e.g., it violates the individual's autonomy). Without abandoning the emphasis on intention and proportionality or neglecting the focus on the way actions display an agent's motives and character, focus should include the motivational structure and good character of the agent as a preeminent part. A morally good person with the right configuration of motivation and moral character is more likely than others to understand what should be done based on principles as well as moral ideals.

VIRTUE ETHICS

Virtue-based moral theory provides an additional focus for moral justification and proportionate reason. Finnis (1991), in arguing for the importance of intentions, emphasized the reflective character of action, whereby acting shapes not only the world but also the character of the agents. Garcia (1993) suggested that accounts of moral justification turn inward, seeking the source of an action's morality or immorality not in its total effect, but in the quality of the sensitivities, decisions, and plans it embodies and how it fits or deforms the human relationship between caregiver and patient. In effect, these proposals focusing on the virtue and character of the actor serve as a complement and balance the principle of double effect.

There have been those who challenge the assumption that ethics should be focused primarily on decisions and principles (Meara, Schmidt, & Day, 1996; Braybrooke, 1991; Spohn, 1992; Oakley, 1996; Keenan, 1992). They argue that it is a mistake to separate questions of the rightness or goodness of an action from the character of the agent performing the action. A virtuous person is predisposed by character to be guided by relevant principles and rules designed to bring about what is judged to be morally right but also to be generous, caring, compassionate, sympathetic, and fair, and the one we hold up as a moral model.

Health care has at its core the doctor– or caregiver–patient relationship. The trust, care, and compassion that are essential to the therapeutic relationship are virtues intrinsic to health care. Pellegrino (1985) wrote that physicians must have a capacity for compassion to feel something of their patients' experience of their illness and what is worthwhile to them. He continued:

> Not every virtue is required in every decision. What we expect of the virtuous physician is that he will exhibit them when they are required and that he will be so habitually disposed to do so that we can depend on it. He will place the good of the patient above his own and seek that good unless its pursuit imposes an injustice upon him, or his family, or requires a violation of his own conscience. (p. 246)

Veatch (1985) argued that virtue theory was not suited to medicine. He stated that modern medicine must be practiced as "stranger medicine," that is:

> Medicine that is practiced among people who are essentially strangers. It would include medicine that is practiced on an emergency basis in emergency rooms in large cities. It would also include care delivered in a clinic setting or in an HMO that does not have physician continuity, most medicine in student health services, VA hospitals, care from consulting specialists, and the medicine in the military as well as care that is delivered by private practice general practitioners to patients who are mobile enough not to establish long-term relationships with their physicians. (p. 338)

Veatch goes on to argue that "there is no reasonable basis for assuming that the stranger with whom one is randomly paired in the emergency room will hold the same theory of virtue as one's self" (p. 339).

Veatch's argument that doctor– or caregiver–patient relationships are best characterized by principles alone without consideration of virtues suggests that the principles themselves justify moral solutions. Using principles in this way vests the principle with unwarranted authority while degrading the agent's role to that of a messenger. Recall that meeting the conditions of the double effect is necessary but not sufficient for the adoption of a course of action as morally right. Aristotle, in his classic work, *Nicomachean Ethics,* provides the second requisite for the adoption of a course of action that is morally right:

> Acts are called just and self-controlled when they are the kinds of acts which a just and self-controlled man would perform; but the just and self-controlled man is not he who performs these acts, but he who also performs them in the way that the just and self-controlled men do (p. 1105).

Principles guide us; however, as Aristotle (1962) suggests, we need to assess a situation and formulate an appropriate response. The assessment and response flow from character as much as from principles.

Virtue ethics is about subjective qualities that lead an individual to a given choice and action that addresses the question, "Whom shall I be?" Keenan (1992) succinctly points out that in addressing this question one must determine whether it is the act or the one acting that ultimately determines the answer. If the act the agent performs is the determining factor, then the act is under appraisal and the question should be: What acts are permissible and what are prohibited? Under conditions where an action has two effects, one good and one bad, the principle of double effect serves to answer the above question. However, this answer is incomplete. Consideration must be given to the agent performing the action. This involves elements of virtue ethics.

Contemporary virtue ethics, in addressing both the action and the agent, seeks to avoid fitting moral experience into preestablished rules (Thomas, 1996; Teehan, 1995; Keenan, 1992; Braybrook, 1991). Virtue ethics' prescription for right action entails the agent asking, "What action will make me a better person now and in the future?" Intrinsic to this orientation is the assumption that one becomes the agent of the act one performs; and therefore, self-understanding is necessary for determining the right action (Punzo, 1996; Thomas, 1996; Keenan, 1992; Braybrook, 1991).

PRINCIPLES AND VIRTUES

Frankena (1973) echoed Aristotle when he wrote that principles without traits (virtues) are impotent and traits without principles are blind. However, he also said that virtues do not provide concrete directives that point the way for right conduct, but rather, stimulate agents with good motivations. Frankena's ideas give rise to the consideration of virtue and principle ethics (principle of double effect) as potentially compatible systems.

Principle ethics encompass five prima facie duties: nonmaleficence, beneficence, fidelity, justice, and autonomy (Beauchamp & Childress, 1994; Bersoff & Koeppl, 1993). The principle of double effect may be seen as a method of establishing a set of prima facie obligations in situations where there is more than one effect associated with a given action. In moral reasoning, this appeal to applying principles (flexibly) to concrete situations provides an array of potential choices that can be applied in relation to dictates or specifics of the dilemma. The *principle of double effect* typically focuses on acts or choices, and the question, "What shall I be?" is answered through the application of what are taken to be objective, rational standards. *Virtue* takes a slightly different perspective, emphasizing the agent who is acting, and asks, "Whom shall I be?" This question is answered through the formation of internal qualities, traits, and/or mature habits. This union gives potency to virtues and sight to potentially blind principles.

The community has been cited as being of primary importance in the understanding of virtues (MacIntyre, 1981; Hauerwas, 1985). The community determines how the principles of nonmaleficence, beneficence, fidelity, justice, and autonomy are defined. However, too much reliance on tradition and community definitions can create ethnocentric and potentially immoral decisions. The poor, the very young, the elderly, the disabled, and minorities are all potentially at risk from undue pressures involving end-of-life decisions.

Some claim that toleration of certain actions or policies as ethically allowable will lead to unwanted consequences and this is a justifiable point of consideration. The argument for tolerance is persuasive only if the act proposed does not violate any ethical principle and, apart from the unintended consequence, would be ethically acceptable. Arguments against such tolerance are often based on the premise that acceptance of such tolerance is contagious because people are psychologically inclined to move to ever-wider interpretations. Serious abuses are not seen as occurring immediately, but as growing increasingly over time. What begins with caution and severe restrictions can be revised and expanded to include unjustified killing. The ultimate success or failure of this argument depends on the possible progressive erosion of moral restraints. Meara, Schmidt, and Day (1996) note that the inclusion of virtue ethics allows professionals to keep norms flexible and not relative to societal or community whims.

Braybrooke (1991) proposed an interesting thesis: no rules without virtues and no virtues without rules. Ethics, according to Braybrooke, is a bifurcating process where virtues and rules are closely related branches originating from one trunk. He noted that the existence of any rule implied the prior existence of some virtue that the rule exemplifies. In a similar manner, Braybrooke noted that *epieikeia,* the virtue of adjusting actions to the circumstance, could not be manifested without rules to adjust to. The rules, although aimed at promoting the common good, are seen as inevitably incomplete in their formulation and require the special virtue of adjusting rules to circumstances.

We can and should protect others from harm as well as avoid causing harm to them. However, there exists conceptual and moral uncertainty surrounding the distinction between the obligation to avoid harm to others and the obligation to benefit them. The principle of double effect and virtue ethics have different emphases, but they are complementary and mutually reinforcing. This complementarity has a significant place in the process of end-of-life decision making.

The gestalt principle of figure and ground is most applicable in addressing how indissolubly the principle of double effect and virtues are entwined in addressing end-of-life decisions. Figure is what occupies the center of the caregiver's attentive awareness; ground is the part of the perceptual field that is not figure and does not occupy attentive awareness. Taken together, figure and ground constitutes a gestalt. The conditions of the double effect are necessary but not always sufficient conditions for the adoption of a morally correct course of action. Embedded in the uniqueness of each situation are also the virtues from which the principles in question are spawned. So in cases where caregivers are confronted with a course of action that has two effects, one good and the other bad, should decisions regarding the moral course of action be made using the principle of double effect or virtue ethics? Or should the decision not be made using both—either one capable of being figure on the other's ground?

QUESTIONS FOR THOUGHT
AND REFLECTION

1. How do you decide whether an action is ethical? Is it all relative, or are there any guiding principles?

2. How do you decide whether your action is correct when the action has more than one outcome or result?

3. Which of the following ethical principles (respect for autonomy, beneficence, nonmaleficence, and justice) is most important to you? Why?

4. Does a terminally ill (adult) individual have the right to refuse life-saving treatment and in effect decide to end his or her life? What factors influence your answer, and why?

5. How would your answer to the above question change if the patient were a child or an adolescent? Why?

4

⁓◯⁓

Attachment Theory

Implications for Understanding Grief and Loss

Before venturing into and attempting to understand the significance of a loss and the human behavior associated with it, one must have some familiarity with and an understanding of the meaning of attachment. The understanding of relationships, from an attachment perspective, has been strongly influenced by the seminal work on attachment and loss of John Bowlby (1969, 1973, 1980). However, Bowlby may not have been the first attachment theorist. The following quotation suggests that perhaps that credit should go to Charles Darwin.

> It has often been assumed that animals were in the first place rendered social, and that they feel as a consequence uncomfortable when separated from each other, and comfortable whilst together; but it is a more probable view that these sensations were first developed, in order that those animals which would profit by living in society, should be included together, . . . for with those animals which were benefited by living in close association, the individuals which took the greatest pleasure in society would best escape various dangers; whilst those that cared least for their comrades and lived solitary would perish in greater numbers (Darwin, 1871/1981, p. 80).

One can easily see the parallel between Darwin's focus on "society" and Bowlby's significant others in an individual's life. Another parallel may be seen in Darwin's concept of "comrades" and Bowlby's attachment figures.

Ironically, Darwin, in his adult life, suffered from a perplexing set of ailments (physical and psychological) that may have been triggered by stressful psychological events. Although it is impossible to ascertain the true etiology of Darwin's illnesses, possibilities include the loss of his mother when he was 8 years old. Bowlby was an ardent admirer of Darwin and ultimately one of his biographers. In his biography of Darwin (Bowlby, 1990), he attributed Darwin's illnesses to suppressed grief following his mother's death. He [Bowlby] believed that the suppression of grief inhibits a natural sequence of painful emotional reactions that, unless allowed to progress naturally, can lead to psychological and physical illnesses.

Bowlby went on to explore the process by which bonds of affection are formed and broken, and developed a grand theory of personality development across the lifespan—attachment theory. Although his ideas about loss changed and developed, he viewed unresolved and suppressed grief as important pathogenic forces and viewed grief itself as a natural part of the human pre-disposition that discourages prolonged separation between individuals and their primary attachment figures.

THE NATURE AND FUNCTION
OF ATTACHMENT BEHAVIOR

Bowlby (1973) defined attachment behavior as ". . . any form of behavior that results in a person attaining or retaining proximity to some other differ-entiated and preferred individual, usually conceived as stronger and/or wiser." (p. 292) Infants of many species, including humans, require protection and care in order to survive. Infants have developed physical adaptations (sucking) and behavioral adaptations (crying) to attract the attention of potential care-givers and elicit protective and/or caring responses. In addition to these basic adaptations, Bowlby posited the infant possesses a motivational system (attach-ment system) designed by natural selection to maintain proximity between infants and their caregivers. The goal of the attachment system is what Stroufe and Waters (1977) called *felt security*. This occurs when the caregiver or attach-ment figure(s) is judged to be sufficiently close and accessible. During this period the infant is more likely to explore the environment and engage in playful interactions. However, when the attachment figure(s) are judged to be absent or inaccessible, the infant experiences anxiety and exuberantly protests, attempting to reestablish contact.

According to Bowlby (1969, 1982), these protests promote the infant's survival in that they help to ensure proximity between the infant and the attachment figure. The anxiety motivates the infant to continue to seek the missing attachment figure until all efforts have been exhausted. Viewed from this perspective, many of the perplexing reactions to separation and loss (e.g., continued searching, protest, even when the attachment figure is objectively lost) emerge as reasonable. Bowlby (1973) hypothesized that attachment behavior forms an organized behavioral system (e.g., smiling, crying) that serves the function of maintaining proximity to the attachment figure. Examples of attachment behaviors are looking to see if the other person is there, greeting, following, clinging, crying, and calling. These behaviors begin in infancy and childhood and are displayed in various forms through the life cycle. They serve to form the development of attachments with others. Feedback in this system provides the mechanism by which the attachment behaviors are modified. When the system is stressed, the individual may display more attachment behaviors, which serve to elicit a comforting response by the attachment figure. High levels of emotion (such as anger, anxiety, agitation, or sadness) may result from threats to the attachment bond. Early experiences with attachment affect the patterns used from then on. The attachment system was seen by Bowlby as one of several interrelated behavioral systems (e.g., exploring, caregiving, and sexual mating) designed to ensure survival. These behavioral systems were described by Bowlby as homeostatic control systems that maintain a relatively steady state between individuals and their environment.

Although Bowlby defined attachment behaviors in terms of the goals of proximity maintenance, other interrelated functions of attachment have been identified. The attachment figure, as we have seen, serves as a secure base from which the infant may explore and master the environment. On one hand, in situations where the attachment figure is present in reasonable proximity and no apparent threat exists, the infant is likely to engage in exploration as opposed to attachment behavior. On the other hand, attachment behaviors are likely to be exhibited when the infant perceives a threat in the immediate environment.

Bowlby regarded the process making up the attachment system to be a universal part of human nature. He went on to complement this normative view of attachment behavior by addressing the issues of individual differences.

Individual Differences in Attachment

Issues of individual differences can be seen in the following propositions of attachment theory:

1. When an individual is confident that the attachment figure is available whenever he or she desires it, that person is much less prone to either intense or chronic fear than an individual who for any reason has no such confidence.

2. Confidence in the availability of the attachment figure or lack of such confidence is built up slowly during the years of immaturity (infancy, childhood, and adolescence); whatever expectations are developed during those years tend to persist relatively unchanged throughout the rest of life.

3. The varied expectations of the accessibility and responsiveness of the attachment figure that individuals develop during the years of immaturity are tolerably accurate reflections of the experiences those individuals have actually had. (Bowlby, 1973, p. 235)

As one can clearly see, the individual's expectations of the attachment figure are paramount. Expectations about the availability and responsiveness of attachment figures are thought to be integrated into the individual's paradigm of attachment. These paradigms reflect memories, perceptions, and beliefs that develop from the individual's early experiences of the attachment figure and caregiving. They are carried over into new relationships where they play a major role in perception and related behavioral responses.

Ainsworth, Blehar, Waters, and Wall (1978) conducted the first detailed studies of individual differences in attachment theory. Ainsworth et al. conducted naturalistic observations of mother–infant interactions. On the basis of these observations they suggested three patterns of attachment: secure, anxious-ambivalent, and avoidant. Each attachment pattern reflects a different contingency strategy designed to solve adaptive problems posed by different rearing environments.

Mothers of securely attached infants are available and responsive to the needs and signs of their infants (Ainsworth et al., 1978, Grossmann, Grossman, Spangler, Suess, & Unzner, 1985). They are highly attuned to signs that their infants are distressed (Crockenberg, 1981); provide moderate and appropriate levels of stimulation (Belsky, Rovine, & Taylor, 1984); are synchronous in interactions with their infant (Isabella & Belsky, 1990; Isabella, Belsky, & von Eye, 1989), and behave in a warm, involved, and consistent manner (Bates, Maslin, & Frankel, 1985). In large part because their attachment figures respond to them in a caring and consistent manner, securely attached infants need not worry about the availability and responsiveness of their caregivers. Therefore, they are free to attend and focus on issues other than attachment.

Anxious-ambivalent infants were seen to have attachment figures who behave in an inconsistent manner. Caregivers of anxious-ambivalent infants tended to respond erratically to the needs and signals of their infants, often appearing underinvolved as parents (Belsky et al., 1984; Isabella et al., 1989; Lewis & Feiring, 1989; Smith & Pederson, 1988). These children exhibited a demanding nature, coupled with vehement protests, which may reflect a strategy designed to obtain, retain, and improve the amount and quality of responsiveness from habitually inattentive caregivers (Cassidy & Berlin, 1994; Main & Solomon, 1986).

Avoidant infants have attachment figures who are consistently cold and rejecting (Ainsworth et al., 1978). Mothers of avoidant infants are less responsive to their infants' distress (Crockenberg, 1981), use overstimulating styles of interaction (Belsky et al., 1984), and have a disdain for close body contact (Ainsworth et al., 1978). Main (1981) theorized that avoidant behavior may allow the infant to maintain reasonably close proximity to belligerent or overwhelmed caregivers without driving them away.

Main and Hesse (1990) have identified a fourth attachment pattern, disorganized/disoriented. This group tends to show contradictory behaviors, confusion, or apprehension in response to the approaching attachment figure. This pattern is witnessed when attachment figures are highly abusive, depressed, or emotionally disturbed (Crittenden, 1988, Main & Hesse, 1990).

Patterns of attachment behavior exist as products of the establishment or absence of a secure base accessible to the individual in times of need or perceived threat. The establishment of a security base influences how the individual as an infant, child, adolescent, and adult relates to others and to the world. A secure child, as we have seen, will venture out and explore the environment, knowing that the caregiver will be accessible upon return. Likewise, autonomy-seeking behavior in adolescence may be viewed as part of the exploration process (Allen, Kuperminc, & Moore, 1997). Without such exploration, accomplishing the tasks of social development in adolescence and young adulthood such as long-term relationships and productive vocational careers may be difficult, if not impossible. Allen, Hauser, Bell, and O'Conner (1994) suggest that the presence of adolescent autonomy-seeking behavior tends to be highly correlated with evidence of an underlying positive relationship with parents. As independence increases, so, too, will the emotional distance between parent and child as the nature of the attachment relationship is reworked. This reworking is critical to resolving difficulties in the relationship with parental attachment figures and allows for the potential development of secure relationships with others and ultimately the possibility of becoming an attachment figure to one's own children.

Attachment and Bereavement

One of Bowlby's most important contributions to the literature was an ethnological perspective on attachment and loss. According to Bowlby (1969, 1982), protest reactions during periods of separation serve to promote the infant's survival by helping to ensure proximity to the caregiver. During the protest phase of separation infants generally react vigorously to their plight. However, the intensity of these reactions eventually wanes if the separation is extended, as in the death of a caregiver. Emotional protests (anxiety, crying, and anger) eventually give way to despair, sadness, and withdrawal. Bowlby viewed this second phase as resulting from the failure of protesting to protect the infant by bringing about the return of the lost attachment figure.

Detachment and a gradual renewal of interest in previous activities and social relationships is the third phase. *Detachment,* as in indifference, is a somewhat misleading term. Bowlby found that reunion with the lost attachment figure can, following a period of reassurance of the individual's permanent return and affection, bring about reactivation of the attachment system and related behaviors (e.g., crying, following, clinging). The apparent detachment, Bowlby thought, was not a wearing away of the attachment bond but, rather, a defensive suppression of attachment responses that have failed for a lengthy period to produce the return of the attachment figure.

Although Bowlby was primarily concerned with infant–caregiver attachment, he viewed adult romantic or pair-bond relationships within the same framework he used to explain infant attachment. Bowlby, along with Parkes and Weiss (1983), observed that adults who are separated from or lose their romantic attachment figures experience a series of reactions similar to those observed in infants who have been separated from or have lost attachment figures. Parkes and Weiss in their book *Recovery from Bereavement,* describe the protest reaction of a woman whose husband died in the hospital from cancer:

> I went over to him. I remember my brother-in-law taking me away from him because he said I kept holding on to him and patting his head. I cried my heart out. But I remember my brother-in-law coming to me and taking me away from him. (Quoted in Parkes & Weiss, 1983, p. 78)

They note that when a loss is prolonged or permanent, the protest phase is often accompanied by a preoccupation with the missing person. An adult often experiences an intense yearning for the lost mate and continues for some time following the loss to be surprised when aspects of their normal routine reawaken a conscious absence of the attachment figure. Parkes and Weiss again use the bereaved woman's experience as an example:

> The hardest thing for me I think is at night. We have a neighbor [who] works the second shift and we hear his pickup truck every night. And my husband always says something like, "When's he going to get his brakes fixed?" And every night I'm sitting here when he comes along, and that's when I really think about my husband because he would always say something, (Quoted in Parkes & Weiss, 1983, p. 87)

Eventually the realization transpires that the loss is permanent and that the partner will not return. When this occurs, despair and disorganization are concomitant factors. Depressive symptoms such as sleep and appetite disturbances, social withdrawal, intense loneliness, and heartfelt sorrow are also common in both adults and children. Weiss (1973) noted that the feelings of loneliness are related specifically to the absence of the attachment figure and cannot be alleviated by the presence of others. Social support from family and friends is comforting, but it does not fill the void left by the loss. This phase can be brief or can last for years. Bereaved individuals generally agree, echoing as in a chorus a remarkably similar statement, "You don't get over it, you just get used to it."

Bowlby's later work (1980) on adult loss identified a new initial phase, that of *numbing.* Research indicated that the bereaved often fail to acknowledge the loss of the attachment figure in the initial stages of grief, presumably because the loss is too painful and overwhelming. Parkes and Weiss (1983) provide an example of this psychological numbing in the response of a woman to the sudden and unexpected death of her husband:

> I didn't believe it. I stayed there for twenty minutes. I rubbed him, I rubbed his face, I patted him, I rubbed his head. I called him, but he didn't answer. And I knew if I called him he would answer me because he's used to my voice. But he didn't answer me. They said he was dead, but his skin was just as warm as mine. (Quoted in Parkes & Weiss, p. 84)

Continued work with adults led Bowlby to change his final phase from detachment to reorganization. This change reflects Bowlby's belief that bereaved individuals do not detach from the lost attachment figure, but rather, they reorganize their relationship to the lost figure so that a continuing bond and adjustment to the existing circumstances are both possible.

Animals as well as humans demonstrate perplexing reactions to separation and loss. For many animals born without the capacity to initially care for themselves, the loss of a primary attachment figure evokes extreme anxiety and protest. Early studies (Seay, Hansen, & Harlow, 1962) on attachment in rhesus macaques separated five-month-old rhesus infants from their mothers for a three-week period. The infants initially responded with excessive signs of protest and agitation, screaming and attempting to break the barriers separating them from their mothers. When these and repeated attempts failed, the infants became lethargic and withdrawn. More recent studies by Plimpton and Rosenblum, (1987) and Reite and Boccia, (1994) provide additional support.

Similar attachment behaviors have also been seen in nonmammalian species. Konrad Lorenz described the perplexing behavior of a greylag goose in response to separation from its mate:

> The first response to the disappearance of the partner consists in the anxious attempts to find him again. The goose moves about restlessly by day and night, flying great distances and visiting places where the partner might be found, uttering all the time the penetrating trisyllabic long-distance call . . . . The searching expeditions are extended further and further and quite often the searcher itself gets lost, or succumbs to an accident . . . . All the objective observable characteristics of the goose's behavior on losing its mate are roughly identical with human grief. (Lorenz, 1963, cited in Parkes, 1972, p. 40)

THE PHASES AND STAGES OF GRIEF

A death loss, according to Bowlby (1980), is a disruption in the attachment bond a person has with a significant other in their environment. As such, the system must reorganize to a different level. He described the process as involving four phases.

Phase I is characterized by emotional numbing and an initial disbelief that the death has actually occurred. This numbing provides the bereaved an opportunity to temporarily suspend the emotional surge of pain that is associated with the loss. This usually lasts from a few hours to a week or more and may be interrupted by outbursts of extreme emotion. Self-protection comes at a high cost of energy mobilization and, if prolonged, the individual may reach a level of exhaustion and display debilitating physical decline and subsequent illness.

Phase II includes yearning and searching. Here the realization of the loss begins to be faced. The numbness begins to wear off. Individuals may be restless, preoccupied with thoughts of the deceased and prone to initially interpret events (phone ringing, door opening) as coming from the deceased person. Energy levels, if not depleted from prolonged periods of numbness, are high. Crying, calling to the person and paying attention to stimuli that suggest the presence of the person are also common. Bereaved individuals may or may not be aware of their search. Anger is common as the grieving person searches for a responsible party and/or experiences frustration from searching without success for the lost person. These attachment behaviors may last months or years and are seen as attempts to regain the object of the attachment relationship.

Phase III is the experience of disorganization and despair. It will become apparent that attachment behaviors that were effective in maintaining the attachment bond while the deceased was alive are no longer working. The reality of the loss is now complete. Withdrawal and isolation are common behaviors, as are the experiences of fatigue and symptoms of depression. Energy levels that were previously high in phase II are now low, and it may take great effort just to get out of bed in the morning. The person begins to wonder if any part of his/her prior life is salvageable. This can create an overwhelming sense of despair. The self without the deceased person must be reevaluated and redefined, and this requires full acceptance of the loss, along with all the disruption and upheaval that it brings.

Phase IV involved a greater or lesser degree of reorganization. Once the bereaved individual has come to a realization that life must go on, various changes may begin to take place. This process does not consist of sudden jumps (ahas!) but rather, is a gradual process. Thoughts of the deceased begin to take a different place in the bereaved person's life. There is a small but growing recognition of the possibility of a new life. Social relationships and responsibilities may also begin to change to accommodate a world without the person who was lost.

It should be understood that grief is fluid, and most people do not begin with stage one and progress in an orderly fashion to completion. Nor is grieving an all-or-none experience. There is a great deal of movement among and within the stages, and the degree of resolution necessary to move on is highly variable. Often one stage is revisited several times as the journey progresses. The journey is more often than not a labyrinth of redundant visits to the various stages and is a normal part of the grieving process.

Bowlby, however, was not the first to attempt to describe the grief process. In 1917, Freud published his classic paper, "Mourning and Melancholia," in which he undertook to define the normal process of grief. He wrote:

> The reaction to the loss of a loved person, or the loss of some abstraction which has taken the place of one, such as one's country, liberty, an ideal, and so on . . . . It is also well worth notice that, although mourning involves grave departures from the normal attitude to life, it never occurs to us to regard it as a pathological condition and to refer it to medical treatment. We rely on its being overcome after a certain lapse of time, and we look upon any interference with it as useless and even harmful.
> (Freud, 1957, pp. 243–244)

Freud astutely noted that grief is prompted by a loss and that the loss need not involve a death. Losses may be of two types: physical or symbolic. A physical loss may include losing a cherished possession or having a friend die.

A symbolic loss may include a loss of status caused by a demotion or lack of promotion. Usually a symbolic loss is not identified as a loss per se, and one may not experience it consciously as such, nor realize grieving is necessary. Nonetheless, it will initiate a process of grieving just as a physical loss will. It is a normal and expected reaction that under normal conditions will occur and resolve itself over time. Freud described four grave departures from the normal attitude to life that are associated with grief:

1. A profound painful dejection
2. Cessation of interest in the outside world (insofar as it does not recall the lost loved one)
3. Loss of the capacity to love
4. Inhibition of activity by withdrawal from any activity not connected with thoughts of the lost person

In a landmark study following the tragedy of the 1942 Coconut Grove Night Club fire in Boston, Erich Lindemann, a pioneer in grief studies, wrote about acute grief as a normal reaction to a distressing circumstance. He described three stages of grief:

Stage 1. Shock and disbelief, which is characterized by the inability to accept the loss. Lindemann noted that periodically there could be a complete denial that the loss has occurred.

Stage 2. Acute mourning, which begins with the acknowledgment and acceptance that the loss has occurred. He noted that as a sequel to this acceptance there may be a disinterest in daily affairs, tearfulness and weeping, pervasive feelings of loneliness, insomnia, and loss of appetite. There may also be an intense preoccupation with the image of the deceased.

Stage 3. Resolution of the grief process is typified by a gradual reentry into the activities of daily living and a reduction in preoccupation with the image of the deceased.

Lindemann's work provided insight into the fact that grief, although usually conceived as a psychological reaction to loss, has a somatic sequel. He, along with Parkes (1964, 1970, 1972), observed that there are also a number of common physiological symptoms that occur in reactions to loss. They include loss of appetite, gastrointestinal disturbances, weight loss, insomnia, lack of strength, physical exhaustion, heart palpitations and other signs of anxiety, loss of sexual desire or hypersexuality, shortness of breath, and nervousness and tension.

It is important to remember that grieving is a holistic reaction to loss and may involve not only the psychological but the physical and the spiritual. Symptoms are present and indicate the grieving process remains unresolved. This is most likely normal, though individuals may seek therapy for help in achieving resolution.

Westberg (1962) reported 10 fairly common experiences for people in grief. Again it should be understood that grief is fluid and most people do not begin with stage one and proceed in an orderly fashion to Stage 10. The bereaved will often comment that after a week or two of "progress" they have reverted back to the beginning or square one. It is important to remember that the grieving process contains the emotional illusion of regression; when, in fact movement is most always forward. At worst, usually one is merely standing still. As long as the grieving process is not diluted or interrupted, there is progress, however slow.

1. *Shock.* The shock of death is to be expected, even after a long terminal illness and months of anticipatory grief. People often describe the first few weeks of grief as having been on "auto-pilot." There is little actual memory of specific details, merely the knowledge that one did what had to be done. Shock usually wears off after five or six weeks, but may last much longer, depending on the person's skill at self-protection from painful feelings and the significance of the relationship that has been lost.

2. *Emotional release.* It is not uncommon to see intense emotional release at the time of the death, and then have it seem to dry up for a number of weeks. When the shock finally dissipates, the bereaved will often find strong, possibly unsettling emotions such as anger, fear, remorse, and extreme loneliness present in great quantities. Lives are often reviewed during this period, and people are amazed to discover the degree of dependence (psychological, social, and physical) they felt for the person who died. This can lead to loss of self-esteem and feelings of inadequacy.

3. *Depression.* Depression takes the emotions mentioned above and intensifies them, adding to them feelings of helplessness and hopelessness. The bereaved may complain of not feeling their loved one close to them anymore, or of wanting to be with their loved one. There are fears of suicide from friends and family, but the bereaved will usually express it as: "I won't do anything to myself, but if death comes for me tonight I won't fight it."

4. *Physical symptoms of distress.* This is a very common phenomenon, especially in children. If the deceased died of a heart attack, the survivor(s) might experience tightness in the chest, pain radiating to the jaw and down the left arm, and other symptoms associated with a heart attack. A woman whose fiancee was murdered by a gunshot to the face developed a persistent sore on her face. When it was pointed out to her that the sore was the mirror reflection of the entry wound (opposite cheek) the sore healed and did not return.

5. *Anxiety.* The bereaved may experience vivid dreams, waking and sleeping, in which they see or hear their loved one. There is also spiritual anxiety, which is expressed as, "Where is my loved one now? Is he (or she) happy? How can he (or she) be at peace knowing I am suffering so much?" There may also be a fear that the anger being felt toward God will bring about punishment in the form of additional losses. Many bereaved individuals experience deep anxiety over the possibilities of forgetting their loved

ones and will express concern that they can no longer recall how the person smiled or how their voice sounded.

6. *Hostility.* Anger usually surfaces sometime between the sixth and eighth-week after death. This rage is sometimes random, sometimes specific. God, medical professionals, clergy, and the deceased are frequent targets. Usually the individual is confused by the intensity of the anger, seeing it as inappropriate or irrational, but feeling unable to defuse it.

7. *Guilt.* Guilt is sometimes real, often imaginary or exaggerated, but should always be taken with great seriousness. Death amplifies whatever problems existed in the relationship, and little issues that were virtually ignored in life may now be insurmountable obstacles for the survivor. The *shoulds* seem to rule the world of the bereaved: I should have done this; I should not have done that. Rational explanations may soothe for a time, but usually the guilt will return until resolution is achieved. (No one can punish better than we can punish ourselves, and the instrument of choice is guilt).

8. *Fear.* Fear wears many faces with the bereaved. There may be a fear of sleeping in the same bed or room. There may be a fear of leaving the house or of staying in it. People are generally afraid of the aloneness (physical and existential) that comes after a death; however, they are also afraid of beginning new relationships, however platonic these may be. There is a fear of never knowing joy again or not being able to laugh without guilt. The act of living becomes fearful for the person who feels so lost without his/her loved one and each day is a burden to be endured. As one woman said, "I can only go on because each day I live brings me one day nearer to him."

9. *Healing through memories.* The bereaved move back and forth between good memories and bad. At times it seems that there is a need for self-punishment and so all the negative aspects of the relationship are resurrected and relived. The happier moments often seem too painful, and it may take many months before these can be faced, but there is healing in remembering. As the memories become less painful to remember, there is an ability to begin to face the world once again.

10. *Acceptance.* There is a difference between accepting the reality of death, (thereby letting go) and forgetting the person who has died. As with the healing of any serious wound, there will always be a scar to remind one of the injury. With time will come a lessening of the pain, until finally the injury can be touched, remembered, and accepted as a new part of the life being lived. This acceptance may take years or longer to achieve, depending on the depth of emotional investment (attachment) one made in the relationship with the deceased.

Within these phases and stages, there is a continuum of behaviors ranging from normal and/or healthy to dysfunctional for the person who is grieving. Westberg's theory suggests that the patterns of loss following a death are similar (but not identical in duration or intensity) regardless of age, gender, or relationship to the deceased.

Engel (1964) identified five characteristic features of grief: (1) interruption of automatic or taken-for-granted aspects of living, such as awareness of the innumerable ways in which the deceased supported and gratified the bereaved; (2) attempts to deny or dispute the reality of the loss; (3) communication of various (behavioral) cries for help to solicit the response of others and express feelings of impotence, loss, and helplessness; (4) attempts to construct a mental representation of the deceased to replace the physical presence; and (5) personal, social, and institutionalized experiences of grief that serve to detach the survivors from the dead and restore them to their place in the social community. Engel describes the normal sequence of grief as following this sequence:

Phase 1. Shock and disbelief characterize the initial process. The bereaved attempts to protect him/herself from the recognition that the loss has occurred and the overwhelmingly painful feelings associated with the loss.

Phase 2. Developing awareness that the loss has occurred begins as the shock wears off. The reality of the loss and its implications for the bereaved are felt as a growing wave of anguish. Tearful lamenting involves acknowledgment of the loss and related feelings of helplessness. Anger, guilt, impulsive acting out, or self-destructive behavior may occur in response to the impotent feelings of helplessness.

Phase 3. Restitution is thought to be the work of ritual mourning occurring in various aspects of the wake and/or funeral that help to initiate the recovery phase. These involve social support, give emphasis to the reality of the loss, elicit the expression of feelings, and induce a process of identification with the deceased, aiding the bereaved in coping with the loss. Religious rites and spiritual beliefs offer meaning to help the bereaved cope with the loss.

Phase 4. Resolving the loss involves attempting to deal with the painful void created by the absence of the deceased. This may be reported as feeling an absence of wholeness or intactness. There may also be an increase in awareness of bodily sensations, which may be identical with the symptoms experienced by the deceased. The bereaved's thoughts are almost exclusively focused on the deceased; initially, emphasis is on the personal experience of the bereaved and later on the deceased. An extensive review of the relationship and associated ventilation of feelings occurs repeatedly. The bereaved begins to erect an image of the deceased that is devoid of all negative or undesirable appearance.

Phase 5. Idealization involves the repression of all negative and hostile feeling toward the deceased. This may lead to fluctuating feelings of guilt or remorse for past acts or thoughts toward the deceased. There may even be an unrealistic sense of responsibility for the death. The recurring thoughts and reminiscences about the deceased serve to establish and to cultivate identification through conscious and unconscious taking on of the deceased's qualities and attributes. Over time, this preoccupation with the deceased gradually lessens. Fewer reminders evoke feelings of sadness; ambivalent memories can be tolerated with less guilt. Desire to be with the deceased is slowly replaced with involvement in life while the identification with the deceased's ideals and aspirations provide an impetus to continue life. Interest in new relationships may begin as the psychic dependence on the deceased diminishes.

Phase 6. The outcome of successful mourning takes time (possibly a year or more). Successful healing is evident in the ability to remember the deceased without overwhelming or undue sadness or pain and to do so in a realistic light, acknowledging both the positive and negative aspects of the relationship.

Kubler-Ross' five stages of dying discussed in Chapter 2 have frequently been applied to the grieving process. When people become aware of their impending death, they are faced with the task of cognitively and emotionally coping with this reality and at the same time beginning to mourn their own death. The phases or stages identified by Kubler-Ross (1969), and Doyle (1980) may be used as a framework to understand the normal grieving process of both the dying and the bereaved.

Stage 1. Shock, denial, and isolation; attempts to limit awareness. Shock and its associated numbness serves to protect the bereaved from the overwhelming devastation associated with their new reality. Denial is usually a temporary defense and slowly abates, giving way to at least partial acceptance of the loss, which increases over time. Isolation may also occur frequently, and is seen as a self-protective action in which the bereaved withdraws from others who through the nature of their relationship with the deceased and/or the bereaved may trigger overwhelming emotional responses overriding attempts to limit awareness.

Stage 2. Awareness and emotional release. As shock and denial abate and are replaced with conscious awareness, emotions erupt. Feelings including a range of possible emotions; however, anger and guilt are among the most common. Anger, if present, generally results from helplessness and frustration over the inability to control or change the situation. Anger may be expressed toward the deceased, self, family members, or others such as medical personnel. Guilt is a common theme and may result from a variety of factors (i.e., outbursts of anger, real or perceived culpability, relational factors or unfinished business).

Kubler-Ross included in her stages of dying the stage of *bargaining,* which follows the stage of anger. Bargaining may be seen as the bereaved's way of attempting to avoid the finality of the loss and the associated intense emotions by attempting to make a deal with God, promising to change beliefs or behavior if the loss can be reversed or avoided.

Stage 3. Depression. Depression, in response to feelings of hopelessness, ensues when denial can no longer be maintained, and protest (anger) and bargaining have failed to stave off the reality and finality of the loss.

Depression after a loss is a normal reaction; however, a prolonged reaction and/or severity of associated symptoms may suggest a complication by a major depressive episode.

Wolfelt (1988) discusses some possible distinctions between normal depression associated with grieving and other forms of depression. In a normal grief response the bereaved is responsive to offerings of support and comfort, whereas in other forms of depression individuals may be unable or willing to accept support. There is also a difference in the affect presentation, with the bereaved individual presenting as acutely sad and empty, whereas in other forms of depression these feelings are chronic and have associated generalized feelings of hopelessness and helplessness. Additionally, bereaved individuals are able at some point to experience moments of happiness, whereas in other forms of depression this is not possible.

Stage 4. Acceptance and resolution. In the final stage of grief the bereaved comes to terms with reality. Acceptance is seen in the bereaved individual's ability to talk about and remember the deceased without experiencing severe emotional upheaval. Resolution includes the reinvestment in life and social activities. There is an acknowledgment that life will continue and there exists some hope for the future.

Schneider (1984) developed an eight-stage model, which he called *The Grieving Process.* His goal was to create a holistic model that integrated the physical, cognitive, emotional, behavioral, and spiritual components of the individual.

Stage 1. The initial awareness of the loss. Schneider saw the initial impact of the loss as creating a threat to the body's sense of homeostasis. Response to loss may be seen in physical, cognitive, emotional, behavioral, and spiritual dimensions. Shock, numbness, and confusion are a few of the multitude of the behaviors and emotions an individual may experience as a normal, adaptive response accompanying the acknowledgment of a significant loss.

Stage 2. Attempts to limit awareness by holding on. Limiting awareness reduced the imbalance created by threats to homeostasis. The strategy is to provide time to put the loss into perspective without being completely overwhelmed. Coping strategies effective in past losses are now employed. Schneider noted behaviors such as muscular tension, sleep disturbance, belief in internal control, and bargaining as accompanying attempts to hang on.

Stage 3. Attempts at limiting awareness by letting go. Letting go involves recognizing one's personal limits with regard to the loss and letting go of unrealistic goals, assumptions, and illusions. In this stage Schneider saw individuals separating themselves from dependent attachments to the attachment figure. Characteristics associated with this stage include: depression, rejection, disgust, anxiety, shame, self-destructive behaviors, and hedonism. It is during this stage that individuals may decide to give up formerly held beliefs and values.

Stage 4. Awareness of the extent of the loss. This is the stage of painful mourning. The individual may experience a flooding into consciousness feelings of deprivation, guilt, and a feeling of defenselessness against the overwhelming reality of the loss. Typical feelings and behaviors associated with this stage are aloneness, fatigue, preoccupation, helplessness and hopelessness, and existential loss.

Stage 5. Gaining perspective on the loss. This involves making peace with the individual's past, thus allowing some perspective to be achieved. Schneider saw this as taking two forms. The first is discovering a balance between the positive and negative aspects of the loss; the second is gaining perspective on the personal limits of responsibility. Typical behaviors and emotions seen here are acceptance, forgiveness, openness, reminiscence, and peace.

Stage 6. Resolving the loss. Schneider saw grief as being resolved when the bereaved can move on with life without it being a condition of holding on or letting go of the attachment figure. This is a time of self-forgiveness, finishing unfinished business, and saying good-bye. Characteristic emotions and behaviors are self-care, forgiveness of self and others, and peacefulness.

Stage 7. Reformulating the loss in the context of growth. This stage Schneider sees as an outgrowth of resolving grief. Facing and resolving grief allows for growth potential through the recognition of the individual's strengths, limits, mortality, and the finiteness of temporal existence. Characteristic behaviors and emotions include enhanced sensory awareness, integrity/ balance/centeredness, and spontaneity.

Stage 8. Transforming loss into new levels of attachment. Ironically, out of one of life's greatest losses emerges a reformulation and transformation that produces a greater capacity for growth and attachment. Accompanying this stage are behaviors and emotions such as unconditional love, creativity, wholeness, empathy, and commitment.

A recent model by Marrone (1997) highlights and incorporates existential change and psychospiritual transformation as a significant part of the process. The four-phase model includes the following:

Phase 1. Cognitive restructuring. This involves reorganizing and restructuring of the bereaved's thoughts and concepts, allowing for the death of the loved one to be assimilated.

Phase 2. Emotional expression. This requires the bereaved to begin to identify and accept, and in some way, express the emotional turmoil and cognitive confusion related to the loss experienced.

Phase 3. Psychological reintegration. This involves developing new coping behaviors and cognitive strategies that allow the individual to adjust to a world in which the deceased is absent.

Phase 4. Psychospiritual transformation. This is a penetrating growth-oriented spiritual/existential transformation that may fundamentally change the individual's central assumptions, beliefs, and attitudes about life, death, love, and God.

Many individuals seem to go through some form or fashion of these phases. Evidence of the phases has been found in grief responses of children exposed to extremely violent deaths (Pynoos & Nader, 1990). Case studies have shown it is beneficial to encourage the expression of distressful emotions (phases I and II) and to facilitate an appropriate relationship with the deceased (phases III and IV) (Shuchter & Zisook, 1990; Worden, 1991).

Regardless of which stage or phase theory one accepts or adopts as a guide, malleability, flexibility, and the realization that individual behavior exists on a vast continuum must temper the outcome. The model or theory embraced must respect individuality as well as universality. There is no "correct way to die or to grieve a loss," there is only the human way.

ANTICIPATORY GRIEF

Certain types of deaths provide the bereaved a pre-death grief process, which may affect the nature, course, and duration of the grieving process. Death due to chronic or prolonged illness may include an anticipatory or forewarning period in which the survivors may begin the process of grieving prior to the actual loss. Lindemann (1944) first observed this phenomenon as a lack of grief response or symptoms of grief in bereaved individuals who had recently experienced the death of a loved one. They reported that they had experienced many of the stages of grief prior to the actual death of their loved one. Fulton and Fulton (1971) describe four aspects of anticipatory grief: (1) depression; (2) heightened concern for the terminally ill person; (3) rehearsal of the death; and (4) attempts to adjust to the consequences of the death.

Anticipatory grief may allow for the gradual absorbing of the reality of the loss over time as opposed to all at once, as in the case of acute loss. Relationship issues such as resolving past conflicts or expressing previously unshared feelings may be done prior to the loss, thereby helping to eliminate unfinished business. Plans for the future may be made with the dying person, potentially eliminating the guilt associated with decisions that could not be discussed. Although anticipatory grief allows for the grieving to be well under way at the time of death, the mourning is rarely, if ever, completed. It should also be noted that the grief experience following the anticipated loss is no less painful than when the loss is not anticipated.

Anticipatory grief may also play a role in grief and adjustment in advance of losses that are other than death. Irving Janis in 1958 noted how the "work of worry" [a form of anticipatory grieving] prior to surgery was associated with better psychological and physical outcomes. Anticipating a specific loss may allow time to prepare psychological and/or physical coping mechanisms that can aid in the post-loss adjustment.

Anticipatory grief can also be seen as a two-edged sword. Some individuals or families during the period of anticipatory grief will have worked successfully toward letting go, detaching emotionally and starting to move on with their lives prematurely. Having done so, they now find it difficult to maintain their involvement and continued investment with the person who they regard as already dead. In yet other cases, the expected loss might not occur. The bereaved might have already grieved the anticipated loss and might have to a large degree emotionally detached from the individual.

Because of this detachment mixed emotions result if there is a change in prognosis. Terminally ill patients who were expected to die sometimes go into remission or recover. In these cases, known as *the Lazarus syndrome,* the family may have made significant headway in resolving the loss, and might experience difficulty reinvesting in the relationship. Ambivalent feelings including anger, frustration, and resentment at having been put through this process are not uncommon.

Anticipatory grief depending on many factors (e.g., its length, intensity of the relationship) can be either helpful in the quest for resolution of the grieving process or present yet another hurdle for the bereaved to negotiate. As in all aspects of the grief experience, there is both danger and opportunity.

In some situations, prolonged terminal illness may alter the existing relationship in such a way as to heighten attachments between individuals, disallowing anticipatory grief and heighten the experience of living. Shuchter (1986) in his book, *Dimensions of Grief: Adjusting to the Death of a Spouse,* provides some excellent examples:

> Melinda's struggle with Jim's cancer intensified their relationship in many ways. Melinda became inseparable from Jim physically, attending to his moment-to-moment needs on a 24-hour-per-day basis, nursing him with greater degrees of intimacy and greater exposure to his most private moments. At the same time she fought furiously to deny his illness, to preserve hope, and to maintain a positive spirit. All these actions conspired to make their relationship more real to her and deeper than it had ever been.

> During the years after the onset of his illness and before his death, David and Carol became much closer. They talked about all aspects of living and dying, and they got to know each other's innermost thoughts and feelings in a way that they never had before. "We had a much deeper communication than we had all of our married life." (1986, p. 70)

QUESTIONS FOR THOUGHT
AND REFLECTION

1. Do you remember your first day of school or day care when you were a young child? What was it like being separated for the first time from your parents? How did you react when they left? How did you act when they returned?

2. Who is the person with whom you feel most secure?

3. What would it be like for you if the person with whom you feel most secure were not there?

4. Describe your relationship with the above-noted person. Are there any attachment behaviors that you can identify?

5. Describe a death loss you have experienced. What were the stages of recovery you progressed through?

6. Describe a non-death loss you have experienced. What were the stages of recovery that you progressed through?

7. Have you ever had a best friend move away? Were you able to maintain the relationship as it was prior to the move? What factors contributed to the outcome?

8. Have you ever thoroughly prepared yourself for something that was about to happen, only to have it not happen? What was your reaction? Did you experience mixed or ambivalent feelings?

5

❧

Grief: The Reaction
to Loss

Psychiatrist George Engel in 1961 wrote in the journal *Psychosomatic Medicine* that the loss of a loved one is traumatic psychologically to the same extent as being wounded or burned is physiologically. Grief to Engel represents a departure from a state of health. Just as healing is necessary in the case of a physiological departure from a state of health in order to reestablish the body to a state of homeostatic balance, similarly a period of time is needed to return the bereaved to a similar state of psychosocial homeostasis. The grieving process can be seen here as the mechanism that brings about healing. As with any healing process, physiological or psychosocial healing may be complete or partial. Mourning, or more specifically, what Lindemann (1944) called *grief work,* appears to be a necessary part of the healing process. However, before going on to explore the work required for healing it is important to know what we are working with or what constitutes normal grief responses.

MANIFESTATION OF NORMAL GRIEF

Lindemann (1944) in his classic paper, *The Symptomatology and Management of Acute Grief,* described what he called the *pathogenomic characteristics* of normal or acute grief. The list since then has been extensively expanded and is quite varied. Worden (1991) arranges normal grief behaviors into four general categories: (1) feelings, (2) physical sensations, (3) cognitions, and (4) behaviors.

Feelings

Sadness appears to be the most common feeling associated with grief. Tearfulness or crying is frequently associated with sadness. Parkes and Weiss (1983) speculate that crying is a gesture that evokes a sympathetic and protective reaction from others and establishes a social situation in which the normal laws of competitive behavior are suspended.

Numbness or shock is also important to note because after a loss it is not uncommon to feel nothing, *numb*. This may be a normal defensive reaction to protect the bereaved from being overwhelmed and otherwise incapacitated by the plethora of feelings and related demands pressing to be allowed into consciousness. Blocking of sensation as a defense against what would otherwise be overwhelming pain would seem extremely normal (Parkes & Weiss, 1983).

Anger is frequently associated with loss. It can be a very confusing emotion to the bereaved and can present a significant hurdle to be overcome. Anger may result from a loss of faith in God: "How could he allow this to happen?" It can also stem from a sense of injustice and disillusionment—"This is not fair." Anger at the deceased is also common. A frequent response to the presence of this anger in the bereaved is, "How can I be angry? He didn't want to die." Anger might or might not be a "rational feeling;" however, the bereaved are often angry at their loved one for dying and leaving them. Anger can be viewed as the result of a potentially volatile mixture of frustration—the inability of attachment behaviors to bring back the attachment figure—and helplessness—the painful acknowledgment that death is the finale and we are powerless to do anything about it.

The anger, as we have seen, may be displaced or directed at others in the environment. This behavior follows the *death-denying* logic that there has to be someone or something to blame, someone to take responsibility. After all, this did not have to happen.

Guilt is a very common emotion in the bereaved and is not limited to those who are prone to feeling guilty. Relationships by their very nature contain some variable amount of ambivalence, positive and negative feelings. As a result, guilt may well be a specter associated with a loss. It is not unusual for survivors to need to pay a price for surviving or to extract a toll for the right to continue to live and possibly be happy. The bereaved might feel guilty about still being alive while the loved one is dead. This is known as *survivor's guilt*. Regardless of the source, guilt represents a hurdle in the path to healing.

Most guilt has an irrational basis and as such, will yield in the light of reality testing. For example if the bereaved says, "I didn't do enough," the obvious questions that may follow are, "What did you do?" and, following the reply, "What else did you do?" Through this process, more and more things will be recalled, and at some point a tenable conclusion is usually entertained; "Maybe I did all I could do under the circumstances."

There are situations in which the survivor is culpable and guilt is real. In such instances confession is good for the soul, as is the realization that the task is in front of us, not behind us. What that means is, if one has responsibility, then one needs to remember that in the future. The past is unreconcilable; however, the future is up to us. An interchange with Jerry provides an example:

> Jerry was a retired physician with a secret. When he was 19 he was out driving with friends and, while distracted, struck a motorcyclist. The cyclist, though injured, did recover. He required a metal plate to be inserted in his head and had some mild residual deficits. Jerry felt extremely guilty about this for his entire life. However, as a result, he never had so much as a parking ticket following the incident. He admitted that the incident had made him an extremely careful and defensive driver. Following his story, I questioned Jerry about how many lives he thought he had saved by being so careful a driver. He acknowledged there were probably many, to which I asked what he felt so guilty about.

A great deal of good came out of what could have been a very bad choice—to remain mired in guilt but not to change any behavior. Jerry made a decision oriented toward the future; he just didn't recognize it that way when he made it. In working with the bereaved, we can help them make their decision regarding how to handle their guilt a conscious one.

Anxiety and, to some degree, even a sense of panic is a common reaction to a loss and comes from several sources. Confronting the loss has the reciprocal effect of confronting us with the fact that we are alone. Regardless of the number of people around us, and the support we have, there is a growing existential awareness that we are alone. An immediate question consciously or unconsciously that confronts the bereaved is, "How am I going to live without my loved one?" This anxiety is often compounded by the heightened awareness or realization of our own mortality. We spend most of our lives denying the fact that we will ultimately die while living a *vital delusion,* one that is fractured by a death loss.

Other feelings that might be included on the list of normal reactions to loss include fatigue, helplessness, feelings of being overwhelmed, loneliness, emancipation, relief, irritability, and depression.

In reviewing this list, remember that it is not all-inclusive, as there are few if any feelings that would be outside the realm of normal. However, the span of time that the feelings are present and the related intensity of them may foretell a complicated grief reaction. This topic will be dealt with in a future chapter.

Physical Sensations

Lindemann, it was noted earlier, described not only the psychological grief reactions of people but also the physical sensations associated with their grief reactions. Physical sensations are frequently overlooked but may be key indicators of a bereaved individual's grief reaction. Many times it will be the physical sensations that will prompt the bereaved to seek assistance initially with their physician. The following is a list of commonly reported sensations associated with grief reactions:

1. Hollowness in the pit of the stomach
2. Tightness in the chest or throat

3. Muscular weakness

4. Lack of energy

5. Dry mouth

6. Insomnia

7. Loss of appetite

8. Depression

9. Generalized anxiety

10. Anhedonia (absence of pleasurable experience)

11. Sense of depersonalization (nothing seems to be real, including me)

Frequently with the passage of time, *somatic symptoms* (without other cause) are the only indicators that grief is still unresolved.

Cognitions

A natural cognitive response to a death loss is preoccupation with the deceased. This occurs as a wish to undo the loss and may take the form of obsessional thinking. This may be viewed as mentally hugging and holding the deceased tightly before acknowledging that one must let go, say good-bye, and part. Some preoccupation may be in the form of intrusive thoughts. These may be may be related to guilt or other unresolved issues.

Hallucinations (both visual and auditory), though normally associated with severely disturbed functioning, are included because they are frequent experiences of the bereaved. They are usually transient and occur within a few weeks or a month of the loss. The following is a normal experience of an olfactory hallucination following a loss:

> A woman in grief therapy reported being overwhelmed with the smell of blood everytime she entered her fiancee's car. Her fiancee had committed suicide (gun shot to the head) in his car and was found by his girlfriend. The car was cleaned and given to her by his family. Shortly thereafter in session she reported what was to her a bizarre experience, and questioned if she was losing her mind. The incident was normalized as one frequently experienced by the bereaved, and the hallucinations abated shortly thereafter.

Other cognitions may include disbelief, confusion, and passive suicidal thoughts. It is important to remember that what is dysfunctional in one individual or circumstance is not for another individual or in another situation.

Behaviors

A number of specific behaviors are frequently associated with normal grief reactions, some of which have already been mentioned. This section will focus on those not yet covered.

Dreams of the deceased are quite common and can be a source of comfort or concern. The following is an example of both. Conway (1988) describes a son who thought his mother was going crazy. The woman said that on occasion, her husband, deceased two years previously, still visited her at night in her dreams, and that during his visits she found sexual satisfaction. The woman was well adjusted in her work, social, and family life, and active in the community. When the son understood that seeing a deceased loved one and experiencing sexual satisfaction in dreams are normal, he saw his mother's experience in a different and more positive light. Existentially speaking, dreaming is as close to death as the living can get; viewed another way, dreaming can serve as a bridge to those otherwise unreachable.

Some bereaved individuals find it necessary to avoid places and things that trigger painful feelings of grief. They avoid the place where the person died, the cemetery, and even objects that remind them of the deceased. This behavior is counterbalanced by those who need to visit the cemetery daily and carry the deceased's picture with them constantly, fearing that they will forget his or her face. Still others will treasure objects of the deceased and find it difficult to part with them. Other behaviors include social withdrawal, absentmindedness, sighing, restlessness, and crying.

It is important for those who work with the bereaved to be well acquainted with the characteristics of the normal grief reaction. This knowledge will enable them to reassure those who experience these often-disconcerting but normal reactions and not pathologize behavior that should be considered normal.

GRIEF WORK: TASKS OF GRIEVING

Many new theories of coping with bereavement have been proposed by researchers (Cook & Oltjenbruns; 1998, Neimeyer, 1998, 1997; Rubin & Schechter, 1997; Sanders, 1989). However, a helpful concept for both the bereaved and the caregiver is the tasks of mourning. The bereaveds' awareness of these needs or tasks of grief work can give a participative, action-oriented outlook of the experience of grief as opposed to a perception of grief being a phenomenon that is experienced in a passive manner. This also provides a framework for outlining a significant portion of the caregivers' role. Several researchers have described these tasks.

Lindemann, in his 1944 seminal work, described three tasks that he saw as constituting grief work: emancipation from the bondage of the deceased, readjustment to the environment in which the deceased is missing, and formation of new relationships.

Task 1. Emancipation from the bondage of the deceased. When two people form a relationship there is an investment of self that is made with the other person. They are intertwined emotionally, investing psychic and emotional energy in the loved one. When one of the individuals dies, the remaining individual has to withdraw the psychic and emotional energy that was invested in the person who is no longer alive. Attachments to the deceased person must be relinquished and a new altered status developed. Untying the attachments, the ties that bind, does not mean disregarding or forgetting the deceased; rather, it means that the emotional energy that was invested in the deceased is withdrawn and modified to allow the bereaved to invest it in others for emotional satisfaction.

This process is often confused with being disloyal or betraying the deceased. The relationship is changed but continues to exist in the heart and in the mind of the bereaved, but in an altered form. What changes is the bereaved's ongoing relationship, the investment in and attachment to the deceased as a living person who can return the investment. The energy investment that went into keeping the relationship with the deceased alive must now be reinvested where it can be returned. As painful as this process is, it is because life is indeed for the living.

Task 2. Readjustment to the environment in which the deceased is missing. To accommodate the world without the deceased attachment figure is the task at hand. Roles as well as identity may have to be redefined. For example, the surviving spouse must shift from thinking about "we" to thinking about "I," and face the fears associated with one's new autonomy. Adjustments will be required in all areas: emotionally, physically, socially, and financially.

Task 3. Formation of new relationships. This is not a quest to replace the person who has died; however, it will establish a new and different attachment with another person who can return the energy investment. The time required for this reinvestment in someone or something else will depend on a host of factors. Ideally, at some time the bereaved will be able to reinvest in life again.

Parkes and Weiss (1983) saw three tasks as necessary in order for recovery from grief to take place: intellectual recognition and explanation of the loss, emotional acceptance of the loss, and assumption of a new identity.

Task 1. Intellectual recognition and explanation of the loss. Parkes and Weiss saw anxiety and vigilance against threats of new loss as problematic for the bereaved individual's recovery. Only by developing an adequate explanation of how the loss happened that answers all their questions and identifies an inevitable cause of death can the anxiety and related vigilance be overcome.

Task 2. Emotional acceptance of the loss. Obsessive preoccupation with the deceased serves to bring about emotional acceptance. It is only through repeated confrontations with every detail of the loss and obsessive review of memories, thoughts, and feelings that the pain abates and gradual acceptance is achieved.

Task 3. Assumption of a new identity. The bereaved, according to Parkes and Weiss, develop new identities over time that reflect their new circumstances. This is a process brought on by an awareness and discomfort with the way the world is now and the way it was. Just as the handicapped learn to adapt to the loss of a limb or sight, so do the bereaved learn to stop including the deceased in their everyday thoughts and plans as if they were not dead. Each time the bereaved mistakenly includes the deceased, as if they were living, in thought or plan, the inevitable confrontation with reality occurs and the pain of grief, frustration, and absence of security is felt. It is only when the bereaved has established and no longer forgets the new identity that the painful reminders end. The speed of acquisition is not as important as progress itself.

William Worden (1991) in his book, *Grief Counseling and Grief Therapy,* posits four tasks of mourning: accept the reality of the loss; work through the pain of grief; adjust to an environment in which the deceased is missing; emotionally relocate the deceased and move on with life.

Task 1. Accept the Reality of the Loss. When a loved one dies, regardless of whether the loss was anticipated, there is a tendency to not believe that this has happened. Before mourning can occur, before anything connected to the loss can happen, there must be an acknowledgment; a coming face to face with the fact that the person has died. Worden noted that this includes admitting that reunion with the deceased, at least in this life, is impossible. It is during this first task of mourning that Worden believes the searching behavior of which Bowlby and Parkes write are exhibited.

The opposite of acceptance of the reality of the loss is to not believe or deny it. Worden notes that this can be accomplished in many different ways. Denying the meaning of the loss allows it to be seen as less significant than it actually is. This may be done through statements like, "We weren't close, I don't miss him;" or, "She wasn't my mother, she was only my stepmother."

Gorer (1965) described a process of denial that he called *mummification.* The bereaved retain possessions of the deceased in a mummified condition ready for use when their loved ones return. In this way, they deny that the death has occurred and act as if they expect the return at any time. Removing all the reminders of the individual as if they never existed is the opposite of mummification, but also serves to minimize or deny the loss. The bereaved attempt to protect themselves from things that would remind them of the individual and confront them with the reality of their loss.

Selective forgetting is yet another technique Worden describes as a way to avoid the reality of the loss. Here the bereaved selectively remove all memory of the deceased, thereby eliminating them and the associated loss from reality.

Coming to accept the loss is both an intellectual and an emotional process. The bereaved may have an intellectual acceptance that a death has occurred long before they can allow the related emotional impact to be felt and fully integrated.

Accepting the reality of the loss carries with it a significant consequence—pain. It is this pain that is the focus of the next task of mourning.

Task 2. Work through to the pain of grief. Parkes (1972) wrote, "It is necessary for the bereaved person to go through the pain in order to get the grief work done, then anything that continually allows the person to avoid or suppress the pain can be expected to prolong the course of mourning." (p. 173)

Culture and society can greatly influence the time and ultimately the difficulty experienced in progressing through to the completion of the second task of mourning. In general, Western society is uncomfortable with the strong emotions associated with mourning. Subtle and not so subtle messages have been sent to us since our youth. Big boys/big girls don't cry. Now, as the bereaved, one might receive the message that mourning is feeling sorry for yourself, or, that giving way to feelings like that is unhealthy. The socially correct thing to do is often seen as distracting the bereaved from their grief, and a strong message is sent—don't feel.

Task 1 has a significant bearing on task 2. If the bereaved accept the reality of their loss, pain will be the consequence. The reverse is also true. If survivors can deny, ignore, or distract themselves from the reality that a loss has occurred, then pain can also be avoided.

Some individuals do not understand the necessity of experiencing the emotional pain associated with a loss and attempt a traveling cure. Traveling from place to place accomplishes two things. First, it distracts them from the reality of the loss, and second, it is hoped that upon return everything magically will be all right. Another variation of this theme is to believe that the deceased is now in a better place than they were before death. However true this might be for the deceased, the focus distracts the bereaved from feelings they might have about being left behind alone.

Time knows no limits when it comes to the pain associated with mourning a loss. Bowlby (1980) wrote that "sooner or later, some of those who avoid all conscious grieving break down, usually with some form of depression." (p. 158) Bowlby's words have rung true many times. The author, while leading groups for survivors (family and friends) of suicide victims, noticed that many participants have acknowledged the loss that occurred 20 or more years ago, and they came to the group because they are tired of feeling so depressed.

Task 3. Adjust to an environment in which the deceased is missing. This means different things to different people. The bereaved are often not consciously aware of all the roles that the deceased played in their lives. This does not occur all at once but is generally an unfolding process that occurs over time. The example cited in an earlier section of Mrs. X, the woman whose husband was killed in an automobile accident, has relevance here. The first morning following the accident included a small but highly significant revelation for Mrs. X related to this third task of mourning. Upon waking, she went into the kitchen, intending to make coffee. Her painful awareness was that she did not know how. She became consciously aware that for the 48 years of their marriage, Mr. X had made the coffee and had done most, and, recently following his retirement, all of the cooking.

Although Mrs. X developed this skill and many others, she did so reluctantly and with some resentment.

Mr. X's death also had implications for Mrs. X and her sense of self. The "we" that had existed for 48 years was now an "I." The world socially was a different place, and also required new behaviors from Mrs. X. All of these painful realizations contributed to an acknowledgment of her changed circumstance and elicited from her an adaptation to the way things are now, as opposed to the way things were then.

Compromising the third task would be not adapting to the loss. Well-intentioned caregivers and family members work against successful completion of task 3 when they do too much and promote helplessness. Coping and adaptation are difficult; however, as Viktor Frankl purports, the power of the human spirit, if allowed, can overcome any obstacle.

Task 4. Emotionally relocate the deceased and move on with life. The relationship must be moved from one of the present to one in memory. Doing this allows room in one's life for something other than grief. It was as a result of the emotional investment in life with the deceased that the bereaved feels the pangs associated with the tasks of mourning. Without this emotional investment, life would have been but a hollow shell. To live in the world without being able to reinvest will also be a hollow shell. To live in a world without love is to not live. However, loving again does not mean you did not truly love the one who died, although it often seems so. Finding a proper and fitting place for the memory and emotions one has for the deceased and mustering the strength to move on can truly be a formidable task. Nietzsche, the German philosopher, reminds us that those who have a *why* to live for can find a *how.* Viktor Frankl often reminded those whom he taught that life does not offer you happiness, it offers you meaning.

Reinvesting has benefits, of course, but it also has consequences; and the bereaved are all too familiar with those. Fearing additional loss can make reinvesting an anxiety-provoking thought. For many bereaved, this final task is the most difficult. Some get stuck here, often accompanied by a realization that their life also stopped at the time of the loss they grieve. This, however, need not always be the case.

SYNOPSIS OF THE TASKS OF MOURNING
AND SUGGESTIONS FOR COUNSELORS

The first task of mourning is to experience and express outside of one's self the reality of the death (Lindemann, 1944; Parkes & Weiss, 1983; Worden, 1991). This involves confronting the reality that the person has died and will not be coming back. To do this requires talking about the death. Using, not avoiding, the word *death* helps to establish this reality. Discussing how and where the death occurred and the funeral experience is facilitative of this process.

Questions to ask yourself as a counselor working with the bereaved might include:

- Where is the person in terms of confronting the reality that his or her loved one has died?
- How might I help the person talk about his or her loss?
- Do I need to respect the person's need to avoid the full reality of the loss for a period of time while attempting to help the person cautiously confront this new reality?

The second task of mourning is to tolerate the emotional suffering that is inherent in the grief while nurturing oneself both physically and emotionally (Parkes & Weiss, 1983; Shuchter & Zisook, 1990; Worden, 1991). The thoughts and feelings (pain of grief) resulting from this encounter with death must be absorbed. It is important to note that some feelings such as anger, guilt, and helplessness might be difficult to acknowledge and/or appropriately direct. Interpreting feelings and related behaviors as normal is often of great relief to the bereaved, who might feel as if they are going crazy.

Questions to ask yourself as a counselor working with the bereaved might include:

- Has the person allowed his/her self to experience the pain of grief? If so, with whom has the person shared this grief?
- Was the bereaved person provided with a sense of feeling understood in the expression of grief?
- How might I help this person find a balance between negative and positive feelings felt toward the deceased? Facilitative questions might be, "What do you miss about the deceased? What do you not miss?"

The third requisite of mourning is to convert the relationship with the deceased from one of the presence to a relationship of memory (Lindemann, 1944; Parkes & Weiss, 1983; Rando, 1987; 1993; Ruskay, 1996; Sable, 1991; Worden, 1991). This requires the bereaved to develop a new relationship with the deceased. Mourners must work to modify and detach the emotional ties to those who have died in preparation to live in an altered relationship with them. The bereaved should not be expected to relinquish all ties to those who have died. However, an alteration of the relationship must be accomplished. Important here is the concept of time. Allow the bereaved time to grieve and say good-bye as part of making the necessary changes in converting the relationship.

Questions to ask yourself as a counselor working with the bereaved might include:

- Where is the person in the process of converting the relationship from one of presence to one of memory?

- Is the bereaved resisting any change in viewing the relationship as one of presence? If so, what contributing factors may be influencing this (i.e., nature of the relationship with the deceased, personality of the deceased or of the bereaved)?

- Does the bereaved think he or she must give up all forms of bonding with the deceased?

- How may I assist the bereaved in saying a final good-bye?

The fourth task of mourning is to develop a new sense of self-identity based on a life without the deceased (Lindeman, 1944; Parkes & Weiss, 1983; Ruskay, 1996; Worden, 1991). Role confusion involves the struggle between the "we" and the "I" and fears associated with one's new autonomy. Again, time is a critical factor, and individual differences will dictate how quickly or slowly this task is performed. Remember also to provide for continuing support as indicated (e.g., follow up counseling or support groups) Questions to ask yourself as a counselor working with the bereaved might include:

- Where is the bereaved in the process of forming a new self-identity? Is time a factor that is influencing where this person is currently?

- What are the role changes that this person is experiencing? Is the person aware of the specific changes needed?

- Are role models of persons who have gone through similar experiences available?

Finally, to complete the work of grief one must relate the experience of loss in a context of meaning. The bereaved will typically question their philosophy of life and values in seeking an answer to the question *why?* As Nietzsche said, "It was not the suffering that was his problem but that the question was wanting to the outcry, '*Why* the suffering?' "

Questions to ask yourself as a counselor working with the bereaved might include:

- Where is the person in the process of relating the experience of loss to a context of meaning?

- What were the person's religious and philosophical beliefs about life before the loss? How has the loss altered these beliefs?

- What is standing between this person and acceptance of fate?

Having examined the various tasks associated with grief and mourning, an obvious question emerges: "When is mourning finished?" One might say it is when the final task is completed. There is no concise answer. When asked, I usually reply that you know you have completed the mourning process when you can remember the deceased without the gut-wrenching sadness you feel now. As for a time frame, a year and often much more are common estimates.

TIME INTERVALS AND IMPLICATIONS
FOR COUNSELORS

Time, like the stages of grief, is fluid. People move within the stages quickly, sometimes going back to the first hours, and then jumping well ahead of where they actually are feeling as though they have finally finished resolving their loss. The following is included as a general descriptive guide based on the author's work with survivors of a loved one's loss:

During the first 48 hours the shock of the death can be intense, and denial is often strong in the first hours. However, the initial emotional response can be frightening to the bereaved and friends and family members.

During the first week, the necessity of planning the funeral and making other arrangements usually takes over, and the bereaved may function in an automatic manner. This may be followed by a feeling of letdown and emotional and physical exhaustion.

In the second through fifth weeks there may be a general feeling of abandonment as family and friends return to their own lives after the funeral. Employers often expect the bereaved to have recovered and to be fully functional on the job. The insulation of shock may still be in effect, and there may be a sensation of "well, this isn't going to be as bad as I first thought."

It is during the sixth through twelfth weeks that the shock finally wears off, and the reality of the loss sets in. The range of emotions may vary widely, and the person might feel out of control. Family and friends are often not as supportive as previously and may think, "That was three months ago, why are you feeling bad now?" Experiences during this time may include radical changes in sleep patterns, onset of fear (sometimes paranoia), changes in appetite with significant weight gain or loss, mood swings, changes in libido, periods of uncontrollable weeping, desire for social withdrawal and isolation, inability to concentrate or remember, and an increased need to talk about the deceased.

The cycle of good and bad days begins during the third and fourth months. Irritability increases, and there is a lowering of the frustration tolerance. There may be verbal and physical acting out of anger, feelings of emotional regression, and an increase of somatic complaints, especially flu and colds, as the immune system is depressed.

Depression sets in as the sixth-month anniversary approaches. The event of loss is relived and the emotional upheaval seems to be starting all over again. Anniversaries, birthdays, and holidays are especially difficult, bringing about renewed depression.

The first anniversary of the death can be either traumatic or the beginning of resolution. This will depend on the amount and quality of grief work done during the year.

Eighteen to 24 months is the time for resolution. The pain of separation becomes bearable, and the bereaved is able to proceed with living. There is an emotional letting go of the deceased, a recognition that, while the person will never be forgotten, the pain of the death will no longer need to be the focal point of the life of the bereaved. It is during this phase that the terms *bereaved* and *grieving* are eased from the vocabulary, and the process of living begins in earnest.

Grief and mourning are uniquely individual processes, and no one has the correct timetable for their completion. The process of healing might take a year, or it might take a lifetime. Whatever the time, the bereaved should not travel alone.

Bowlby (1980) suggests that clinicians sometimes have unrealistic expectations about the progress that people should be making as they grieve. He quotes one widow as saying, "Mourning never ends: only as time goes on it erupts less frequently." (p. 101) Sable (1991) reports similar feelings in widows that were not showing signs of pathologic grieving. The common notion that time is the best healer is not supported in much of the research (Conway, 1988; Gray, 1987; Kaffman, Elizur & Gluckson, 1987; Wortman & Silver, 1989; Zisook, Shuchter & Lyons, 1987). Widows and widowers showing gradual improvement over a period of two years still faced loneliness and adjustment to their new roles (Lund, Caserta & Dimond, 1986). Rando (1983) describes a V configuration with bereavement intensity decreasing in the second year and increasing in the third year. This suggests that patterns of grieving fluctuate over time in a nonlinear fashion (Gray, 1987). Even so, some of the literature proposes that time since bereavement is the best predictor of adjustment (Campbell, Swank & Vincent, 1991; Farnsworth, Pett & Lund, 1989; Worden, 1991).

FACTORS INFLUENCING
THE GRIEF REACTION

It is true that some aspects of grief are universal. It is, however, equally true that each person's grief reaction will be uniquely idiosyncratic. The uniqueness will be, in large part, determined by a combination of psychological and social factors.

Psychological Factors

To appreciate the idiosyncratic meaning that a loss has for a given individual, one must know something about who or what was lost. The death of a grandparent may have different impact on a bereaved child than the death of a parent. Likewise, the death of a spouse may be grieved differently than the death of a parent. It cannot automatically be assumed that a parent's death will bring about more grief or a grandparent's death less grief. In determining what was lost, it is important to note the difference between role-loss and an object-loss. A *role-loss* is a symbolic loss and is associated with a loss of status or function. An *object-loss* is a physical loss and involves the loss of a particular person or object. A widow may sustain both types of loss. She experiences an object-loss, the loss of her husband. She also sustains a role-loss in that she is no longer a couple, "we" is now an "I." In some cases, a role-loss might be more difficult to grieve than an object loss. The empty nest syndrome may bring about more grieving because of a role-loss (i.e., loss of being able to directly parent and nurture) than the loss of the child (object-loss). Because the child is alive and well, the physical loss is therefore less than the role-loss.

The nature of the relationship, the strength of the attachment, and the role the deceased occupied will all have significant impact on the grief reaction of the bereaved and his or her capacity for grief work. It is logically self-evident that the intensity of the grief reaction is, in part, determined by the intensity of the love the bereaved had for the deceased.

The strength of the attachment is in part determined by how important the deceased was for the sense of well-being of the bereaved. If the relationship was such that the bereaved individual needed the deceased to maintain a sense of self, then this may lead to a more difficult grief reaction and possible complicated bereavement. The strength of the attachment is also determined by the degree of ambivalence in the relationship. Positive and negative feelings coexist as part of any relationship. Usually the positive far outweighs the negative. However, in significantly ambivalent relationships, the negative and positive feelings are more equally proportioned. Ambivalent relationships generally contain significant quantities of guilt and anger that are both exacerbated by the loss. Unfinished business in the form of unresolved conflicts is also an important detail. Any or all of these factors can lead to a more difficult grief reaction or a complicated bereavement.

Parkes (1972) noted the complexity of the multirole phenomenon in bereavement and wrote:

> Even bereavement by death is not as simple a stress as it might, at first sight, appear to be. In any bereavement it is seldom clear exactly what is lost. A loss of a husband, for instance, may or may not mean the loss of a sexual partner, companion, accountant, gardener, baby-minder, audience, bed-warmer, and so on, depending upon the particular roles normally performed by this husband. (p. 7)

Parkes succinctly points out that the roles vacated by the deceased place new [role] demands and responsibilities on the bereaved, which, depending on the ability and desire to compensate for these changes, can profoundly influence the grief reaction.

Personality Variables

Bowlby (1980) recommended that the bereaved's personality structure be taken into account when attempting to understand the individual's grief reaction. Variables of concern might include individual coping styles and behaviors, personality, and overall mental health.

People do change over time; however, coping behaviors are usually familiar responses and in situations of crisis or extreme stress are generally predictable. If an individual has consistently coped with stress by fleeing and running away, then it is predictable that the person will exhibit the same behavior in reaction to grief. Knowledge of past coping behaviors can be helpful in establishing reasonable expectations for an individual's grief experience. It is also helpful in that the caregiver can be prepared to support healthy and adaptive coping behaviors and offer or help the bereaved develop alternatives for less adaptive ones. Normal coping behaviors may include

- Avoidance of painful stimuli including not talking about the deceased, temporarily removing pictures or other mementos
- Distracting oneself through preoccupation with work, school, or social activities; constantly reading or watching TV
- Minimizing the loss through rationalization

Unhealthy coping behaviors may include

- The use of alcohol and/or drugs as a means of blocking out reality
- Acting out, hypersexuality, or self-destructive behaviors

Various aspects of personality also affect the individual's reaction to a death loss. Highly dependent persons and persons who have difficulty forming relationships may be at risk for complicated bereavement. Other personality factors such as self-esteem, conscious and/or unconscious conflicts, needs, attitudes, and beliefs will all play a role in the person's grief reaction. Assessment of these factors is important, not only for developing accurate expectations, but also to allow for the identification of potential deficit areas and the development of support strategies.

A history of current and past mental health is important in that it can significantly influence the individual's capacity for and ability to deal with the grief experience. A history of depressive illness, for example, would be important. Symptoms will need to be monitored so that medical help may be sought if necessary to prevent a significant exacerbation of the illness. Similarly, individuals diagnosed with certain personality disorders may have a difficult time handling a loss.

Past Experience with Loss

An individual's past experience with loss will affect expectations for the current experience and may influence the selection of coping strategies. A negative or extremely painful past experience may inhibit the individual's acceptance of the grieving process and lead to a strong desire to deny the loss and/or associated emotions. Past avoidance or the incomplete grieving of a past loss may also give rise to old unresolved issues or conflicts that interfere with effectively grieving the current loss.

The magnitude of prior losses can influence the current course of mourning. An individual who has experienced too many death losses may be in a state of overload and have no emotional reserves with which to adequately grieve the current loss. The deaths may have been experienced serially one after another, as is often the case with the elderly, or singularly with multiple victims such as a disaster, natural or man-made. Regardless of the situation, past experience with loss may not allow the individual the resources needed to adequately grieve the current loss.

Mode and Timeliness of Death

Death can occur as the result of natural causes, an accident, suicide, or homicide. Each may have implication for the survivors and will affect the course of how the loss is grieved. A salient factor influencing the course of grief is the bereaved's perception of the circumstances of the death. This may include who died, how death occurred, and also the reason (culpability if any) and whether the death was sudden or expected.

The "who" is related to the psychological acceptability of death for a given person at a given time. The death of a child in our society is always viewed as psychologically unacceptable; it stands against the natural order of things that dictates the elderly should be the first to die. The death of a young mother or father with small children is always untimely. However, the natural order of things also has rules for the elderly and the psychological acceptability of death. For example, it is unfair and psychologically unacceptable for an individual to die immediately or shortly after retirement. Regardless of the fact that the person may be in the age group where death is psychologically acceptable, just *beginning* to partake of the fruits of his or her labor makes death unacceptable. Death, according to the natural order of things, is supposed to occur when it is scheduled, and here it can be seen that death just did not occur when it was supposed to.

How death occurs, whether naturally, by accident, suicide, or homicide may influence how the loss is grieved. Suicide and homicide will be dealt with in Chapter 7. The primary factor influencing the course of bereavement in deaths from natural or accidental causes is culpability. The perception of death as preventable is a significant factor in the length and intensity of bereavement. Perception may be based on both rational and irrational expectations of self and others. As is often the case with parents whose children experience what is perceived to be a preventable death, blame and guilt are inescapable, usually directed at self and/or spouse, destroying relationships and significantly complicating the grieving process. The American Psychiatric Association notes that in cases of post-traumatic stress disorder, symptoms are of longer duration and greater intensity when the traumatic event is of human origin.

A final influencing factor is whether the death was sudden or expected. As we have seen, anticipatory grieving can be, but is not always, a positive factor influencing loss. The forewarning of a loss may allow time to resolve previously unresolved conflicts and/or express unshared feelings as well as providing time to gradually accommodate the reality of the impending loss. The impact of a sudden unexpected loss depending on the mode, timeliness, and other factors can render the bereaved in a state of recoverable shock or overwhelm the survivor compromising his/her ability to cope and complicating the bereavement process.

THE ROLE OF SOCIAL
AND EMOTIONAL SUPPORT

The tasks of mourning require social and emotional support (encouragement, empathy, positive relationships). The bereaved's responses to spoken condolences are considered a reliable indication of how the grieving is progressing. Grateful acceptance of consolation is a positive sign of progress. Conversely, insistence upon silence in all matters related to the dead person may be evidence of prolonged absence of grieving (Gorer, 1965, cited in Bowlby, 1980).

Weiss (1975a, cited in Bowlby, 1980) believes that there is a difference between social and emotional loneliness. Social loneliness can be overcome through friends and support groups, but the assuaging of emotional loneliness and isolation requires the sense of security found in a dedicated interpersonal relationship (Sable, 1991). This seems to apply regardless of the loss sustained.

Gray (1987) looked at social and emotional support and depression following loss. He examined the likelihood of depression in adolescents six months after a parent's death and found that individuals with low levels of social support, when combined with a dependent personality type, were more likely to experience depression. Adolescents that had emotional support at home from the surviving parent had significantly lower depression scores and lower incidence of physical ailments. Similarly, Lasker and Toedter (1991) found that women with emotional support from family after a pregnancy loss had lowered long-term difficulty with feelings of despair. Sable (1991) found that elderly bereaved women who had found new partners had lower psychological distress scores than those who remained alone. Emotional loneliness was even reduced in women who had dogs or cats for companionship.

Social support networks that allow for the expression of emotions and review of the relationship have been identified as a factor in positive bereavement and physical health outcome 13 months after a death loss (Maddison & Walker, 1967, cited in Raphael & Middleton, 1987). A perceived lack of social support may be related to poorer outcomes of bereavement (Rando, 1993; Worden, 1991).

There is some evidence that intervention and support in the grieving process may be especially effective in the early days of bereavement. Bowlby (1980) found that simply being interviewed for a research study immediately after bereavement by suicide appeared to lead to a more favorable long-term outcome. Support from others might have the effect of providing a temporary replacement of the previously supportive attachment bond that has just been broken. This might alleviate some of the despair encountered as the bereaved realizes that, while the lost person cannot be regained, there are others available with whom bonding is possible. Research indicates that the nature of the support relationship in the very early stages of grieving is important. "On-call help . . . beginning with the stage of acute crisis, is better received by the grieving family than continued and prolonged therapy or help offered at later stages" (Kaffman, Elizur & Gluckson, 1987, p. 73). Pynoos and Nader (1990) found that children who have witnessed a violent death seem to benefit from early intervention.

USE OF MEDICATION

The use of medication in the management of normal grief has undergone much discussion. The general consensus is that medication ought to be used sparingly and then on specific symptoms such as overwhelming anxiety, insomnia, or significant loss of appetite and not for what is typically regarded as "normal" depressed mood. The obvious exception would be in the case of major depressive episodes.

There are at present no controlled studies supporting the above thinking; however, it seems logically contradictory to mask or attempt to elevate strong emotions brought on by a normal grief reaction. If acknowledging the loss brings about pain and anguish, then these symptoms appear to function much like the symptoms of acute appendicitis. The pain of acute appendicitis dictates that one seek medical attention and not attempt to simply avoid the pain through the use of analgesics. Similarly the cognitions, feelings, physical sensations, and behaviors one experiences as the result of a loss need to be given a voice and not silenced if the grieving process is to progress.

It is noteworthy to acknowledge that the duration and expression of "normal" bereavement varies considerably; however, the presence of certain symptoms that are not characteristic of a "normal" grief reaction may be helpful in determining the existence of a major depressive episode. According to the DSM-IV these include the following:

- Guilt about things other than actions taken or not taken by the bereaved at the time of death
- Thoughts of death other than the bereaved feeling that he or she should have died with the deceased or would be better off dead than without the deceased
- Morbid preoccupation with worthlessness
- Marked psychomotor retardation
- Significant and prolonged impaired functioning
- Hallucinatory experiences other than thinking that the bereaved hears the deceased voice or transiently sees the deceased person's image

QUESTIONS FOR THOUGHT
AND REFLECTION

1. Have you ever experienced the breakup of a significant relationship? Describe what occurred. What did you experience?

2. Related to the above experience, was the passage of time enough to facilitate your recovery, or did you have to do something? Were there tasks involved in your recovery? Describe what you experienced.

3. Think about your current relationship. How many identities do you have in that relationship? How many related roles are included in your relationship?

4. How does your family deal with strong emotions? What influence has this had on you and how you express or do not express strong feelings?

6

Unresolved Grief

There is no correct way to grieve; therefore, the grieving process takes on many forms and faces. A multitude of factors combine to determine an individual's unique grief reaction, and it is therefore not surprising that there are a number of variants on the normal grieving process. Recall also that the grieving process may contain an emotional illusion of regression, a feeling that the bereaved is slipping backward and returning to square one. This is only an illusion, because as long as the grieving process is not diluted or interrupted, then progress, regardless of how slow, can continue. At worse, the bereaved's progress is momentarily static. However, there are some variants that result in the disruption or disturbance of the normal progress toward resolution of the grieving process. This disruption is sometimes referred to as pathological or abnormal grief. Horowitz et al. (1980) saw this disruption as involving the intensification of grief to the level where the person is overwhelmed, resorts to maladaptive behavior, or remains interminably in the state of grief without progression of the mourning process toward completion. It involves processes that do not move progressively toward assimilation or accommodation but, instead, lead to stereotyped repetitions or extensive interruptions of healing. (p. 1157)

Lindemann, in his article, *Symptomatology and Management of Acute Grief,* wrote about his involvement in treating the survivors of the Coconut Grove Night Club fire in Boston in 1942 in which 492 people died. In the article he describes cases that he considered normal grief reactions and several he considered morbid or abnormal grief reactions.

The following case Lindemann described as being a normal grief reaction with a very successful adjustment.

A man of 52, successful in business, lost his wife, with whom he had lived in a happy marriage. He responded with a severe grief reaction, with which he was unable to cope. He did not want to see visitors, was ashamed of breaking down, and asked to be permitted to stay in the hospital on the psychiatric service, when his physical condition would have permitted his discharge, because he wanted further assistance. Any mention of his wife produced a severe depressive reaction, but with psychiatric assistance he gradually became willing to go through this painful process, and after three days on the psychiatric service he seemed well enough to go home.

He showed a high rate of verbal activity, was restless, needed to be occupied continually, and felt that the experience had whipped him into a state of restless overactivity.

As soon as he returned home he took an active part in his business, assuming a post in which he had a great many phone calls. He also took over the role of amateur psychiatrist to another bereaved person, spending time with him and comforting him for his loss. In his eagerness to start anew, he developed a plan to sell all his former holdings, including his house, his furniture, and give away anything that could remind him of his wife. Only after considerable discussion was he able to see that this would mean avoiding immediate grief at the price of an act of poor judgment. Again he had to be encouraged to deal with his grief reaction in a more direct manner. He made a good adjustment. (pp. 143–144)

Lindemann's writing also includes cases he thought represented distortions of normal grief, or what he referred to as morbid grief reactions.

A young man aged 32 had received only minor burns and left the hospital, apparently well on the road to recovery, just before the psychiatric survey of the disaster victims took place. On the fifth day, he had learned that his wife had died.

He seemed somewhat relieved of his worry about her fate: impressed the surgeon as being unusually well-controlled during the following short period of his stay in the hospital.

On January 1 he was returned to the hospital by his family. Shortly after his return home he had become restless, did not want to stay at home, had taken a trip to relatives trying to find rest, had not succeeded, and had returned home in a state of marked agitation, appearing preoccupied, frightened, and unable to concentrate on any organized activity. The mental status presented a somewhat unusual picture. He was restless, could not sit still or participate in any activity on the ward. He would try to read, drop it after a few minutes, or try to play ping-pong and give it up after a short time. He would try to start a conversation, break it off abruptly, and again fall into repeated murmured utterances: "Nobody can help me. When is this going to happen? I am doomed, am I not?" With great effort it was possible to establish enough rapport to carry on interviews. He complained about his feeling of extreme tension, inability to breathe, generalized weakness and exhaustion, and his frantic fear that something terrible was going to happen. "I'm destined to live my life in insanity or I must die. I know that it is God's will. I have this awful feeling of guilt." With intense morbid guilt feelings, he reviewed incessantly the events of the fire. His wife had stayed behind. When he tried to pull her out, he had fainted and was shoved out by the crowd. She was burned while he was saved. "I should have saved her or I should have died, too." He complained about being filled with an incredible violence and did not know what to do about it. The rapport established with him lasted for only brief periods of time. He then would fall back into his state of intense agitation and muttering. He slept poorly, even with large sedation. In the course of four days he became somewhat more composed, had longer periods of contact with the psychiatrist, and seemed to feel that he was being understood and might be able to cope with his morbid feelings of guilt and violent impulses. On the sixth day of his hospital stay, however, after skillfully distracting the attention of his special nurse, he jumped through a closed window to a violent death. (p. 146)

As can be seen in this case example, major psychiatric illnesses can result from grief reactions that are unresolved. It is noteworthy to stress that major psychiatric illnesses can result as a consequence of unresolved grief. This is different than saying the grief reaction was pathological or abnormal.

Possibly a more descriptive and certainly less stigmatizing term for what Lindemann describes is complicated or unresolved grief. Prigerson et al. (1996) found that complicated (unresolved) grief differs from symptoms of bereavement-related depression and anxiety, supporting the idea that symptoms of unresolved grief form a separate dimension. Horowitz (1998) agreed that we do not want to pathologize unnecessarily and that we can use psychotherapy as an opportunity to work through a mourning process, even when no diagnosis is warranted. The bereaved struggle with what at times seems like an insurmountable task, and labeling their attempts to cope as pathological or abnormal seems counterproductive. The variants prevent or impede resolution; therefore, the term *unresolved* seems appropriate and will be used here.

Two of Bowlby's major categories of unresolved grief were chronic mourning and prolonged absence of mourning, which were seen as exaggerations of a normal grief response (Bowlby, 1980). These responses are attempts to deny the loss and hold onto the person who has died (Rando, 1993).

CHRONIC UNRESOLVED MOURNING

Chronic mourning is characterized by intense and prolonged reactions, which are associated with the early phases (I & II) of loss (Chapter 4). Phase II and/or III cannot be completed and acceptance of the death does not happen. It might appear as though the bereaved is attempting to keep the deceased alive or at least deny the reality of loss through the repetition of select behaviors seen as normal in the first phases of loss. Indications predictive of chronic mourning may appear early in the process, usually within the first three to six weeks. These include little or no response in the weeks after the loss, followed by intense and continuous yearning, looking forward to death, persistent anger and bitterness, long-reaching guilt, and self-reproach (Parkes, 1975b, cited in Bowlby, 1980). Anniversary and/or holiday reactions are common for years, even decades; however, this by itself does not constitute chronic unresolved grief. Chronic unresolved grieving appears to be a neverending task that is never satisfactorily resolved. Despite being aware of the cycle of grieving, the bereaved find themselves unable to resolve it. Chronic grief reactions are not uncommon and generally require professional counseling to be resolved (Raphael & Middleton, 1990). Counseling might focus on accepting that the deceased is dead and will never be returning, at least not in this life, or on sorting out confusing and ambivalent feelings toward the deceased. Still others might need assistance accepting and dealing with the loss of an idealized relationship that was desired but never existed.

PROLONGED ABSENCE OF GRIEVING

In *prolonged absence of grieving,* the bereaved acts as though nothing has happened; therefore, there is no death to accept. Essentially, the person never leaves Phase I. Although it might appear that the individual is functioning as before, there might be physiological difficulties or depression in the future.

Clues to the prolonged absence of grieving are harder to see. In a culture where self-control is highly valued, the temptation will be to maintain a facade of strength and independence. Forced cheerfulness, withdrawal, contempt for consolation, lack of feelings at many levels, not allowing others to speak of the deceased, being tense or short-tempered, and the presence of physical symptoms such as headaches, bodily pains, and insomnia are indications of absence of conscious grieving (Bowlby, 1980).

Rando (1995), drawing on the work of Averill, Parkes and Weiss, and Raphael, added five types of unresolved grief: inhibited, delayed, conflicted, unanticipated, and chronic.

Inhibited grief includes an inhibition of many of the normal behaviors displayed in the normal grieving process. Somatic complaints and ailments appear in their place. Bereaved who do not allow themselves to experience the pain of grief directly may develop some type of somatic complaints or illnesses. They may experience symptoms and behaviors that cause them difficulty but seldom recognize that these are related to the loss. Zisook and Devaul (1976) reported on several cases where the physical symptoms experienced by the bereaved were similar to those suffered by the deceased. They referred to these as *facsimile illnesses.* Inhibited grief can also manifest itself in aberrant or maladaptive behavior. Again the bereaved may realize that there has been a change in their behavior, but they do not associate it with the loss they have experienced.

Delayed grief may result from pressing responsibilities (real or perceived) that survivors feel they must attend to immediately or because they feel unable to process the loss at the current time. The delay may last for years; however, a full grief reaction may be triggered by another loss or event related to the original loss. Geller (1985) provides an example of a lengthy delayed grief reaction occurring in the case of a woman who lost several of her children in an accident. She was pregnant at the time and was advised by her physician not to get too upset because it could jeopardize her pregnancy. She heeded her doctor's advice and mourning was delayed. Years later she had an intense grief reaction when her last child left home.

Conflicted grief involves the exaggeration of one or more of the behaviors displayed in the normal grieving process, while suppressing others. Anger and guilt are two common patterns. In this pattern anger and guilt are prolonged while other normally occurring emotions are absent. Anxiety is another common response to a loss. It is sometimes exaggerated and experienced as panic attacks or phobias. Underlying this anxiety may be such things as unconscious feelings of survivor's guilt or ambivalent feelings regarding the relationship with the deceased. Problems with alcohol and/or drugs may develop, or existing problems may be exacerbated. This is an attempt to self-medicate. This type of grief reaction may also include major psychiatric disorders that develop following a loss. Lindemann's earlier case of a morbid grief reaction is such an example.

Unanticipated grief occurs in response to an unexpected loss. The loss is experienced as coming out of the blue, and is so overpowering that the adaptive capacities of the bereaved are overwhelmed. Statements such as, "I can't believe this has happened, but I know it did," are common and reflect the incomprehensibility of what has happened. There is great difficulty accepting the loss; and, regardless of intellectual awareness that death has occurred, it continues to be inscrutable.

Chronic grief, as the name implies, is grieving that is intense, at the level expected in the early stages of loss, and is continuously experienced long after the loss. The expected course of mourning toward completion never occurs, and there is little or no progress. Pining or intense yearning is symptomatic of this type of grief and may be associated with extremely dependent relationships where the bereaved feels that he or she has sustained the loss of an irreplaceable relationship or relationships in which there is an extraordinary emotional investment.

Abbreviated grief is often mistakenly seen as a form of unresolved grief. Actually, it is normal grief experience, albeit short-lived, in which grief is abbreviated or shortened, usually because the lost attachment figure is quickly replaced (e.g., remarrying quickly following the death of the spouse). Anticipatory grief may also play a part in that sufficient grieving occurs prior to the actual death. A lack of or insufficient attachment to the deceased may also be a factor that lessens or abbreviates the time necessary for mourning. If there was actually little or no attachment to a spouse, parent, or significant other, then mourning will be minimal to unnecessary.

SYMPTOMS OF UNRESOLVED GRIEF

Siggins (1966) asserted that there were three primary variables that differentiate unresolved grief from normal grief. They are absence of a normal grief reaction, prolongation of a normal grief reaction, and distortion of a normal grief reaction. Lindemann (1944), Lazare (1979), and Worden (1991) all have identified symptoms associated with unresolved grief. Symptoms may be unremarkable during the acute phase of grief; however, when they are evidenced beyond what seems to be an expected time they constitute signs of incomplete grief. The more symptoms the bereaved has, the more likely grief is to be unresolved.

Lindemann (1944) noted the following symptoms associated with unresolved grief:

- Overactivity without a sense of purpose
- Acquisition of symptoms belonging to the last illness of the deceased
- Development of a psychosomatic medical illness
- Alteration in relationships with friends and relatives
- Furious hostility against specific persons somehow connected with the death
- Wooden or formal conduct that masks hostile feelings and resembles a schizophrenic reaction in which there is no emotion
- Lasting loss of patterns of social interaction
- Acts detrimental to one's own social and economic existence (e.g., giving away belongings or making foolish economic decisions)
- Agitated depression with tension agitation, insomnia, feelings of worthlessness, bitter self-accusations, an obvious need for punishment, and suicidal tendencies

Lazare (1979) developed what he considered diagnostic criteria for unresolved grief that included one or more of the following symptoms that occur after a death loss and continue beyond six months and up to a year. The greater the number of symptoms, the greater the likelihood of unresolved grief.

- A depressive syndrome of varying degrees of severity since the time of the death, frequently a very mild, subclinical one often accompanied by persistent guilt and lowered self-esteem
- A history of delayed or prolonged grief, indicating that the person characteristically avoids or has difficulty with grief work
- Symptoms of guilt and self-reproach, panic attacks, and somatic expressions of fear such as choking sensations and shortness of breath

- Somatic symptoms representing identification with the deceased, often symptoms of the terminal illness
- Physical distress under the upper part of the sternum, accompanied by expressions such as, "There is something stuck inside," or "I feel there is a demon inside of me"
- Searching that continues over time, with a great deal of random behavior, restlessness, and moving about
- Recurrence of symptoms of depression and searching behavior on specific dates, such as anniversaries of the death, birthdays of the deceased, and holidays (especially Christmas), that are more extreme than those anniversary reactions normally expected
- A feeling that the death occurred yesterday, even though the loss took place months or years ago
- Unwillingness to move the material possessions of the deceased after a reasonable amount of time has passed
- Changes in relationships following the death
- Diminished participation in religious and ritual activities that are part of the mourner's culture, including avoidance of visiting the grave or taking part in the funeral
- An inability to discuss the deceased without crying or having the voice crack, particularly when the death occurred more than a year ago
- Theme of loss

Worden (1991) suggested the following symptoms:

- Inability to speak of the deceased without experiencing intense grief
- A relatively minor event triggering a major grief reaction
- Loss as a repetitive theme
- Inability to part with possessions of the deceased after a reasonable period
- False euphoria subsequent to the death or a long history of subclinical depression
- Overidentification with the deceased, leading to a compulsion to imitate the dead person, particularly if it is unconscious and the mourner lacks the competence for the same behavior
- Unaccountable sadness during various time of the year; may coincide with holidays or special dates shared with the deceased
- Self-destructive impulses
- Radical change in lifestyle
- Exclusion of friends, family members, or activities associated with the deceased
- Avoidance of the gravesite or participation in death-related rituals or activities
- Phobias about illness or death

The reader is cautioned to remember that these lists are not all-inclusive. There is also no substitute for experience that will develop over time and be used to assess the relative importance of symptoms in context of a survivor and the person's unique situation.

FACTORS RELATED
TO UNRESOLVED GRIEF

In the previous chapter we saw that various psychological and social factors exert significant influence on the normal grief reaction. Some of the same factors are influential in contributing to complicated or unresolved grief.

Psychological Factors

The most frequent type of relationship that hinders people from adequate grieving is one involving extreme ambivalence, coupled with unexpressed hostility. The difficulties associated with unresolved relational ambivalence in life are now carried over and inhibit grieving. Anger and associated guilt are predictable and, as they were in life, they will be a source of adjustment difficulty and complications in the grieving process.

Bowlby (1980) suggests that relationships characterized by a high degree of dependence or ambivalence might be more prone to complicated bereavement reactions. In this type of relationship the bereaved loses a source of sustaining strength, and the result is an overwhelming sense of abandonment and helplessness. The sense of helplessness and loss of self-concept tend to overwhelm any other feelings related to healthy grief (Horowitz et al., 1980). In dependent relationships, each member takes a significant portion of identity from the other person. The tie that binds ambivalent or angry relationships is one of fear of loneliness. In both cases, when the other person dies, the remaining individual is left with "A self-definition [that] is challenged by the absence of someone whose psychological contiguity served as a partial self-referent. Dysfunctional responses to death will be associated with distorted definitions of self." (Rynearson, 1990a, p. 301) These responses may be manifested in a range of dysfunctional behaviors from chronic grieving (Bowlby, 1980; Conway, 1988; Parkes, 1990; Rando, 1993; Raphael & Middleton, 1990; Rynearson, 1987; Zisook, Shuchter & Lyons, 1987) to mummification and even to suicide (Bowlby, 1980).

There also exist factors that are idiosyncratic to the individual, such as a unique mindset that runs counter to the mourning experience. Some individuals pride themselves on being highly analytical and unemotional; others have been socialized to avoid feelings, and still others fear that once the emotions associated with grief are felt, they will never cease. It is universally accepted that regardless of the rationale, avoiding feelings will interfere with the normal grieving process and result in unresolved grief.

Finally, personality factors are also related to how well or poorly a person copes with emotional distress. Inability to tolerate extreme emotional distress leads to defensive withdrawal and can forestall the grieving process. Simos (1979) wrote the following related to complicated grief reactions:

> Because the resolution of grief demands the experiencing of universal feelings of helplessness in the face of existential loss, those individuals whose major defenses are built around avoidance of feelings of helplessness may be among those likely to have dysfunctional reactions to grief. Thus individuals who normally function most competently on the surface may be the very ones thrown most heavily by a major loss as it strikes at the core of their defensive system. (p. 170)

Circumstantial Factors

Circumstantial factors surrounding a loss may preclude or make completion of the grieving process difficult or impossible. Uncertainty of the loss—not knowing if a person is truly dead—precludes adequate grieving (e.g., soldiers who were listed MIA during the war or disaster victims whose bodies are not recovered, or missing children). Where no concrete evidence of death is found, mourning can be unresolved. As the saying goes, hope springs eternal, especially in the absence of proof of the finality of the loss. Without a true reality to accept, many will find it impossible to avoid unresolved grief.

Situations where multiple losses occur (e.g., Oklahoma City bombing, 9/11) can make grieving difficult due to the sheer volume involved. Where there are multiple losses in close proximity, it becomes easier and sometimes necessary for the bereaved to shut down completely.

A history of mental illness, such as major depressive illness, can predispose one to complications that inhibit or even prevent adequate grief response. Also, a history of early parental loss may have implications for the grieving process. Likewise, factors such as insecurity related to inadequate parenting also appear to be factors. Finally, people who have experienced complicated grief in the past are seen as having a higher probability of having complications again following a loss owing to the same or other factors.

The influence of psychological and circumstantial factors were supported by a study at Scott and White Clinic and Memorial Hospital on predictors of intensified mourning. Gamino, Sewell, and Easterling (1998) found three factors, age of decedent (younger), relationship quality (conflictual, ambivalent, or overly dependent), and mourner liability (history of mental health problems) were associated with greater grief misery.

Social Factors

Mourning is the outward expression of grief, and social settings provide the bereaved an opportunity to find support and reinforcement in their reactions to the loss. Lazare (1979) cites three social conditions that tend to give rise to complications in the grieving process: the loss is socially unspeakable, the loss is socially negated, or there is no social support network. William James (1890) recognized our need for social recognition and the consequences associated with such a predisposition when he wrote the following:

> We are not only gregarious animals liking to be in sight of our fellows but have an innate propensity to get ourselves noticed favorably by our own kind. No more fiendish punishment could be devised were such a thing physically possible than that one should be turned loose in society and remain absolutely unnoticed by all the members thereof. (p. 292)

Doka (1995) notes that there are circumstances in which an individual experiences a loss but does not have a socially recognized right, role, or capacity to grieve. In these cases he refers to the grief as disenfranchised. He defines disenfranchised grief as the grief that individuals experience when they incur a loss that is not or cannot be acknowledged publicly, openly mourned, or socially supported. This lack of social acknowledgment and/or support is predicated on mostly unwritten but nonetheless accepted social norms that specify who, when, where, for whom, for how long, and what mourning behavior and rituals are acceptable. Some rules for grieving are written, as in the case of personnel policies. These rules dictate how long and for whom an individual may be allowed time off following a death. This type of codification permeates our society and functions to define whom and under what circumstances an individual has a legitimate or recognized right to grieve. Doka points out that in any given society these rules might not correspond to the nature of human attachments, the sense of loss, or the experience of the bereaved. Consequently, the grief is disenfranchised. He notes that this may occur for three reasons: the relationship is not recognized, the loss is not recognized, and/or the bereaved is not recognized.

In our society, families, their related roles, and their relationships are considered to be of paramount importance. The assumption being made here is that family ties are the closest attachments one has and that all others wane by comparison. Therefore, those outside the family are not understood, recognized, or accepted as possibly having the same grief experience. As such, these individuals might not have the opportunity or social support for a public display of mourning. The role of nonfamily is usually defined in terms of offering support to the bereaved family members.

There are also relationships that exist but for one reason or another are not publicly recognized (e.g., extramarital, closet homosexual, or pets). Other relationships existing primarily in the past may also be affected by the loss and experience grief but are publicly unrecognized (e.g., ex-spouses, lovers, or friends having limited contact). If the relationship does not fit the proper definition or for other reasons is not publicly recognized, then there exists a perception that though a loss has occurred, it should not cause any significant reaction.

Society also has rules regarding what is socially significant and thus what loss may be recognized. Perinatal death sometimes involves intense grief reactions; however, the loss might be perceived as relatively minor to many. Abortions might also constitute serious losses, both at the time of the abortion and years later, yet this loss may also be unrecognized.

Sudnow (1967), in a previous chapter, introduced us to the fact that there are many types of death (social, psychological, biological, and physiological). In each type of death the bereaved experiences a profound sense of loss; however, the loss may not be publicly acknowledged. Recall from Chapter 1 the story of Mr. and Mrs. X. Mrs. X experienced the psychological death of Mr. X in the SICU upon the realization that no matter what the outcome psychologically, she had lost her husband. This loss went unacknowledged publicly, although the effects were felt by Mrs. X. Similarly, the loss experienced at the time of Mr. X's physiological death was socially unacknowledged. If it does not meet the accepted definition of being socially significant, it might not publicly be recognized.

Finally, societal rules exist that dictate who has the capacity to grieve and who is therefore recognized as a mourner. Often the very young are perceived as having little understanding or comprehension of death and therefore no noteworthy reaction to the death of a significant other. As a result, they are excluded from the rituals involved in the mourning process. Similarly, the mentally disabled may also be perceived as not able to understand what has occurred and also excluded from the mourning process.

Those working with the bereaved will likely have exposure to many cases of disenfranchised grief. This topic will be discussed further in chapter 7, p. 98 on grieving special types of losses.

ASSESSING AND WORKING THROUGH UNRESOLVED GRIEF

As has been seen in the chapter on normal grief, the goal of grief work, whether normal or complicated (unresolved), is to resolve the conflicts associated with attachment and separation and to complete the tasks associated with grieving. This requires experiencing the thoughts and feelings that the bereaved has avoided. In facilitating this experience, the bereaved must be given permission to grieve. In the case of unresolved grief, many thoughts and/or feelings may be experienced as foreign and inherently unacceptable or bad. Consequently, permission must be given (not necessarily verbally) to experience what is there, but heretofore not acknowledged, accepted, or seen as socially unacceptable. To achieve this end, the counselor must listen for the bereaved's voice to crack, and watch for facial muscles to quiver, eyes to water, or other telling signs to emerge. At this critical moment the bereaved will begin to assess both his or her and the counselor's ability to allow (give permission) and accept the previously denied thoughts and feelings. If the counselor can accurately recognize and then empathize with the bereaved's plight, then permission to begin to experience the process of grieving may be given; and, if other factors are present, received.

Counseling is obviously not a prescriptive interaction; however, understanding of the dynamics of a given protocol applied within the framework of the counselor's own theoretical orientation is useful. Raphael (1983) outlined what she referred to as a therapeutic assessment. Its purpose is not only to provide information but also to facilitate the expression of emotion, thus promoting the mourning process. Questions and their purposes are outlined as follows:

- Can you tell me a little about the death? What happened that day? Related questions may include: How did you find out about the death? Where were you when your loved one died?

These questions open up the topic and allow the bereaved permission to talk about the loss. It further provides information related to the nature and circumstances of the death and whether death was anticipated or unexpected. The bereaved's capacity to discuss the death and availability of emotional response will be evident. Denial and other related defense or coping mechanisms may begin to emerge. Also guilt, feelings of culpability, or illogical thinking may become apparent.

- Can you tell me about your loved one? Can you tell me about your relationship with your loved one?

These questions allow the counselor to get a history of the deceased and the relationship the bereaved had with the person. The counselor should listen for information that indicates the quality of the relationship, expectations (real and ideal), needs (relating to independence and dependence), conflicts, rules governing the expression of feelings, or other related aspects of the relationship. The history, as well as the degree of agreement between content and affect (sadness or tears associated with sad memories), will be a clue to the existence of ambivalent or conflicted feelings. Finally, the emotions associated with the grief experience may be assessed and will indicate the bereaved's progress in this area of the grief process.

- What has been happening since the death? How have things been with you and your family and friends?

These questions allow for the exploration of family and social patterns of interaction (availability of social support) following the loss as well as sociocultural norms that may influence the grieving process. Listening for terms of inclusion of the deceased will help to further assess the acceptance of the permanence of loss.

- Have you been through any other bad times recently or prior to the loss?

This inquiry allows for the assessment of prior and/or additional recent losses that might have an impact on mourning. Not only should normal losses be explored, but also the possibility of disenfranchised losses.

Worden (1991) has outlined a set of nine procedures involved in working through unresolved grief:

1. Rule out physical disease.
2. Set up the contract and establish an alliance.
3. Revive memories of the deceased.
4. Assess which grief tasks have not been completed.

5. Deal with effect (or lack of) stimulated by memories.

6. Explore and defuse linking objects.

7. Acknowledge the finality of the loss.

8. Deal with the fantasy of ending grief.

9. Help the patient say a final good-bye.

   Let's look at each procedure more closely.

Rule Out Physical Disease

If the bereaved presents with physical symptoms (including depression) it is important to rule out physical disease. It is true that physical symptoms are compatible with grief; however, it is also true that physical disease such as hypothyroidism might also be compatible with symptoms of depression. All physical symptoms should be checked out medically prior to accepting them as grief related and entering into a course of counseling.

Set Up the Contract and Establish an Alliance

A specific contract to re-explore the bereaved's relationship with the deceased is made. The contract provides reinforcement or face validity to the belief that this endeavor will indeed be helpful and serves as a tool to establish an alliance with the bereaved to accomplish the stated goal.

Revive Memories of the Deceased

It is imperative that the bereaved talk about the person who has died. Discussion should focus on who the person was, what he or she was like, and what the bereaved enjoyed doing with the deceased. It is helpful to begin with positive memories, as these are likely to elicit less resistance and this will serve as a counterbalance that will support the bereaved later when acknowledging negative attributes of the person and/or the relationship. Should a person present with mostly negative memories, the process can be reversed.

   In the case of bereaved who have experienced multiple losses, it is necessary to deal with each loss separately. Following the logic of least resistance, it is generally helpful to deal with the loss that has the fewest complicating factors first and then move to more complicated relationships or variants.

Assess Which Grief Tasks Are Not Completed

This assessment allows the intervention to be focused. If the first task of grief, accepting the loss, is not completed, then the focus of counseling is on accepting the reality of the death and letting go of the deceased. This may prove to be a multitask problem and also involve task 2, working through the pain of grief. Acknowledging the loss oftentimes result in immediate pain that may be too intense to bear. If this should happen, the bereaved's coping strategy might be to deny the loss in an attempt to escape the pain. Movement may be back and forth. In this case, the counseling intervention will be much like peeling an artichoke one leaf or layer at time until the heart is slowly and carefully exposed.

In the cases where the loss is accepted but feelings associated with the loss are not, conflicted or ambivalent feelings should be suspected and a careful balance will need to be constructed. The ultimate goal may be a redefining of the bereaved's relationship to the deceased.

Difficulty in task 3, adjusting to an environment in which the deceased is missing, may involve helping the bereaved define what has been lost, acquire a new role, or overcome feelings of helplessness. Problem solving will be the main focus. This occurs in a supportive setting that allows for progress to be measured in the appropriate context of time. For Mrs. X, this was a major task in her grief work, learning for the first time and then relearning many social skills and related activities of daily living. Her work also involved the difficult task of developing a new self-identity. This required her to struggle with and to establish herself as an "I." The accompanying difficulties included questioning her self-worth, doubts about the future, and fears related to a new-found autonomy.

Moving on with life, the fourth task of grief, is sometimes viewed as being disloyal. It may also be symbolically saying that final good-bye and accepting the finality of the loss. The bereaved may need permission to stop grieving and a reason, a why to continue with life. Helping the bereaved to find meaning in an otherwise meaningless situation may be seen in the following example.

> An elderly man, Mr. P, was referred to me for therapy following the death of his wife of 50+ years. As may be expected, Mr. P was experiencing significant depression, and his family thought therapy might help. In talking with him, I learned that he and his wife had a very traditional marriage with he being the bread-winner and she the wife and mother. In the course of our discussion, I asked Mr. P what would have happened if he rather than his wife had died. He explained how terrible that would have been and all of the difficult trials and tribulations she would have had to face alone in his absence. In light of his comments, I suggested that it was a gift that his wife had been allowed to die first. However, as I pointed out, the gift does not come without a price. The price was that now he, not she, would have to endure the difficult trials and tribulations as well as the sadness and grief he now felt. This was a novel idea to Mr. P, and it gave him a reason to accept his fate. More than that, it allowed him to see his suffering as a final gift of love he was able to give his wife. In subsequent meetings, I also queried Mr. P on how he thought Mrs. P might want him to live life. Again, he told me of plans they had and things that they enjoyed together. I asked how he felt about Mrs. P not being able to experience those things. He naturally responded that he wished that she could. I suggested that since she could not partake, he as the surviving mate should take the aforementioned opportunity he had wished for her. With help, Mr. P was to find his answer to why and move back into life.

Deal with Effect or the Lack
of Effect Stimulated by Memories

In the beginning when the bereaved talk about the deceased, their description is of the "best person who ever lived." This description may indicate or suggest the existence of unexpressed anger or other conflicted feelings. The bereaved might be recalling what they wish or idealize the deceased to have been. It is important to listen and to allow the bereaved to describe the deceased in this manner. This allows the bereaved to have a supportive platform from which to gradually explore the angry or conflicted feelings they have toward the deceased. In dealing with the presence or absence of feelings triggered by memories of the deceased, remember not to use a machete when a scalpel will do.

Explore and Defuse Linking Objects

Linking objects are defined here as symbolic objects that the bereaved keeps that allow them to maintain a relationship with the deceased. As such, Worden views their function as being contrary to effective resolution of grief through denial of the actual loss. The object is seen as being invaluable, and its whereabouts must be known at all times. Linking objects are more than keepsakes or mementos and are invested with much more meaning. The loss of a linking object may produce a great anxiety in the bereaved. Linking objects may be seen as similar to transitional objects that young children hold onto as they first venture away from their parents (e.g., crib blankets or stuffed animals). The concept of linking objects was identified by Volkan (1972, 1973) and is seen as playing a role in the irresolution of mourning.

Following the death the bereaved sometimes invest an inanimate object with symbolism that establishes a link between them and the deceased. The bereaved are most often aware of the object and the symbolism that they have invested in it but without comprehending all of the implications. Volkan (1972) noted that linking objects are chosen from one of four areas: (1) Some belonging of the deceased, such as something they wore like a watch or a piece of jewelry; (2) something with which the deceased extended his or her senses, like a camera, which would represent a visual extension; (3) a representation of the deceased, such as a photograph; and (4) something that was at hand when the news of the death was received or when the bereaved saw the body. Volkan believes that these types of linking objects are used to handle anxiety and that they provide a "token of triumph" over the loss. The linking objects mark a blurring of psychic boundaries between the bereaved and the deceased, as if representations of the two individuals or parts of them are merged through the use of the linking object.

Volken (1972) described a patient whose linking object was a tiny stuffed animal that he and his deceased wife had given a particular name. He kept the object with him, especially when he was on trips. Once, returning home from a business trip, he noticed it missing. Seized with panic and desperation, he pulled up the auto seat and the carpeting in an effort to find the lost linking object. He never found it, and his anxiety was the focus of many therapy sessions following its loss.

It is important to ask the bereaved about items or objects they have saved; and, if it is determined that are using something as a linking object, this should be a point of discussion and focus. Using the object as a point of focus can help facilitate mourning. Defusing of the linking object does not mean the object is no longer desired or retained; rather, it is kept for the happy memories it represents and no longer as a source of comfort.

It should be clear that Worden's use of the term *linking objects* refers to those objects whose function it is to deny the loss and ultimate separation of the bereaved from the deceased. Not all "linking" objects (i.e., momentos and other keepsakes) serve this purpose, and those that are kept for sentimental value representing happy memories or shared meaning are considered normal.

Acknowledge the Finality of the Loss

In most cases, this is accomplished early on following the loss; however, there are some bereaved who hold on to the belief that the deceased is coming back in some form or another. Volkan (1972) called this a *chronic hope for reunion*. In these cases it is important to assist the bereaved in discovering the source of the continued attachment and inability to acknowledge the finality of the loss.

Deal with the Fantasy of Ending Grief

Fantasies sometimes provide us a glimpse of reality. It might be helpful when grieving has gone on for prolonged periods to have the bereaved fantasize about what it would be like to finish grieving. This exercise should take the form of experiencing both the pros and cons of grieving. Fully examine and experience what life would be like without grief and what the bereaved would be giving up by not continuing to grieve. Simple gestalt exercises can prove to be a powerful tool in the resolution of mourning.

Help the Patient Say a Final Good-bye

As noted previously, what is meant by saying good-bye to the deceased can be confusing. (Does it mean I give up all contact with the deceased and forget the person?) *Good-bye* is a good-bye to the corporal relationship. Attempting to hang on to that which no longer exists leads only to pain and suffering. That which was central to my life must now be reordered to allow for other things or individuals to become more central. On a trip to a local public library I found a writing that caught the sentiment well:

> I am standing on the seashore, a ship spreads her white sails to the morning breeze and starts for the ocean. I stand watching her until she fades on the horizon, and someone at my side says, "She is gone." Gone where? The loss of sight is in me, not her. Just at that moment when

somewhere someone says, "She is gone," there are others who are watching her coming. Other voices take up the glad shout, "Here she comes." And this is dying. (Anonymous)

This anonymous writer captures the essence of the process that the bereaved go through saying good-bye and at the same time saying hello, again. Both the voice that utters, "She is gone" (good-bye to the corporal relationship) and the one that proclaims, "Here she comes," (hello to a new transformed relationship of memory and unfolding meaning) are one and the same for the bereaved. And this is the task of emotionally relocating the deceased and preparing to move on with life.

QUESTIONS FOR THOUGHT
AND REFLECTION

1. Define the words *normal* and *abnormal*. What makes something normal and something else abnormal? How does this apply to grieving?

2. As a child, did you ever play pretend? Have you ever pretended that you were not scared when you really were? How was this beneficial? How does this apply to grieving?

3. How long, in your opinion, should mourning last? What factors are influential in your answer?

4. Is it possible to both love and hate someone at the same time? What effect does this have on the relationship? If this were not resolved, how might it influence the grieving process?

5. Does everything, every problem, ultimately come to resolution? If so, how? If not, why not?

7

❧

Grieving Special Types
of Losses

T hus far, our introduction to grief and loss has been somewhat generic. However, we have seen how different circumstances can affect the grief experience. In this chapter three specific bereavement situations, suicide, homicide, death of a child (including miscarriage, abortion, stillbirth, young child, adolescent, and adult child) and the diverse issues that arise related to the different circumstances will be explored. As we have seen, not all grief reactions are the same, nor are the circumstances that spawn them.

SUDDEN AND UNEXPECTED DEATH

Before moving into our specific bereavement situations, it may be helpful to identify issues inherent in sudden and unexpected death. Sudden death obviously occurs without warning and may categorically include suicide, homicide, accidental death, and health-related death due to such things as heart attacks or strokes. Rando (1993) identified 11 issues inherent in sudden, unanticipated death that may complicate mourning:

1. The capacity to cope is diminished as the shock effect of the death overwhelms the ego at the same time new stressors are added (e.g., heightened personal threat and vulnerability).

2. The bereaved's assumptions about the world are violently shattered without warning and the violation of these assumptions (e.g., the world is

safe, predictable, orderly) causes intense reactions of fear, anxiety, vulnerability, and loss of control.

3. The loss does not make sense, and cannot be understood or accommodated.

4. There is no chance to say good–bye and complete unfinished business with the deceased.

5. Symptoms of acute grief and of physical and emotional shock persist for a prolonged period of time.

6. The bereaved obsessively reconstructs events in an effort to comprehend the death and to prepare for it in retrospect.

7. The bereaved experience a profound loss of security and confidence in the world, which affects all areas of life and increases anxiety.

8. The loss cuts across experiences in the relationship and tends to highlight what was happening at the time of death, often causing these last-minute situations to be out of proportion with the rest of the relationship and predisposing the bereaved to problems associated with unrealistic recollections and guilt.

9. The death tends to leave the bereaved with relatively more intense emotional reactions, such as anger, ambivalence, guilt, helplessness, death anxiety, vulnerability, confusion, disorganization, and obsession with the deceased, along with strong needs to make meaning of the death and to determine blame and affix responsibility for it.

10. The death tends to be followed by a number of major secondary losses, owing to the lack of anticipation.

11. The death can provoke post-traumatic stress responses (e.g., repeated intrusive memories, increased physiological arousal).

Sudden, unexpected death creates a crisis situation and, as such, principles of crisis intervention may be appropriate. Remember that an individual in a state of shock or numbness cannot always ask for help or may respond in a negative way if asked. Generally, it is helpful in dealing with victims of sudden, unanticipated loss to say something like, "I work with people who have had such a loss and I'm here to talk and work with you." Initial facultative responses to the bereaved should include being physically present and providing empathic understanding and acknowledgment of the loss.

Survivors of Suicide and Grief

Death by suicide can be one of the most difficult and complicated losses to grieve. Suicide is usually sudden, unexpected, often violent, possibly preventable, and always self-inflicted. Edwin Shenidman, the founder of the American Association of Suicidology, estimates that for each death by suicide, six other persons are intimately affected (1969). A 1990 study in Quebec suggests that an average of 10 individuals are affected by each completed suicide (Association

Quebecoise de Suicidologie). Kastenbaum (1977) noted that although the deceased from suicide are neither more nor less dead than those who die after a long, debilitating illness, the phenomenon of suicide itself has a special set of meanings for us.

Evidence is emerging that suggests individuals bereaved through suicide (survivors of suicide) will likely experience a more complicated grief reaction than will those in which the death is the result of natural causes or accident (Silverman, Range, & Overholser, 1994, Calhoun & Allen, 1993; Tedeschi & Calhoun, 1993; van der Wal, 1990; Calhoun, Selby, & Selby, 1982).

Stillion & McDowell (1996) noted three promising areas of research relating to the grief experience of survivors of suicide: (1) attitudes toward survivors; (2) the experience of suicide survivors; (3) postvention with suicide survivors.

Attitudes toward survivors of suicide are influenced by many factors. One of the strongest of these is the cultural tradition that regards suicide as a sin. This position has been held for centuries by members of the Judeo-Christian faiths. Catholics, Protestants, and Jews generally have been taught that suicide is morally wrong and that salvation may be imperiled as a result. Negative attitudes may also be related to fears aroused by confronting or acknowledging our own potential for self-destruction. Regardless of the source, research (Silverman, Ramge, & Overholser, 1994; Reed & Greenwald, 1991; Barrett & Scott, 1989; Saunders, 1981) has shown that survivors of suicide are viewed more negatively than are those bereaved through natural death or accident. This finding, however, did not appear to hold true in persons who knew someone bereaved through suicide (Calhoun, Selby, & Steelman, 1984).

Those who experience bereavement have a need to express and talk about their thoughts and feelings in a safe environment where they will not feel judged. This is especially true of those bereaved through suicide. Paradoxically, funeral directors have noticed that visitors to families bereaved through suicide react differently from others; they expressed compassion but appeared uncomfortable in expressing their sympathy (Calhoun, Selby, & Abernathy, 1988). These and other factors contribute to the suicide survivor's unique experience.

Survivors of suicide report experiencing greater guilt, shame, and rejection than did survivors of accidental death (Reed & Greenwald, 1991). Shneidman said the following about survivors of suicide:

> I believe that the person who commits suicide puts his psychological skeletons in the survivor's emotional closet—he sentences the survivor to deal with many negative feelings, and, more, to become obsessed with thoughts regarding their own actual or possible role in having precipitated the suicidal act or having failed to abort it. It can be a heavy load. (Quoted in Cain, 1972, p. X).

Guilt can sometimes manifest itself as blame, and since death by suicide is an intentional act, there is often inclination for survivor's to blame themselves for failing to prevent the suicide. In the search for understanding, survivors may look back and see in light of the death hints or cues forecasting the impending suicide. Guilt, as we have seen, is a normal feeling following any type of death; however, in the case of death by suicide, guilt can be exacerbated exponentially. Guilt can also be increased by the fact that there may be no external source to blame. Death was not inevitable, caused by a terminal disease, or the result of an unforeseen and unexpected accident. The experience of relief that the deceased's suffering is over can also be the source of great guilt and self-recrimination. Owing to the severity of guilt experienced, some bereaved may experience a need to punish themselves or to be punished. Children and/or adolescents may engage in acting out or delinquent behavior as a means of eliciting self-punishment.

Blame can also be assigned or inferred by others. Research findings suggest suicide survivors often isolate themselves from friends and family following the death, refusing to discuss the death or lying about the cause of death (Rudestam, 1977; Solomon, 1982). They report feeling uneasy in the aftermath of the suicide in dealing with police officers, coroners, and physicians, and often report feeling blamed by other family members for the suicide (Cain & Fast, 1972; Nees & Pfeffer, 1990; Solomon, 1982). Range and Goggin (1990) found that when the person who died by suicide was younger, the family was more often thought to be of blame for the suicide.

As we have seen, our society attaches a social stigma to suicide, and it is the survivors who have to suffer the shame associated with the act. This may be seen in the fact that obituaries may be altered to avoid stating the cause of death or completely omitted. Insurance companies often have suicide clauses, and claims may be disallowed. The experience of shame can also be influenced by the reactions of others. As one bereaved mother said, "I want to talk about my son, but no one will talk to me. They act as if he never existed." This collateral emotional burden may influence the survivor's interactions with both friends and family, leading to further isolation and feelings of shame and complicating the grieving process.

The dynamics of a loved one choosing to die and separate him or herself from the survivors can lead to intense feelings of rejection and anger. Lindemann (1953) wrote, "To be bereft by self-imposed death is to be rejected." (p. 9) Survivors often speculate that the deceased did not love them enough, or the individual would not have committed suicide. Feelings of rejection may fuel feelings of guilt and shame. Survivors might experience lowered self-esteem, feelings of unworthiness, or a feeling that something about themselves is wrong or bad, might develop as they struggle to understand the perceived rejection. The repetitive question, "Why?" is frequently heard, although the real question might be, "Why did you do this to me?" This question has, more often than not, anger, possibly bordering on rage, associated with it. This anger may be directed toward the deceased, God, the world, or the survivors themselves. It is not uncommon to hear an utterance such as, "If you weren't dead I'd kill you." Angry outbursts, although therapeutic, can also be the source additional guilt and shame.

It is also not uncommon for suicide survivors to develop a fear of their own self-destructive impulses and develop a preoccupation with suicide. Questions about the inheritability of suicidal thinking and action are not uncommon.

Finally, in some instances, there is another feature unique to survivors of suicide, a conspiracy of silence. This conspiracy grows out of a need to deny that the deceased's action was a suicide and to see it as an accident. Myths might develop about what happened that involve a single individual or an entire family. Those who call the death by its real name are usually met with strong resistance, including anger. This denial distorts and prevents both the intellectual and emotional acceptance of the loss, and it might result in communication distortions that affect both family and other interpersonal relations. This form of denial, like most, might be helpful in the short term but is not productive long term and will most likely interfere with bringing the grieving process to fruition. An example of the development and perpetuation of a family myth may be seen in the following:

> A 16-year-old adolescent died following a self-inflicted gunshot wound to the head. His mother discovered the gruesome sight when she went to explore the loud noise she heard coming from her son's room. The victim was an only child, and the loss was devastating to the parents. Despite emotional support being offered immediately, symptoms of severe depression and PTSD were evidenced by the mother. In the first weeks that followed, the parents began to question the reality of the death being a suicide, despite the almost indisputable facts. In short order their questioning developed into a complete story of how the "accident" happened. Any comment or failure to accept the death as an accident was met with masked resentment and social withdrawal. Within nine months of the suicide, the parents had terminated almost all previous social relationships and withdrew into a social cocoon. Though they continued to live in the community, they discontinued virtually all social contact.

Postvention with survivors of suicide is extremely important, especially when the population is adolescent. Adolescents respond to what is called *cluster* or *copycat suicide* more often than do older groups (Stillion & McDowell, 1996). Cluster suicides occur when a group of people, usually adolescents, living in the same geographic area commit suicide over a relatively short period of time. Cluster suicides have been seen as having a contagious effect in adolescent suicide (Carter & Brooks, 1990).

In working with survivors of suicide, remember that suicide is one of those unmentionables and there may be hesitation on the part of the survivors and others to discuss the death. It is important to talk about and to face the reality of the suicide in order to work through it. Using the words suicide and/or killed him/herself, as painful as they may be, may facilitate this work. As in the above example, individuals who have witnessed the suicide may be plagued by intrusive images of what they have seen. Exploring and talking about the graphic images is a difficult task; but, again, it is part of the healing process. These images usually dissipate with time; however, when they do not special interventions may be necessary.

Guilt, shame, and blame all may be present in varying degrees of intensity. Most of these feelings will abate in light of reality. Reality testing irrational guilt is nothing more than cognitively confronting the often-heard statement, "I should have done more." Repetitive questioning of what was done, what else could have realistically been done will often result in an awareness and acceptance that maybe s/he did all s/he could under the circumstances. Recall from Chapter 5 that some guilt is deserved; however, the resolution lies in front of the bereaved and not behind them. Helping the bereaved make their decision on how to handle their guilt a conscious one facilitates their not making the same mistake in the future that they feel guilty about making in their past.

Recall that it is common to feel anger when someone dies. This is especially true in the case of suicide. Sometimes, however, anger is elusive. Often it is not socially acceptable, or there are other prohibitions against it. Recall from a previous chapter that a technique for facilitating a balancing of emotions is to ask what the bereaved missed about the deceased and later what they did not miss. This may be a back door way to help the bereaved to acknowledge and then express anger. However anger is exposed and expressed, it is important and empowering for the bereaved to express strong emotions while maintaining a sense of personal control over these feelings.

Noted earlier was the bereaveds' need to express and talk about their thoughts and feelings in a safe place. For this reason, many of the programs involved in work with suicide and those bereaved through suicide have group sessions with people who share the common experience of having lost a friend or relative through suicide. Group work is perhaps the first choice as a vehicle through which to facilitate the survivors' of suicide search for understanding and resolution (Moore & Freeman, 1995; Freeman, 1991; Calhoun, Selby, & Steelman, 1984). Utilizing the therapeutic (curative) factors of group identified by Yalom (1995), the facilitator can focus on a guided interplay of experience culminating in movement of the bereaved through the grieving process. The use of group as a therapeutic intervention will be examined in greater detail in Chapter 9.

SURVIVORS OF HOMICIDE AND GRIEF

It was a weekend. Her son was, as usually was the case, out with a group of friends. In retelling the horrible trauma she experienced, she became confused as to what night [Friday or Saturday] the murder occurred. It was late. They had dined out and were returning to their car from a local pub when they were confronted by a man with a gun. Her son was well to the rear of the group, actually some distance back, and the robber was demanding money from the others as he approached. A physically large man, her son began to struggle with the robber. In the course of the struggle the gun went off several times, striking her son. The assailant fled the scene. Her son died before the ambulance arrived. The call every parent fears came in the wee hours of the morning—the hospital official offered little information other than stating, "You need to come to the hospital immediately."

Needless to say, this woman was beyond devastation, and suffered unending torment. There was no preparation for this sudden and violent assault on her son. There was no way to comprehend that death could come so swiftly and violently at the hands of another human being.

Homicide is always considered to be an act of violence. Deaths involving violence are particularly traumatic in that they evoke feelings of terror, shock, helplessness, vulnerability, threat, fear, violation, hyperarousal, and victimization in the survivors (Rando, 1996). Rynearson (1987) noted that violence is highly associated with post-traumatic stress, which includes among its many sequela post-traumatic imagery that can be overwhelming. Additionally, Rynearson (1988) found that because of personal attachment to the deceased, surviving family members of those who died these types of death are compelled to work through an internalized fantasy of grotesque dying that not only increases their own fears, but also complicates their mourning by presenting them with tasks of assimilating the violence. In the case of homicide, assimilating as well the transgression implicit in the death further complicates grief.

Cognitive dissonance is one of the special features that should be noted when working with this special group of bereaved. The death under these circumstances does not make sense. The event violates the "rules," and no amount of struggle brings about something that will make sense. This cognitive dissonance might continue for some time—months or even years—and create problems with unresolved grief; specifically, delayed grief reactions.

Anger and rage are often significantly exacerbated in cases of homicide. Both are normal reactions, but for the homicide survivor, they may intensify to previously unknown levels. Worden (1991) sees rage as the result of frustration and helplessness. Frustration is experienced from the inability to resolve the cognitive dissonance and make sense out of nonsense. Helplessness is spawned from the gnawing awareness that no matter what we do, we, cannot make the situation better or change what has happened. At this emotional intersection there is a tremendous collision that results in rage. This rage is generally directed at the perpetrator. However, finding someone to blame is necessary so that the intense emotion may be felt and justified. The intensity of this rage may be quite disconcerting, and knowing that these feelings are normal may not be enough to quell the additional cognitive dissonance created by the anathema between the murderous rage the bereaved feels and his or her own sense of morality and justice.

The murder of a loved one may threaten the ideals and values the bereaved holds about the world. This is a personal violation that fractures the belief that the world is a good place and that the people in it are also good. The delusion of personal control is also compromised. Recovery and the ability to trust again might be a difficult struggle and might take a long time.

Rando (1996) considered preventability and/or randomness as additional factors that have distinct consequences for the bereaved. She notes that the mourner's perception of the preventability of the death is often an underappreciated factor in the individual's grief reaction. If the bereaved perceives that the death was preventable—that it did not have to occur—then anger is intensified. The perception that the death was not inevitable drives the bereaved to spend intense time and energy searching for a cause or reason for the death and to determine who is responsible so that punishment can be meted out. This has the secondary effect of helping the bereaved to strive to regain a sense of control.

If an event is truly random, it cannot be predicted and therefore cannot be controlled. This thought can be extremely frightening because if it is true, it implies that individuals cannot protect themselves from random acts of violence. In the absence of a responsible party, there is a tendency for the bereaved to blame themselves. It is easier for survivors to cope with a devastating event even if they believe they are responsible, and therefore it is potentially controllable, than it is to cope with or accept an act as random. Again, by identifying events that survivors can control, they can protect themselves or in the future avoid certain situations, thereby forestalling a recurrence.

Michalowski (1976), examining the social meaning of death, writes, "It is the manner of dying, and not the death itself, that determines the social meaning of death." (p. 83) He notes five distinct areas that make homicide more salient than other forms of violent death:

1. *Inevitability.* Homicide is not considered an accident. Traffic fatalities result from circumstances beyond human control, which is not true of homicides.

2. *Controllability.* Homicide is perceived as controllable in that it arises from the willful act of individuals.

3. *Intent.* Homicide by definition involves intent.

4. *Deviance.* Homicide is illegal and considered abnormal, whereas a traffic fatality is perceived as less of a social problem.

5. *Social unity.* Homicide provides no social unity; society will tolerate traffic deaths because the automobile does provide social utility. Death by homicide so sickens our society that, even though most deaths are by other means, homicide assumes prominence in our social world.

Stigmatization follows the bereaved by homicide just as it follows those bereaved by suicide. The bereaved are often avoided, and discussions with them involving the victim are sometimes considered taboo. Again, one may hear the all too familiar proclamation, "I want to talk about my son, but no one will talk to me. They act as if he never existed." This resulting isolation is a revictimization of the bereaved, this time by silent ostracism. It may be that this avoidance is a defense that allows others to shore up their armament, their denial of vulnerability, that something like this could happen to them. Whatever the reason, those bereaved by homicide often suffer disenfranchisement.

Social disenfranchisement is only one part of the problem. The criminal justice system is often perceived as being more concerned with the rights of the accused perpetrator than with finding justice for the victim or the bereaved survivor. The trial itself can be a source of conflict as well as satisfaction. Sitting through long hours of testimony can recreate for the bereaved the trauma of the violent and unexpected loss. It can also, however, provide the bereaved a sense of participation and allow them to feel a degree of power over the perpetrator. Until now, survivors might have perceived the perpetrator as having held sway over their sense of personal power. Active involvement may alleviate this and help to replace it with some sense of security.

Those bereaved by homicide have been noted to experience symptoms of post-traumatic stress. It is therefore important for counselors to be acquainted with appropriate intervention strategies. The following generic approach to treatment of the bereaved experiencing post-traumatic stress was abstracted from Rando (1993):

- Bring into consciousness the traumatic experience. Repeatedly review, reconstruct, reexperience, and abreact the experience until it is robbed of its potency.
- Identify, express, and work through until mastered the effects of the traumatic encounter (e.g., helplessness, shock, anxiety, guilt).
- Integrate conscious and dissociated memories, affects, thoughts, images, behaviors, and somatic sensations from the traumatic experience.
- Mourn relevant physical and psychosocial losses.
- Discourage maladaptive processes and therapeutically address defenses and behaviors used to cope with both the trauma and its aftermath.
- Acquire and develop new skills and behaviors or overhaul overwhelmed ones to promote healthy living again.
- Counter the helplessness and powerlessness with experiences that support mastery, a sense of personal worth and value, and connectedness with others; help others, or minimize the effects of similar traumatic experiences; and the avoidance of further victimization.
- Develop a perspective on what happened, by whom to whom, why, and what one was and was not able to do and control within the traumatic experience. Recognize and come to terms with the helplessness of the trauma.
- Accept full responsibility for one's behaviors as is appropriate and ultimately relinquish inappropriate assumptions of responsibility and guilt after therapeutically addressing survivor guilt.
- Create meaning out of the traumatic experience.
- Integrate the aspects of the trauma and its meaning into assumptions about the world; place the event in psychic continuity within the totality of one's past, present, and future.
- Form a new identity reflecting one's survival of the traumatic experience and the integration of the extraordinary into one's life.
- Reinvest in love, work, and play; reconnect with others and reassure the continued flow of life and development halted by the traumatic event.

DEATH OF A CHILD

There is widespread agreement that the death of a child is one of the most, if not the most, difficult losses that an individual can experience. Osterweis, Solomon and Green (1984) write that any bereavement is painful, but that the experience of losing a child is by far the worst. Sanders (1989) supports this position, noting that the death of a child is an unbearable sorrow, a wound that cuts deeply, ulcerates, and festers. For some, it never heals. Klass (1988) notes amputation of a limb is used as a metaphor to describe the loss of a child. If the limb that is lost is a leg, the individual learns to walk again, but the healed stump is always there as a reminder.

The parent–child relationship is a complex configuration that includes physical as well as psychological bonds. Attachment may begin as soon as the verification of conception and increases as pregnancy progresses. The child is an extension of the parents and represents not only the genealogical future of the family line but also the hopes and dreams of the parents. Both literally and figuratively, children are an extension of their parents that assures their continuing future.

The fact that attachment may begin with the verification of conception means that spontaneous miscarriages may result in significant grief reactions. The potential significance of this loss most often goes unrecognized by others, especially if the miscarriage occurs in the early weeks or months before the fetus is considered viable. In the later stages of pregnancy, especially when fetal movement is detectable and the fetus is regarded more as a "baby" the loss is more likely to be socially acknowledged.

Most often when a miscarriage occurs, concern is first about the woman's health. It is only later that there may be recognition of what has been lost. Well-meaning comments by friends and/or family such as, "You can have another one," or "There must have been something wrong and it's probably a blessing," or "It happened to me, too; you'll get over it," only serve to disenfranchise the loss. As such, there may be little opportunity to acknowledge what was lost and to share thoughts and feelings as the bereaved relinquish the dead child.

Grief may occur immediately or may be delayed, depending on a myriad of factors. Sadness is usually the predominant effect. Guilt may be experienced, especially if there was ambivalence about the pregnancy at some point. Anger may be present, notably if the woman believes the miscarriage should not have happened. Self-blame or questions about personal culpability, such as whether the miscarriage was caused by working, jogging, or other physical activities, often occur.

Pregnancy may be selectively terminated by abortion, which can bring its own unique set of variables to the grief experience. In these situations, the pregnancy is at least somewhat unwanted. This does not mean that the decision to terminate is without conflict or ambivalent feelings. Family and religious moral values may be sources of significant conflict. In these cases, delayed grief from a previous abortion may not be recognized as the source of current psychological difficulties.

The experience of Mrs. G provides an example of this type of delayed grief. Mrs. G, age 36, was referred to me for psychotherapy for depression. Her initial session included taking her history. During this intake, she mentioned an abortion while a college student. In our next meeting, she told me that since our previous session she had become more depressed and could not stop thinking about the abortion. She went on to say that she had lied and that she had actually had two abortions while in college. Grief work became the focal point of therapy, which upon completion also resolved the depressive features she had presented with.

The pattern of grief and mourning following abortion is similar to that following a miscarriage. The most obvious difference is that suppression and inhibition of grief and mourning are more likely to occur and remain for longer periods.

Stillbirth is a tragedy in that it is the theft of the fulfillment of pregnancy. It may occur suddenly, without warning. Others experience some forewarning. They sense that something is wrong—cessation of movement, unexpected sensations, or not "feeling pregnant" anymore. Regardless, hopes and plans constructed over the past months are cruelly dashed. Additional pain comes to those who must wait for the natural onset of labor to deliver a dead baby.

Not seeing or touching the lost infant can complicate mourning. The pregnancy produced a child who died, and the dead child should not be whisked away as if the baby were unimportant or the whole thing did not happen. Giving the child a name and retaining meaningful articles such as pictures, a birth certificate, or nursery bracelet might help make the loss real and assist in resolving the loss. Parents should be encouraged to share in decisions about disposition of the body and should participate in rituals such as a memorial or funeral service.

In families with surviving children, it is important not to forget them. Their understanding of the loss will be influenced by the children's ages and cognitive and emotional development. Acknowledging the loss is important; however, the degree of involvement and explanation should be tailored to the individual child.

During the infant to toddler to early childhood years, the family system changes to accommodate a fully functioning new member. Death during this period is a multidimensional loss that includes both the shared past and the anticipated hoped for the future. Deaths are not common in this age group; however, accidents are by far the leading cause. The unexpected nature of accidental death may be compounded if the parent was in any way involved. In cases where there is parental involvement, guilt and recrimination are usually overwhelming.

Given that accidental death is unanticipated, shock constitutes a large part of the initial reaction. Acknowledging and accepting the loss is often made more difficult by the fact that the death is seen as malapropos. Anger, even rage, about the accident and/or those responsible is not an uncommon response. Recall the dynamic collision between frustration and helplessness. Parents now experience an overwhelming sense of frustration connected to a lack of fulfillment of the potential they dreamed of for their child. This collides with devastating feelings of helplessness (powerlessness, impotency, and dread) that there is nothing they can do now to protect their child. Repetitious consuming thoughts of "if only" are common as all the events leading up to the death are replayed over and over. Commissions and omissions are all sorted through in an attempt to intellectually understand what happened and why it happened.

Death that occurs during the adolescent years is likely to evoke similar parental responses to those of losses that occurred in childhood. However, owing to the often conflictual strivings toward independence associated with adolescence, the quest for resolution may be complicated. Death during this age, as in childhood, is most often the result of accidents. These accidents may frequently occur within the context of family conflict or ambivalence associated with increased independence or adult pursuits on the part of the adolescent. Because driving in adolescence is seen as a rite of passage, death resulting from a motor vehicle accident may frequently be the background for family conflict. Alcohol and/or drug use may also be a source of conflict and be associated with the death.

Regardless of the cause of death, adolescence is often a turbulent time as family boundaries are being negotiated and redrawn to accommodate the individual who will ultimately become an adult member of the family. Grief reactions may be complicated by the heightened ambivalence and conflict associated with this developmental period.

As children become adults, parents are likely to be entering into the "old age of youth" or the "youth of old age" themselves. A degree of separation usually takes place when the children establish their own families. As such, the death of an adult child may be difficult or complicated for yet another set of reasons. Older parents are likely to feel—even more now than at earlier stages of development—that it should have been their time to die rather than their son's or daughter's. The deceased child might have been a parent, and now the surviving parents might be faced with the task of raising their child's children at a time when emotional resources may be significantly diminished. This might necessitate delaying mourning until the task at hand is completed or substantially underway.

Parent–child attachment begins at conception and continues a lifetime. Whatever the age, the death of a child is seen as one of the most negative life experiences that an individual can encounter. Grieving is complicated, owing to the fact that the loss is both internal—a loss of hope for the future—and external—the loss of an individual who is an extension of ourselves. Chronic grief is therefore not uncommon, for even when mourned the child is not forgotten.

In Chapter 5 we examined the tasks of grief. Grieving the loss of a child, while not requiring a new and different model of grief, does require that we examine these tasks again as they pose specific difficulties for the bereaved parent.

The first task of mourning is to experience and express outside of one's self the reality of the death (Lindemann, 1944; Parkes & Weiss, 1983; Worden, 1991). For bereaved parents this task is extremely difficult at best and not possible at worst. The normal difficulty encountered here is compounded by the fact that the loss violates what is seen as acceptable and the natural order of things. To acknowledge or accept this loss also destroys the myth that parents are omnipotent protectors and providers. The eradication of this myth may result in unrealistic guilt and shame. If the dead child is an adult, physical separation is most likely to have occurred and the loss is not as visible as with a younger child or adolescent. This can also contribute to difficulties in accepting the loss.

The second task of mourning is to tolerate the emotional suffering that is inherent in the grief while nurturing oneself both physically and emotionally (Parkes & Weiss, 1983; Shuchter & Zisook, 1990; Worden, 1991). It has been questioned whether the pain of grief associated with any other loss can be as severe as that experienced by the loss of a child. Certainly the anger and/or rage that a grieving parent might experience may not be understood by others and interpreted as a sign of mental instability or other problems. A lack of adequate social support and unrealistic expectations as to time and intensity of mourning can also be special factors to consider.

The third requisite of mourning is to convert the relationship with the deceased from one of the presence to a relationship of memory (Lindemann, 1944; Parkes & Weiss, 1983; Rando, 1987; 1993; Ruskay, 1996; Sable, 1991; Worden, 1991). This task may be compounded when there is one or more surviving children. In this case, parents may overinvest energies and expectations in the surviving child, attempting to somehow deny or compensate for the loss. Still other options include having a "replacement" child. In either situation, there is an attempt to somehow continue the relationship in the present with the dead child.

The fourth task of mourning is to develop a new sense of self-identity based on a life without the deceased (Lindeman, 1944; Parkes & Weiss, 1983; Ruskay, 1996; Worden, 1991). This is especially difficult for parents who have lost a child in that the child was an extension of them and their hoped for future. The bereaved parents may or may not be fully aware of all the losses incurred in this arena and how it related to their identity. The hopes and dreams the parent had for the dead child were a part of them and provided meaning for their lives. A new self-identity will, by necessity, include a new meaning in life.

Finally, to complete the work of grief one must relate the experience of loss in a context of meaning. The bereaved will typically question his/her philosophy of life and values, seeking an answer to the question *why?* The following is an example of a parent finding such meaning:

> Joseph Fabry was a concentration camp survivor and dear friend of the existential psychiatrist, Viktor Frankl. Following the atrocities of the concentration camps he immigrated to the United States and enjoyed a successful professional as well as personal life. That is, until his daughter, Wendy, was murdered. The resulting grief reaction was one of unspeakable devastation. Frankl called his friend from Vienna, Austria, daily for 10 days.

Joe was hardly able to speak, his loss and grief were so profound. However, he was able to proceed with the grieving process and find meaning in the final act of his daughter's life, a gift that Wendy left. In his book, *The Pursuit of Meaning,* he describes this gift of meaning in the dedication, which reads: To Wendy, who taught me what being a father is all about. In acknowledging her death, he was challenged by all of the missed opportunities he had had to be a father to Wendy that now no longer existed. By accepting the loss of his daughter Wendy, he was able to embrace and not lose the opportunities still available to him to be a father to his remaining children. This was the meaning he found in Wendy's death, her gift.

QUESTIONS FOR THOUGHT
AND REFLECTION

1. What are your beliefs about the morality of suicide?

2. What would you say to someone who said to you, "My daughter recently committed suicide." How do you feel talking about this subject? Why?

3. What would you say to someone who said to you, "I have just recently had a miscarriage." How do you feel talking about this subject? Why?

4. What special type(s) of losses have you experienced in your life?

5. From what or where is meaning derived?

8

Children and Loss

Do children mourn? Most theorists would answer yes. However, qualifications are required here. Most are in agreement that mourning requires the child to have achieved a coherent mental representation of the attachment figure, as well as object constancy. Until these requirements are met the image of the attachment figure in the person's absence is ephemeral. It seems logical, then, that the child must have a clear idea about the attachment figure as an independent person before mourning the loss or absence of that person is possible. This is not to say that a very young child will not display strong emotional and visceral reactions to the loss of an attachment figure. This grief reaction, as we have seen, is well documented and may occur in the absence of a mature understanding of death and meaning of the loss. Given these qualifications and the definition of mourning as mental work following the loss of an attachment figure through death, therefore, very young children may not indeed mourn.

What might seem like semantic hair splitting does have a rationale. In the Preface, Bowlby (1980) noted a warning to clinicians not to expect too much from the people with whom they worked. Like society, clinicians may have unrealistic expectations of how and when grieving should be resolved. Similarly, those working with children need to respect their feelings, without expecting more than the child is capable of developmentally. Given this qualifying discourse, we may answer the question, can children grieve, with an unequivocal yes.

With the groundwork established, let us move on to examine children and loss. What should children know about death? When should they know it? From whom or by what method should they acquire the information? Many people embrace the notion of childhood innocence and refrain from any comment or acknowledgment that death even occurs. This conspiracy of silence contradicts the reality of the contemporary child's life, as they, through television and movies, are regularly exposed to literally hundreds of real and fictional deaths. The question, then, is not should they know about death, but rather, what do they actually know?

CHILDREN'S CONCEPT OF DEATH

Understanding death as a concept might seem on the surface a deceivingly simple task; however, as we will see, it is quite a challenge. This is especially true for children. Even at its least complicated level, the concept of death contains several components. For most children, the natural evolution of their cognitive ability leads gradually to a more complete understanding of the concept of death.

Speece and Brent (1996), investigating children's understanding of the concept of death, reviewed more than 100 research studies conducted between 1934 and the early 1990s. They concluded that there are five subconcepts involved in a child's concept of death, each containing other closely related notions necessary for complete comprehension. They are universality, irreversibility, nonfunctionality, causality, and some type of continued life.

The subconcept of *universality* requires children to recognize the fact that death happens to everything that is alive. Nothing that is alive will live forever; however, some things will live longer than others. Even though death is universal and unavoidable, it does not occur on a strict timetable.

Speece and Brent (1996) have explained that *irreversibility* involves both the process that distinguishes the transition from being alive to being dead and the state which results from this. Irreversibility of death means that once dead, the physical body cannot be restored to life.

There are at least two factors not covered by the concept of irreversibility that might occur to children. The first is miraculous interventions, or supernatural (unexplainable) occurrences. There are cases where individuals have been declared dead and yet somehow came back to life, defying explanation of how it occurred. The second is technological advances in medical resuscitation. Many times individuals are brought in to emergency rooms not breathing and without a heartbeat and have been resuscitated. Both of these factors serve to further complicate the understanding and comprehension of the subconcept of irreversibility.

Nonfunctionality refers to the final cession of bodily functions that are typically attributed to a living physical body. Life-defining functions discussed in Chapter 1 can become, by necessity, quite complicated. However, from a child's perspective, life-defining functions are usually external (observable)— such as breathing, eating, or playing—and internal—such as feeling and thinking. Nonfunctionality entails the absence of both internal and external functions.

To fully comprehend *causality* requires the ability to think abstractly. On a concrete level, causality is that which brings about death. But what is a child to make of the statement, "Grandmother died of old age"? To understand what this statement means, one must understand that death can result from external causes, but that even in the absence of external factors death will ultimately result from internal causes or a combination of both. Causality can be a difficult concept even for adults.

The final subconcept is a belief in some type of *continued life after death*. This is commonly reported as a part of both adult and children's concepts of death. Though there is no agreement as to what type of continued life form there is, it is reported often enough and is worthy of inclusion.

CHILDREN'S VIEW OF DEATH

Our understanding of the way children think about death has been greatly influenced by the work of Hungarian psychologist Maria Nagy. In her seminal work she stated the question guiding her research as "What does the child think death to be, what theory does he construct of the nature of death?" (p. 3) To investigate this question she invited 378 children ranging in age from 3 to 10 years old to express their death-related thoughts and feelings. Nagy (1948) found that three age-related stages could be established:

> *Stage 1. There is no definitive death.* This stage includes the youngest children from three to five years of age. In general, these children do not accept death. Death was described like sleeping. They saw death as the same as living but under changed circumstances. The deceased person does not change; however, the child does not see or live with the loved one anymore. The youngest children regard death as temporary and think the dead might return, just as someone sleeping might wake up. The most painful thing about death to these children is separation.
>
> Another notable characteristic of Nagy's youngest participants was their curiosity. To the children, death equaled departure. However, most children were not satisfied with someone merely departing and wanted to know where their loved one went and what that's like. There were many questions about the funeral, the coffin, and the cemetery. The children also decided that death did not sound like very much fun. Specifically, lying around all day and all night in a coffin was seen as boring, and being away from all of your friends might be somewhat lonely and scary, too.

Stage 2. Death equals a man. This stage includes children from five to nine years of age. In this stage, death is personified in some form. Two-thirds of Nagy's subjects imagined death as a distinct personality, a skeleton-man or individually created their own idea of a death-man.

Compared with the first stage, where death is denied, in this stage there is an increasing belief that death is a reality, despite it being contrary to the children's desires. The older the child, the more firm this conclusion. The universality of death is not acknowledged in this stage. In fact, the only ones who die are the ones that the death–man catches and carries off. If you are lucky or smart enough to get away, you don't die.

Stage 3. Death is cessation of corporal activities. This stage includes children 9 and 10 years of age (the age at which Nagy's survey ends). Here, the child understands that death is personal, universal, inevitable, and final. With an increased understanding of death emerges the possibility of an afterlife. The concept of an afterlife requires an understanding and acceptance of death as final and inevitable.

As we have seen, most all of us eventually come to understand and accept the fact that death is universal, irreversible, and inevitable. Most children become aware of these facts by 9 or 10 years of age, owing to their own cognitive development and life experiences. Other children, because they have experienced death in the family or through other factors, may achieve this understanding at younger ages.

The cognitive development of children is a critical factor influencing their understanding of death. Although Piaget's work did not specifically address children's understanding of death, his theories are most applicable:

1. *Preoperational stage: Ages 2–7.* In this stage the child is largely egocentric and views the world from his or her own unique perspective. There may be no distinction made between thoughts and action. One may cause the other (e.g., a child may believe that being angry at a sibling was the cause of her illness and death). Imaginations are also developing, and there is a tendency toward magical thinking. Reality may be distorted to conform to the child's idiosyncratic understanding. Naturally the child believes that everyone else sees the world in exactly the same way. The child does not comprehend the irreversibility of death and therefore does not understand why his or her granddad won't wake up and play or why his or her dead father does not come home.

2. *Concrete operations stage: Ages 7–11.* Residual characteristics of the previous stage still remain to varying degrees, but there is a reduction in egocentricity and an improved capacity for reasoning. Movement from intuitive thinking is facilitated by learning to read, write, and carry out functions required in arithmetic. These budding cognitive abilities also open the child's thinking to a more accurate view of the concepts of death. This is seen in the fact that there is a realization among elementary school age children that death is irreversible. However, with developing

cognitive abilities comes an increase in one's own sense of personal power and control. Therefore, the concepts of inevitability and universality are initially elusive. Initially, children in this age range see death as something that happens to old people or those who cannot run fast enough to escape the pursuing skeleton or death angel. By the end of this stage, most children have developed a more realistic view of death.

3. *Formal operations: Ages 11–.* Piaget's stage of formal operations begins around the age of 11 and builds on the relative success achieved in the preceding stages. Children now have the expanding capacity to think logically and abstractly. They have the capacity to understand the concept of death in its entirety. Still, in this stage and for some years to come, death is only somewhat accepted. It is a detached acknowledgment of something that exists far in the future and is accepted as being in the domain of the old.

Any child, regardless of chronological age or developmental station, that has the capacity of forming attachments, is capable of experiencing a loss. Although the very young may not have the ability to comprehend the total meaning of death, they have in their own idiosyncratic way the ability to respond authentically to a loss. In addition, it is important to remember that children of the same age are not necessarily of the same developmental level cognitively or emotionally. Each child is an individual; therefore, each encounter is unique, and helping requires one to learn the particulars about the unique individual and related circumstance of the loss.

HOW CHILDREN GRIEVE

The bereavement experience of a child is not so different from that experienced by an adult. The intensity of the acute emotional arousal may be similar. The feelings of disbelief, despair, anger, and guilt may also be similar. A major difference in the experience will be that children will probably find it incredibly difficult to identify and express their feelings. Intense feelings related to loss can easily overwhelm an adult. Children often have lesser verbal abilities than adults and can be easily dismayed and possibly alarmed by ambivalent or conflicted emotions they feel. Following a loss, some children display tears of anger, frustration, and/or guilt; however, when questioned about their feelings, they might say, "I feel sad."

Children lacking the cognitive skills to identify and verbal skills to adequately express their feelings often channel emotional disturbances into negative behaviors. It is imperative that those who work with children recognize that following a loss, the behavior exhibited may not necessarily mean that a child is mad or bad. It may indicate that the child is sad and grieving. The following are common behaviors:

■ Children might exhibit temper tantrums, physical and/or verbal aggression toward peers or caregivers. This acting out is usually the result of an inability to express feelings verbally.

- Appetite may sometimes suffer in response to grief reactions (reactive depression). However, overeating may also occur, as food may be used as a source of comfort.

- Sleep disturbances are common, including an inability to get to sleep, frequent waking, nightmares or bad dreams, and fear of going to sleep.

- Children may withdraw from friends or family, or they may exhibit excessive clinging and expressions of fear when adults leave.

- Regression such as thumb sucking, bedwetting, using baby talk, or other regressive behaviors may occur. These are generally seen as a desire to return to a better, safer, more predictable time of life.

- School-age children may refuse to attend school, fearing something will happen in their absence.

- Children who previously had little or no problem with schoolwork may fall behind or have difficulties with peers or teachers. This may be due to inattention or an inability to concentrate.

- Some previously average-achieving children will now completely immerse themselves in school. This can be one way of distracting themselves from their loss.

Usually behavioral changes will need to be dramatic before they are interpreted as symptoms of distress.

Feelings are often a source of confusion for children. Response to a loss is significantly influenced by their perception of themselves, their relationship with the deceased, and their perception of what happened to the deceased.

Children as well as adolescents are egocentric and generally see themselves as potent beings occupying the center of the universe. This is quite normal and usually culminates in a healthy self-concept. However, in the domain of bereavement this natural egocentricity can be the source of irrational guilt. Children believe they were the cause of death because of what they thought or felt about the deceased or because they were naughty.

Anger is a common emotion for both adults and children. A child might be angry at the deceased for dying or at another family member or person for not dying instead. Feeling left out or not being allowed to participate in the funeral or other rituals can be a source of anger in the present or the future. Anger can also be the result of life or lifestyle changes that occur following the death.

Confusion is frequently shared with adults. Adults are often confused and struggle with what to tell a child about a death, especially in cases of suicide or homicide. Further confusion may be encountered in deciding how to explain the complex event in terms that children would understand without being overwhelmed. This can result in confusion for children over what actually occurred and why. Mixed messages in terms of how to react can also be confusing. Dad may say, "You have to be a big girl and not cry to help your mother," while a teacher or school counselor might say, "It's all right to feel sad and cry. If that's how you feel, you can let it out."

Fear and anxiety can accompany a death, especially if the deceased was a parent. In such cases children might worry about who will take care of them or if another family member, possibly the surviving parent, will die next. Anxiety may also be associated with the future and the perceived lack of the guarantee the deceased parent provided. Anxiety related to one's own mortality is also likely, depending on the age of the child.

Children often grieve in pediatric doses appropriate to their age and cognitive/emotional ability. This means that a child might allow feelings to be felt and then be ready to play again, or, after being told his or her mother or father has died, move to his or her room and play with toys. Neither reaction is strange; it's just not an adult response. Children have limited capacities with which to cope and will usually, if allowed, modulate the experience as necessary to avoid being overwhelmed. Similarly, when a child is told something about a loss, he or she might nod to indicate understanding. In adults, correctly or incorrectly, we accept this gesture as a sign of understanding. In communicating with children, do not accept this as an acknowledgment of understanding. Children are excellent observers and imitators. There is a large probability that the child is merely imitating what has been observed in adults. To confirm that a child understands, in a gentle voice ask the child to explain in his or her own words what you just said.

Bereavement for children, as is true for all of us, is influenced by many factors. This includes who the deceased was, their age and relationship to the child, whether the child was present, whether the death was sudden and unexpected, and whether it was the result of violence, homicide, or suicide. Additional factors specific to childhood bereavement include family relationships prior to and following the death, role of the deceased, family communication patterns, and whether a child remains with the surviving parent. All of these factors will influence the feelings and behaviors of the bereaved child.

HOW TO HELP

When children have caring and involved parents, they are the most important resource. Approaching the parent to determine a child's needs, wishes, and expectations following a loss is paramount. Involvement of clergy, if appropriate, teachers, and others is also helpful and should be orchestrated by the parent(s) with whatever assistance is needed.

Don't attempt to fix anything; there is nothing broken. Bereavement resulting from death is a normal although painful life experience. Allow children to be children and be careful not to impose adult expectations on their cognitive and emotional responses. Allow them to ask questions and to be curious; however, listen carefully and help the child to understand what is happening while avoiding overexplaining. Keep in mind, too, that as adults we are often more comfortable with a highly verbal child. Verbalizations, however, do not signify anything about a particular child's coping. Likewise, excessive silence should not be taken as an automatic indicator of greater concern.

Allow very young children to engage in play, as this is a natural form of expression for them. Drawing and storytelling are natural and enjoyable outlets for young children. Reading stories with themes of loss and reconstruction of life after a loss, such as Leo Buscaglia's *The Fall of Freddie the Leaf,* are ways to help children "work through" and make sense out of the separation and loss that death brings.

Recognize that children are excellent observers and they are hard to fool. They will observe how adults around them react to the loss. Rather than attempting to conceal tears, sadness, irritability, and other normal feelings or pretend they didn't happen, explain these things. Being open and honest will comfort children and allow them to accept grief reactions, both their own and others, as natural.

The real work begins following the ceremonies and the memorial services. Feelings intensify and fluctuate as the bereaved experiences thoughts and memories of the deceased. Anxiety may result from a growing awareness that the memory of the deceased is not so clear anymore. Indicators of fluctuating anxiety may be observed in a child's play, drawings, or questions they ask. Ask about what you observe and listen carefully to their questions. Do not be afraid to talk about the deceased or to view pictures and help the child to organize and retain his or her memories.

TASKS OF MOURNING FOR CHILDREN

As noted earlier, grief work may be conceptualized as tasks—specifically tasks of mourning. This has the effect of providing a framework outlining a significant portion of the caregiver role. But do the tasks of mourning apply to bereaved children? Several researchers in the area of childhood bereavement would say yes (Fox, 1988, Baker, et al., 1992; Corr, 1995; Wolfelt, 1983; Worden, 1996).

Worden (1996), who popularized the concept of tasks of grief in his book *Grief Counseling and Grief Therapy,* believes that tasks of mourning apply to children and can be understood in terms of their cognitive, emotional, and social development. Worden lists four tasks of grief in Chapter 3 of that text:

Task 1. To accept the reality of the loss

Task 2. To work through the pain of grief

Task 3. To adjust to an environment in which the deceased is missing

Task 4. To emotionally relocate the deceased and move on with life

Worden believes that children, like adults, must acknowledge the death and believe that the deceased is indeed dead and will not return to life before it is possible to proceed and deal with the emotional impact of the loss. This requires the child to understand, at least in part, the concept of death; specifically, the subconcepts of irreversibility and nonfunctionality (Speece & Brent, 1996). Nagy (1948) found that children ages three to five years generally do not accept death. Falling in what Piaget called the *preoperational stage of development,* the child is unable to comprehend the subconcepts of irreversibility and nonfunctionality.

To negotiate Worden's first task of mourning, children who have the previously noted capabilities need to be told about the death in ways that are both accurate and in language that is age appropriate for the child. This requires patience, as it will probably need to be done repetitively. Parents may remember reading a favorite book to a child for the one hundredth time. Each reading required precision, and each word had to be read or the error was noted. The repetitive questions children ask about death are similar and are their way of struggling with the reality of the death, and a method to test the consistency of that reality. These questions, though tedious, help children accept the reality of the loss. Changes in the story tend to make the reality less credible and may impede the child's grief work.

The second task of mourning requires one to acknowledge and work through the various emotions associated with the loss. In the case of children this might include somatic or aberrant behaviors. Children will, by their nature, usually approach this task gradually in ways that do not overwhelm or surpass their capacity to cope. Capacities vary, and this can be especially seen in the five to seven years old age group. At this age a child might have developed the cognitive ability to comprehend death as final, but lack the emotional development and social skills to cope with the intense feelings brought on by the loss.

Emotions experienced by children in reaction to loss are similar to those experienced by adults. Children, however, often lack the verbal skills necessary to identify and express them. In addition, their emotional response is influenced by adult modeling. There is security in seeing an adult express grief without being overwhelmed. The opposite may be achieved if a child sees an adult exhibit dysfunctional behavior associated with grief. This may lead the child to be fearful of feelings in general, especially their own feelings. This can consequently result in a complete shutdown of grief work.

Grief work associated with the third task is influenced by the roles and relationships the deceased played in the life of the child and in the life of the family. In most families, the mother is the emotional caretaker of the family and probably the child's confidante. Should the mother die, an aspect of grief work includes the child adapting to the loss of the mother in these roles. Similar role adjustments may be required if the death were the father's. The new roles required of the mother may exclude her from functioning as she had previously. The child now must adjust to losses involving roles of both parents.

These adjustments will not be completed quickly, as they will be ongoing over time. As children mature, they will experience new faces to the old loss. Grief related to childhood loss may be revisited at many points along the developmental road. The loss of a mother in childhood may be again acutely felt when there is no mother of the bride to participate in and fuss over wedding details.

The final task of grieving requires the bereaved to make a new appropriate place for the deceased in their emotional lives and to move on with living. Children's questions are often related to this task. When a child asks, "Does everyone die?" he or she is asking more than "Is death universal?" The unspoken question may be, "Where do they go, how do they now fit in my life?" The repetitive questions and conversations about death and loss experienced in childhood as nurturing and reassuring may be the seed that sprouts a tree full of answers to the existential questions of "why" experienced later in life.

Belief in an afterlife may also be an influential factor in grieving. Silverman, Nickman, and Worden (1992) identified various ways children attempt to maintain a representational identification with the dead parent. They included locating the deceased parent somewhere like heaven, experiencing the dead parent watching them, reaching out to the deceased parent, waking memories of the deceased parent, and cherishing objects shared by the child and the dead parent.

Worden (1996, pp. 95–96) notes the following as important mediators in a child's bereavement experience:

- In general, the loss of a mother is worse for most children than the loss of their father. This is especially true as one moves through the second year of bereavement. The death of a mother portends more daily life changes and, for most families, the loss of the emotional caretaker.

- Mother loss is associated with more emotional/behavioral problems including higher levels of anxiety, more acting-out behavior, lower self-esteem, and less belief in self-efficacy.

- Mother loss brings about more connection with the dead parent.

- The functioning level of the surviving parent is the most powerful predictor of a child's adjustment to the death of a parent. Children with a less well-functioning parent will show more anxiety and depression, and sleep and health problems.

- Bereaved children will have fewer emotional/behavioral problems if discipline is consistently administered and if the surviving parent perceives the child's needs and behaviors in a way that are similar to the child's perception. Inconsistent discipline and perceptual discrepancies will lead to higher levels of anxiety in the child.

- Parental dating in the first year of bereavement can be associated with significant problems in the child, including withdrawn behavior, acting-out behavior, and somatic symptoms. This was especially true when the surviving parent was a father.

- The effect of engagement or remarriage after a suitable bereavement period, on the other hand, can be positive, with children in these families experiencing lower levels of anxiety and depression, as well as being less concerned about safety of the surviving parent.

- Having a number of siblings can have a positive effect in child bereavement. This can mitigate against the negative effects of having a less well-functioning parent. Also, larger families provide a context of safety that gives a child the opportunity and encouragement to express feelings.

- Cohesive families will have children who show less acting-out behavior and who feel better about themselves than children who come from less cohesive families.

- Families that experience large numbers of concomitant stressors occurring before and after the death will have parents with more stress and depression and children who show more emotional/behavioral problems.

- The best bereavement outcomes occur in families who cope actively rather than passively and in families who can find something positive in a difficult situation.

- Bereaved children did not have more well-developed understanding of death than did control children, despite having experienced the death of a parent.

ADOLESCENCE AND GRIEF

Adolescence is a distinct developmental period occurring between childhood and adulthood and overlapping both. The developmental uniqueness of adolescence may, in part, come from the fact that it retains elements of both childhood and adulthood while at the same time struggles to remain separate. As an example, adolescents have the mature intellectual development necessary to understand the core concepts of death—universality, nonfunctionality, irreversibility, and causality—and can elucidate fully the details. However, recognition of death as a phenomenon that can and will happen to everyone is often not enough to curtail high-risk (immature) activities of the adolescent who thinks he or she is immortal. A mature adult grasp of and mature approach to this complex phenomenon appears compromised by a clause in fine print of the adolescent's understanding that reads, "but it won't happen to me."

Life-span human development distinguishes between normative life transitions and unanticipated life events. Normative life transitions are turning points in an individual's development that are expected to occur at a certain time, in concert with other life events, and to most, if not all, members of a cohort. Unanticipated events are, as the phrase implies, not expected. They occur randomly in the course of normative life transitions and violate the fine print in the adolescent's rule book that says, "but it won't happen to me."

Understanding the uniqueness of adolescence and the normative developmental tasks they face provide insight into what factors may affect their grief experience and how one may facilitate their journey through grief and loss. A major developmental task of adolescence is identity formation. During childhood, one's family largely defines one's identity. The process of individuation begins in adolescence and involves reformulation of the parent–child attachment relationship that began at conception and integration of other attachment relationships.

Attachment figures, as we learned in Chapter 2, provide a secure base from which to explore the world. Remember that parent–child attachments are not

relinquished during adolescence but are being renegotiated. Attachment relationships are beginning to be transferred more and more from the parents to
the peer group. This has important implication worth noting in that adolescents, more so than children, may encounter a wide variety of loss–related
experiences that do not involve death but may elicit a grief reaction (e.g.,
ending of love relationships or significant friendships).

The adolescent's experience with parental death and loss may have strong
influence on his or her developmental work. Similarly, ongoing developmental
work may exert a strong influence on grief reactions. For example, an
adolescent who is attempting to achieve emotional emancipation from his or
her parents may experience complications (strong irrational guilt or feelings of
abandonment and lowered self-worth) in the grieving process should one or
both parents unexpectedly die. In a similar scenario, the process of individuation
may be impaired due to feelings of insecurity or lack of safety brought on by
the death. This scenario can become more complicated if other factors influencing the grief response such as those discussed in Chapter 2 are included.

A death loss in the peer group, which now serves as a source of attachment relationships, may also jeopardize the adolescent's developing sense of
autonomy and independence and complicate the grief reaction. The sudden
and unexpected death of a member of the peer group who is seen as a gener-
ational cohort shreds the adolescent's cloak of invincibility and immortality.
This seemingly harsh, but true, reality that death can happen to a person of
the adolescent's own age and similar circumstances means that it can happen
to them, too. This can be the source of great anxiety and fear. Coping behaviors can run the gamut from childlike regression to intense introspection and
reorganization.

Adolescence, particularly late adolescence, is also a time to begin to test
and to establish close and intimate relationships. This threshold has been
approached and tested early in adolescence; however, by removing the shack-
les of egocentric thinking, personal fables, and romanticism the adolescent can
begin to determine who their real friends are. Investments now are great; so
too are the rewards, as well as the risks. The old adage, "It is better to have
loved and lost, than to have never loved at all," may be put to the test. If the
adolescent has not experienced a death loss, the significant investment in a
mature love relationship that ends in death can cause them to reel and question the safety (risk to reward) of relationships. Likewise, such an experience
can also be growth producing; the result of struggling with and finding
personal/existential reasons why the adage is true.

It is perhaps most important to appreciate that grief work in adolescence
represents a situational challenge whose outcome will be influenced by the
normative life transitions and developmental tasks appropriate to the
bereaved. Developmental tasks such as achieving emotional separation and
individuation from parents, a mature self-identity, and developing close intimate relationships may influence how grief is experienced and processed. This
means that those who assist the bereaved adolescent will have the additional
task of ferreting out normal developmental work from grief work.

QUESTIONS FOR THOUGHT
AND REFLECTION

1. How was the subject of death treated in your home when you were a child?

2. What most interested or puzzled you about death as a child?

3. Do you remember the death of a pet at some time in your childhood? What happened? How did you feel? How did adults respond to you?

4. Did anyone in your family or extended family die when you were a child? What happened? How did you feel? How did adults respond to you?

5. What do you think is the best way a parent or other significant person in a child's life can respond when a death is experienced?

6. Read Leo Buscaglia's *The Fall of Freddie the Leaf.* Reflect on your experience.

The following is a small sample of literature for children on death, dying, and bereavement. Further recommendations may be obtained from your reference librarian.

The Dead Bird, Margaret Wise Brown (1958). Reading, MA: Addison-Wesley.

When Violet Died, Mildred Kantrowitz (1973). NY: Parents' Magazine Press.

Why Did Grampa Die? A Book about Death, Barbara S. Hazen (1985). NY: Golden.

The Fall of Freddie the Leaf, Leo Buscaglia (1982). Thorofare, NJ: Slack.

Dusty Was My Friend: Coming to Terms with Loss, Andrea F. Clardy (1984) Human Sciences.

9

⚮

Therapeutic
Interventions

Therapeutic work with the bereaved requires an understanding of the
dynamics of attachment, loss, and the grieving process. To facilitate the
movement through this labyrinth that is grief work, intervention strategies are necessary and are based on the following assumptions: distress following a loss by death is a natural expression of the bereaved's personal reality
experience, and this distress is a natural part of the process of reorganization
and adaptation. It should also be understood and accepted that most individuals possess the resources necessary for a healthy adaptation; however, some, for
reasons already discussed, will experience more difficulty than others. Although
it is true that grief is a universal experience, *Allport's* caution is also true that
some individuals are like all others, some individuals are like some others, and
some individuals are like no others. Before moving on and exploring therapeutic interventions we should reflect briefly on individual differences.

WORKING WITH THOSE DIFFERENT
FROM OURSELVES

In the preceding chapters we have seen a plethora of factors that influence the
grief experience. We have also noted that some components of grief are universal; and, in that regard, all people are like all other people. However, in con-
sidering the factors that influence the grieving process we have seen that there

exists a wide variety of factors which apply to some but not to others. In this regard, the grief experience can vary widely among individuals. Finally, we have also seen that it is possible for the grief experience to be idiosyncratic to a single individual and therefore unlike the experience of any other individual.

Mourning is the outward expression of grief; and, in addition to the factors already discussed, is greatly influenced by the individual's world view. Respecting each individual's uniqueness requires that we meet them where they are in their journey. Encountering and working cross-culturally with individuals different from ourselves requires us to be sensitive to stereotypes or preconceived ideas about inter and/or intracultural or group experiences and related world views. In working with the bereaved, it may be helpful to begin by viewing the experience as an existential encounter between members of the same universal human culture. This view acknowledges our connectedness as human beings and the universality of the components related to the (grief) experience.

To be therapeutic, the relationship must be one Buber (1996) described as the I and thou. The I is authentic, present, and, while acknowledging, transcends the world of experience and related differences. This view does not overlook or deny sociocultural influences; however, it moves beyond the mere collection of information, experience, and potential stereotypes (I and it, I and us, or I and them) to the unique subjective experience of the bereaved and the helper. In the I and thou relationship, the helper is authentically present and listens with the third ear to the bereaved's story, which includes his or her world view and related cultural and personal experiences. The journey requires that the bereaved be understood from his or her unique perspective.

Klass, in his 1999 article "Developing a Cross-Cultural Model of Grief: The State of the Field," explored the daunting thought that a concept of grief could be developed that could apply to all cultures. Rather than attempting to answer the dichotomous question, "Is grief a unitary, universal phenomenon or purely a cultural artifact?" Klass points to a constant interchange between cultural models and individual mental models or schema.

Parkes (2000) wrote that while grief itself is not a unitary and universal phenomenon, it is derived from the interaction of several components that are themselves universal. Although accepting the fact that wide differences exist between individuals as well as cultures, Parkes posits that diversity is not difference, at least not as related to the above concept of universals. Similarities that exist between individuals and between cultures qualify them as universals. Parks notes the following as universals:

> All social animals, by definition, tend to make and maintain attachments with each other. Such attachments are historically necessary for survival. As such, these attachments resist severance and when a threat to attachment occurs (i.e., separation) neurophysiologic arousal takes place and behavior tendencies are initiated with the goal of reunification with the object of the attachment. Because attachments have high survival-value attachment behaviors take priority over many other tendencies of

lesser importance. There are however other priorities which can and often do take priority over attachment behavior. These include the perception of other direct and indirect threats to the survival of the individual. If the set-goal of a behavior pattern is not attained, the behavior will gradually diminish and the individual becomes open to other external and internal stimuli. While attending to other situational needs, the individual may also become open to the exploration of alternative means of reaching the set-goal. (pp. 323–324)

While acknowledging the ubiquitous tendency for each of us to perceive differences in reactions to loss and bereavement through our own cultural blinders, Parkes notes, this does not mean that we cannot learn to see them through the eyes of others, and to do this without necessarily discarding those of our existing ideas that are useful and valid. He believes that much of what is relevant and useful to our own culture can also prove relevant and valuable to others.

A final note is in order before moving to therapeutic interventions. Individuals different from ourselves may have ideas, beliefs, and coping mechanisms that are incompatible with our experience or world view. They, however, need to be understood from their perspective, and a good rule to follow is that if the behavior or coping mechanism isn't broken, regardless of how it appears to us, don't attempt to fix it.

INTERVENTIONS

In the early phases of grief the bereaved are often in shock or on automatic pilot and have little energy or motivation to invest in outside contact. Therapeutic intervention here is simply to make contact and to be present. To do this requires more than saying, "Call me if you need anything." Active involvement is often required. We must assess and determine the needs of the bereaved and then offer assistance. This assessment is ongoing and the bereaved's needs as well as our responses to them will also change. Initial offers may be refused; however, this should not keep us from offering assistance again at another time.

Being physically and emotionally present, especially in the initial periods of shock and disorganization, conveys to the bereaved that they are not alone and helps in their attempt to refocus a world that has suddenly gone out of focus with the experience of a loss by death. Initial interventions are usually best focused on problem solving and finding solutions to the immediate demands that present themselves. Progressing to issues at the feeling level will probably be premature at this time. However, having said that, it should also be acknowledged that since grief is often a foreign experience that brings with it socially unacceptable thoughts and feelings, the bereaved will more often than not need permission to grieve. Recall from Chapter 4 that unresolved grief may relate to a lack of permission to experience the emotions of grief. Permission must be demonstrated through verbal nonjudgmental attitudes and behaviors. The bereaved must receive the message that the expression of thoughts and feelings, whatever they may be, will be accepted and received with compassionate support and understanding.

Social support is an important factor and the bereaved should not be allowed to isolate themselves. At a time of intense emotional reaction, it is particularly helpful to have the presence of others to lend security, order, and a sense of objective reality to balance their subjective, often jumbled reality. This is true both in the initial stages of the loss and during the extended periods following the loss when society dictates grieving should be completed and everything should be back to normal. Therapy groups or self-help support groups may be particularly beneficial.

The bereaved may often seem vulnerable, even fragile; and, not knowing what to say or how to say it, many fail to say anything. Finding the right words may seem like a challenge at best; at worst, the wrong words may seem sufficiently volatile as to cause harm. A bereaved father addressed those who struggle with words and wrote:

> What do you say to someone who is suffering? Some people are gifted with words of wisdom. For such, one is profoundly grateful. There were many such for us. But not all were gifted in that way. Some blurted out strange, inept things. That's OK, too. Your words don't have to be wise. The heart that speaks is heard more than the words spoken. And if you can't think of anything at all to say, just say, "I can't think of anything to say. But I want you to know that we are with you in your grief."
> (Wolterstroff, 1987, pp. 34–35)

The message is clear; the meaning of what is said is not carried in the words themselves, rather it is carried in the struggle one acknowledges in attempting to find the words and in the strength and caring demonstrated by speaking, however uneloquently.

Encourage the bereaved to verbalize feelings and memories of the deceased. This may be difficult due to emotional constriction or concerns of the bereaved that others may grow tired of hearing the same things over and over again. The bereaved will require repeated opportunities to express the pain and anguish of separation. Recalling memories of the deceased and past events aids in accepting the loss and also helps to further define what was lost.

It is, however, not enough to grieve the loss of the deceased, the bereaved must also identify and grieve the secondary losses that occur. Too often secondary losses, especially symbolic losses such as unfulfilled dreams, fail to be identified. These losses, once identified, will incur their own grief reaction. Secondary losses may be quite significant and pose greater difficulty to the bereaved than primary losses. Examples of secondary losses include loss of that part of the self that was defined by the relationship the bereaved had with the deceased (wife or daughter or son of); loss of the family as it was; loss of social status or time with children due to the need to work; loss of the home due to financial difficulties.

In assisting the bereaved in understanding and facilitating the requirements involved in recovering from a loss, it is helpful to assist them in knowing when they are done. It facilitates recovery to orient the bereaved toward the future and an awareness of what it would be like if they were no longer consumed with grief. Questions such as, "If you were no longer struggling with your grief, what would you be doing? How would you be feeling? What would you be thinking?" These are the questions of solution focused method and can be useful in refocusing the therapeutic process. However, as with all therapeutic interventions, timing is critical. Implementation of these types of interventions too early in the grieving process may discourage or minimize what would be a normal and healthy grief reaction.

As the bereaved emotionally and cognitively begin to process loss, it is helpful to educate them about normal and usually expected grief reactions. This may be a time to dispel myths about grief (e.g., timetables for recovery or normal feelings). The normalizing of feelings and experiences can be a great source of relief to those who questioned their mental health or were overwhelmed by guilt or shame related to anger or relief. Exposure to the phases and tasks of grieving may help to restore some sense of control or participation in the process to the bereaved.

Those who aid in the facilitation of the grieving process, regardless of their profession, turn most often to the tools of their own discipline and training. Multiple resources, however, can aid the bereavement process. If healing includes the telling and retelling of the stories of a bereaved's life, then literature can be yet another tool to facilitate the grieving process. Literature, essays, and poetry can not only speak to the heart but also allow the bereaved to find the words and phrases that express what is otherwise unsayable. Metaphor-verbal images and symbols give voice to jumbled chaos that many times is the bereavement experience. Stories, first written by others, can become resources for others initially told, and then possibly, retold with different characters, different plots, and different endings.

How literary resources are used varies greatly. They may be offered as a source of comfort or as a challenge, food for thought. Writing one's own story or a journal or diary might be beneficial to some. Whenever one is faced with a task that requires words to express thoughts, feelings, or experiences, literature is a great resource.

Music, like literature, has the power to facilitate the bereavement process. Music meaningful to the bereaved has the capability to transcend the need for (digital) verbal expression and to provide an analogue experience.

Creativity is a tool that education and professional training often either ignores or obliterates. Creative exploration or experimentation can be useful in that the emotion that accompanies the bereavement experience is mostly illogical; therefore, it is often necessary to step outside of the logic of our disciplines or professional training into arenas that exist for the purpose of saying the unsayable or expressing the inexpressible.

BEREAVEMENT GROUP MODEL

Human beings are a gregarious lot, capable of providing social and emotional support and understanding each other's plight, for as Yalom (1995) states, there is no human deed or thought that is fully outside the experience of other people. Employing the therapeutic elements of group (instillation of hope, universality, imparting information, altruism, development of socializing techniques, imitative behavior, interpersonal learning, group cohesiveness, catharsis, and existential factors) as identified by Yalom, the group leader focuses on and conducts the melodic movement that is grieving process.

The goals of group counseling are to facilitate movement of the bereaved through the stages and tasks of grieving by providing a supportive environment in which those directly affected by the loss can progress. Participants are encouraged to express their needs in dealing with their grief and also to set goals as to what they would like to accomplish in the group.

Participants in the group have the common experience of having suffered a loss through death. In bereavement work, homogeneous groups are recommended. Putting people together who have had similar types of losses—for example, bereaved spouses or bereaved parents—generally works best. However, for some programs or in some locations it is not possible to have a homogeneous group. In these situations it would be best if there were at least two individuals in the group who have experienced the same type of loss. Bonding within the group occurs not only in that they share a loss through death, but also through the type of loss that the bereaved experienced.

Groups ideally consist of 8 to 10 participants. Interviews should be conducted prior to actually forming the group with the purpose of identifying any factors related to or triggered by the loss that would make the individual a poor candidate for the group experience. For some individuals, the facilitation of the grieving process is insufficient for their needs, as the loss may have precipitated other psychological or interpersonal problems. Individuals in crisis are another example of poor candidates for this type of group. Their inclusion and related crisis tend to focus the group and its energy on solving external problems rather than the grieving process.

Basic social skills are also a prerequisite for participation. Individuals displaying excessive rigidity or dogmatism, extreme preferences for high or low structure, social avoidance, poor impulse control, or antisocial behavior should be considered highly questionable for inclusion. Although self-disclosure is usually considered a good quality in counseling, excessive self-disclosure could lead to problems with group monopolization. Therefore, these individuals should be considered cautiously. Individuals with histories of mental instability and those who are actively suicidal should be excluded. Individuals who are currently in counseling should consult with their counselor as to the appropriateness of the group experience for them.

The following is an example of a generic closed-end group model that meets for two hours once a week for eight weeks. This is a general session-by-session outline.

Session 1: Introductions

Introductions and stories consume the first session. The nature of the group and the importance of confidentiality are emphasized. Participants are encouraged to tell their story of loss, including whom it was that they lost and how the deceased died. During this time, the focus of the group leader is on providing support and normalizing the feeling experience and related responses of the bereaved. Looking for common themes in stories and linking common experiences and feelings of the members is crucial to effective facilitation.

Beginning in the first session and continuing throughout the group experience, euphemisms such as *passed away* or *passed on* are avoided. This is done to facilitate accepting that the loss through death has in reality occurred. This is a vital prerequisite to the work that remains.

It is important that everyone in the group shares the reality of the loss and the important realization that "I'm not the only one this has ever happened to. Others have had the same or similar feelings and bad thoughts that I do." The therapeutic elements of universality and instillation of hope are already at work. Universality is experienced in the relief that group members experience through knowing that others feel or have felt as they do. There is also an instillation of hope that comes with attending and being a part of a group whose goal is healing and change. Hope also provides the motivation required for participation that will promote the formation of the other therapeutic factors.

The first session is usually intense and may be the first opportunity for the bereaved to begin to express verbally and with emotion the grief that they carry. In closing the first session participants should be told to heed the words of Cervantes, "forewarned is fore armed." With permission to grieve comes more, not less, sadness and related feelings: In the coming weeks, more "bad days" than good may be the rule. However, there is hope that this will change. Until then, have only the best day possible, which may not be a "good" one.

Session 2: Phases and Tasks of Grief Resolution

The second session is divided into four parts. In the first part, participants are asked to share their week's experience, good and bad. The group leader focuses again on supporting and normalizing feelings, reinforcing the fact that their feelings and experience of grief is probably going to get worse before it gets better.

The second part of the group focuses on educating the participants on the grieving process. This is important for many reasons. The bereaved want to know what to expect. Individuals can handle a lot if allowed to prepare for it. They need to know that they are not going crazy. Sometimes with the flurry of intense, often conflicted emotions, they are not sure. The group is a collaborative process, and expectations need to be clear from the beginning.

The first of two presentations is a brief overview of Bowlby's (1980) phases of grief:

1. *Phase one is the phase of numbness.* During this phase, numbness, shock, and denial serve to block partially or totally the awareness of the loss. Though

this is generally accepted as the first reaction, some form of denial permeates further stages.

2. *Phase two is the phase of yearning.* Here there is an intense longing for and preoccupation with the deceased. In this phase, it is the permanence of the loss rather than the fact of the loss that is denied.

3. *Phase three is the phase of disorganization and despair.* Now the permanence and the fact of the loss are both accepted. This phase begins gradually as the intensity of the yearning begins to diminish and depression, apathy, and aimlessness begin to take over.

4. *Phase four is the phase of reorganization of behavior.* It is now that depression, apathy, and aimlessness greatly diminish as a rekindling of interest in the future, the enjoyment of things and others, and a sense of direction is evolving.

The second presentation is a brief overview of the tasks of grief resolution. Although there is generally an awareness of the phases or stages of grief, there is also an acute awareness of the movement or lack of movement through them. It is noteworthy to mention that phases and stages are suggestive of passivity and that tasks suggest action and control on the part of the bereaved to influence the outcome of grief. There are four tasks of mourning:

1. *Experience and express outside of one's self the reality of the death* (Lindemann, 1944; Parkes & Weiss, 1983; Worden, 1991). This involves confronting the reality that the person has died and will not be coming back.

2. *Tolerate the emotional suffering that is inherent in the grief while nurturing oneself both physically and emotionally* (Parkes & Weiss, 1983; Shuchter & Zisook, 1990; Worden, 1991). It is important to note that some feelings such as anger, guilt, and helplessness may be difficult to acknowledge.

3. *Convert the relationship with the deceased from one of the presence to a relationship of memory* (Lindemann, 1944; Parkes & Weiss, 1983; Rando, 1987, 1993; Ruskay, 1996; Sable, 1991; Worden, 1991). This requires the bereaved to develop a new relationship with the deceased. It also involves coming to terms with the unfilled roles played by the deceased.

4. *Develop a new sense of self-identity based on a life without the deceased* (Lindeman, 1944; Parkes & Weiss, 1983; Ruskay, 1996; Worden, 1991). Role confusion involves the struggle between the "we" and the "I" and fears associated with one's new autonomy.

Following the presentations, participants are encouraged to ask questions and to share comments or personal experiences. This is the third part of the session. The emphasis is on understanding and normalizing the grief experience. This empowers each of the bereaved to struggle with their grief toward resolution.

The final part of the session involves asking each member of the group to identify his or her goals and any needs or specific help that they might desire from the group. It is now that universality and instillation of hope are joined by the therapeutic element imparting of information. Implicitly or explicitly, imparting of information serves to satisfy a human need to minimize feelings of uncertainty.

This session ends with the same warning and comment, as did the first: Don't strive to have a *good* day, have only the best day you are capable of at this point in your grieving process.

Session 3: Sharing

The session opens with participants being asked to share how they experienced their prior week. This is followed by a brief review of the phases and tasks of grief and a request of every member, if able, to share the stage of grief in which they experience themselves. Discussion and exchange is encouraged, focusing on how each person has been able to cope with the experience.

It is here that the group leader makes an extended effort to help the participants to identify and express their feelings. The task here is not to identify unique as well as common feelings, but to relate struggles and accomplishments to the tasks of grief where appropriate.

The therapeutic elements of group previously noted continue to function and another, altruism, is added. Those who entered the group in their own heavy self-absorbed shroud of grief may now begin to more fully experience other group members and receive through giving. This phenomenon of self-transcendence cannot be intellectually obtained. It can only be experienced, and it is an important part of the healing process.

The group is concluded with the invitation to bring remembrance or keepsake items, and told that the group will be talking about the funeral next week. As has become usual, the instructions are not to have a good week, but only to have the best week possible.

Session 4: Remembrances

Following an opening in which group members share their experiences, triumphs and tragedies, of the past week, they are invited to share any remembrance or keepsake items associated with the deceased. This is followed by a description of the funeral experience, including what happened and what, if anything, the bereaved wished would have happened. This telling or retelling of the funeral experience reaffirms the reality of the loss, opening the door for further expression of emotions associated with the loss. Additionally, this provides group members additional opportunities to give and receive emotional support from each other.

This session heralds the arrival or solidification of the next therapeutic element, cohesiveness. There is a strong force that began previously and now binds group members to each other. This bond of acceptance and approval provides fertile conditions for self-disclosure examination, and exploration. Group cohesion is not a therapeutic element in the same sense as the others. However, it is the catalyst without which the other factors cannot achieve their full healing potentials.

In closing, participants are asked to bring pictures or family albums containing pictures of the deceased to the next group meeting. The all-too-familiar comment about not having a good week is echoed yet again, but possibly for the final time.

Session 5: Memories

Memories of holidays, special events, and the various roles played by the deceased are facilitated by albums and pictures that are passed carefully and caringly around the group. The group leader helps the participants to focus on what they miss about the deceased and how it relates to the picture. Following acknowledgment of positive memories and attributes of the deceased, the second question is introduced, "What do you not miss?" With the positive balance struck, it is often easier to acknowledge and accept the less-desirable aspects of the person or the relationship. This exposes the door to possibly unexplored emotions, and beckons for its opening.

This session is often the scene of developing socializing techniques, imitation of behavior and catharsis. The nature and extent of socializing techniques varies, but participants, through participation in the group, have learned how to approach others and talk about death losses and associated feelings. To their amazement, most learn that if they are comfortable with the subject or emotions, that others will be, too.

Participants also have the opportunity to directly and indirectly modify their behavior and imitate effective, more desirable behavior of other group members. An example might be risk-taking behaviors such as self-disclosure or the ability to appropriately express a previously denied strong emotion such as anger. Catharsis generally increases in this session. The group is now seen as a safe place for the expression of strong emotions, and previously denied feelings are often seen as normal, and though still disliked, more willingly accepted.

In closing the group, the comment is made to have the best week possible— a good week, if you can. This is a precursor to next week's session that will focus on saying good-bye and moving on with life.

Session 6: Feedback

In this session, participants are asked where in the process of saying good-bye they are. Those who are further along in the process serve as models and beacons of hope for others not yet there. Those experiencing difficulty are invited to share the difficulties and fears they are experiencing. The difficult task of living is openly discussed, and residual pain is often experienced as the (final) reality of the loss is yet again experienced.

Feedback from others in the form of interpersonal learning now frequently takes place in the group. This process of feedback mirrors for the participant the impression they leave with others. The realization is often made that how others respond to them in their loss is influenced by not disclosing what they really think or need.

Session 7: Coping Strategies

How have you coped and how are you coping now are the focal questions of this session. The group leader assists participants to focus on their use of coping strategies and to examine the effectiveness of these behaviors. The element of interpersonal learning now takes center stage and is of paramount importance if growth and healing is to occur.

Examples of questions include what is to be done with the deceaseds' possessions, and what short-term goals the bereaved see themselves having. Goals established back in the second session are also reviewed and reevaluated, with the participants being queried about unresolved issues.

Existential factors relating to loss are also brought to light and discussed. Examples include recognition that life is sometimes unfair and unjust; that ultimately there is no escape from life's pain and death; that no matter how close I get to other people, I still must face life alone; learning that I must take ultimate responsibility for the way I live my life, no matter how much guidance and support I receive from others, and finally, recognizing my limitations and my mortality.

Participants are encouraged to reflect over the past weeks and to remember the unjust and unfair situations each of them has encountered and the pain each has felt. The group leader reminds each member that although they banded together to face a common condition, each member faced his or her nemesis alone.

Session 8: Saying Good-bye

The group members are again asked to evaluate where they are in the phases and related tasks of grieving. Participants are encouraged to comment and to give each other feedback on their experience and to say good-bye. The group leader also gives feedback to each member of the group. The session closes with referral information regarding additional community services, should anyone wish to avail themselves.

Follow-up in the form of another group meeting or meetings to be held some months in the future or telephone follow-up is beneficial.

Group facilitation of the bereavement process involves the interplay of factors such as universality, instillation of hope, altruism, cohesiveness, socialization techniques, imitating of behavior, catharsis, interpersonal learning, and existential factors. As such, group is a most effective and expeditious way to facilitate the bereavement process.

MAINTAINING THERAPEUTIC PERSPECTIVE

Assisting the bereaved requires maintenance of a therapeutic and realistic perspective. To be truly therapeutic requires acceptance of our own helplessness and impotency. To not acknowledge this is to risk intervening in an ineffectual manner because of our needs and not those of the bereaved. Despite our most fervent desires and endeavors, we cannot make it better and we cannot end the suffering of the bereaved. Recall being a child, falling, and skinning your knee. In tears, you may have sought out your mother to make it better. However, in reality she could not make it better. What she could do was hold you and comfort you while you cried. For most of us, it is difficult to suffer in silence and even more difficult to suffer alone. Realizing and accepting that others cannot take away your pain, but that they can be present with you so that you do not have to suffer alone, allows us to take the first step in becoming therapeutic.

Outbursts of emotion in the initial period following a loss are not uncommon. The protest exhibited by the bereaved may be intense and look inappropriate, though it is not. Counselors must be prepared to accept and appropriately respond to the fact that the bereaved may find them and others ineffective and incompetent, since all they want is the return of the deceased or for this to never have happened, and neither is possible.

The loss belongs to the bereaved and regardless of the circumstances must be viewed from their perspective. Interventions, to be effective, must be appropriate to the bereaved, their unique relationship with the deceased, and their unique loss. Assumptions should not be made; rather, the unique story should be allowed to be told by the bereaved. The counselor's task is to assist the bereaved in telling their stories by helping them to identify, define, and decide for themselves what is important and/or problematic and to prioritize.

It is important to show genuine concern. To do this requires us to allow ourselves to be affected (but not overwhelmed) by the experience of the bereaved. Allowing the bereaved to own the loss, but in doing so to validate or confirm the loss experienced through a genuine emotional response, is very therapeutic. Achieving this balance between caring and overcaring requires preparatory work on the part of the counselor.

RITUALS AND CEREMONIES

Rituals are powerful ceremonies or rites that help to preserve the social order and provide a mechanism through which individuals demonstrate a comprehension of complex aspects of human existence within a given social context. The rules of the ritual may provide a vehicle for the expression or containment of strong emotions. The dynamic quality of a ritual provides ways for people to experience themselves in new roles to which they may not be accustomed. Most cultures have prescribed rites of passage that commemorate transitions into different stages of life (e.g., birth, puberty, marriage, death). Ritual celebrations publicly announce transition or change from one state to another and serve to assist the individual and the community in adapting to this new state or role. Mourning rituals may serve several functions. First, they separate the bereaved from the rest of society. Second, they may assist the bereaved in reintegrating into society.

Funerals are by far the most common bereavement ritual. When bereavement rituals are used, they are often used to facilitate the relinquishing of relationships and the transition to a new social role (Rando, 1993). They further provide for the opportunity for the public display of grief, while at the same time the prescribed ritual provides structure in a time of disorder and confusion. Most all cultures have funeral and/or bereavement rituals that acknowledge the finality of death and prescribe some type of socially supported mourning behaviors (Irish, Lindquist & Nelsen, 1993; Rosenblatt, 1996). Some see popular American culture as dominated by a model that minimizes and deritualizes bereavement practices (Klass, Silverman & Nickman, 1996; McGoldrick et al., 1991).

The funeral may be seen as the final rite of passage for the deceased and the public acknowledgment of a change in role for the bereaved. The noted anthropologist Arnold van Gennep (1960) conceptualized what he called the rite of passage and saw it as facilitating social transition through a series of phases. He identified the phases as follows: the separation from a former state, the transition into a new state, and incorporation into the new state. Rituals such as funerals are seen as mediating this transition. These phases van Gennep describes appear to parallel the task of mourning discussed in Chapter 5: Experience and express outside one's self the reality of death, tolerate the emotional suffering of separation, convert the relationship with the deceased from one of the presence to a relationship of memory, and to develop a new sense of identity based on a life without the deceased.

The funeral ritual as a rite of passage provides psychological as well as social benefits to the bereaved and helps to facilitate the tasks of grief. The funeral is a concrete acknowledgment of the loss through death and begins a ritualized separation of the deceased from the bereaved. Viewing the body is often helpful and assists in accepting the finality of the loss. Even if the bereaved is emotionally unable to accept this reality, the memories of the experience will at some later time help to confirm the reality of the loss. The communal involvement serves to endorse this separation and transition back in to the community in a different state. The funeral also allows the bereaved a public and socially legitimate opportunity to mourn and to receive the condolences of others. In addition to condolences, the bereaved and others might begin to review their relationships with the deceased. The experience and release of emotions associated with these memories and the beloved's death are an essential part of the grieving process. These memories may serve as a way to help identify what has been lost and point toward adaptations that will have to be made. A major adaptation that this memorializing promotes is the accepting and converting of the relationship from one of presence to one of memory. Finally, the funeral, in its public confirmation of the loss through death, confirms that the relationship with the deceased has radically changed and further acknowledges the continuing relationships that exist though the bereaved is now in a new and different role.

The ritual of the funeral can be of exceptional importance to the bereaved in that it provides an experience, albeit condensed, that might not be available otherwise due to societal changes that have decreased the time allocated for the grieving process.

The ritual of the funeral serves the process of transformation and transition; however, other rituals also exist and may serve to connect or provide continuity with the deceased in a new way. Religious practices can offer an opportunity for the formation and continuation of a new altered relationship with the deceased (e.g., Catholic anniversary Mass or Rosary; Jewish Yizkor). Catholics, through the celebration of an anniversary Mass or Rosary, remember the dead and remain connected to them through religious rituals. Yizkor books were kept by the leaders of the Jewish communities throughout Europe. When a person in the community died, the person's name and date of death were recorded in the Yizkor book. In this way, memories of the deceased's existence and life are kept alive. Dias de los Muertos (the days of the dead) is an example of a ritual in cultural context that provides the bereaved an opportunity for an ongoing connection with the deceased. This is an ancient festival that has undergone significant transition over the centuries but that was intended in pre-hispanic Mexico to celebrate children and the dead. It is best described as a time when Mexican families remember their dead and the continuity of life. Judith Strupp Green (1972) provides an extensive description of this elaborate celebration and extensive rituals in her article "The Days of the Dead in Oaxaca, Mexico: An Historical Inquiry."

Rituals are a creative encounter and require us to use our imagination and to be open to stepping outside of normal prescribed or accepted social conventions. Individuals who have experienced their stillborn or newborn baby's death have, out of necessity and a lack of socially prescribed ritual, created their own rituals or rites.

When a baby is born, the entire family is usually involved in ritual bonding. The new family member is viewed, held, passed around, and introduced to everyone. In the event of a miscarriage or stillbirth, this is usually not the case. However, the need to express affection and the desire to physically bond and to hold the baby does not automatically disappear. Families may find comfort in the simple act of washing, dressing, and holding the body of their child. Simple acts that are a part of the normal ritual of bonding create remembrances of the baby, allowing the feelings of life and death to combine and move toward completion. The creation of keepsakes is important. Portraits of the dead child might seem morbid to some; however, this may be the family's only image of their child and may become a cherished remembrance.

In Victorian times, mourning quilts were often pieced out of the clothing of the deceased. This tradition has been revived and is utilized as part of the therapeutic milieu in grief work. Selecting the cloth from old clothing or other items allows for great sensitivity to the memories and emotions associated with them. Each block of the quilt represents a part of the deceased person and is unique. The tapestry represents the person and the life that was lived, the good and the not so good. For example, the green may represent an Irish ancestry and the red an Irish temper that could replace an otherwise happy, cheerful mood at the drop of a hat. Quilts serve as both a visual as well as a tactile memory and celebrate the life of the deceased. Keep in mind that this process of ritual remembrance need not be restricted to quilts. The goal is to create an object that serves as both a visual and a tactile memory.

The Native American legend of the Dream Catcher tells of a spider whose life was saved by a young boy's grandmother. In return, the spider spun a web that would snare bad dreams and only allow good dreams to pass through a small hole and be remembered by the dreamer. The making and hanging of a Dream Catcher over the bereaved's bed can serve as a request of the bereaved that the memory of the deceased be retained in good dreams.

Finally, children who have lost a parent often express a desire to talk to or to tell the deceased news of events in their lives. This may be accomplished through a simple ritual, the balloon launch. The child is asked to write a note or card to the deceased, including the news the child would like to share. Then in a special place and with some ceremony the note is attached to a helium-filled balloon(s) and released to ascend to heaven, where the deceased will receive it.

Remember that rituals are individual idiosyncratic creative encounters that require imagination. The comfort and meaning that is derived need only be understood by the bereaved.

QUESTIONS FOR THOUGHT
AND REFLECTION

1. Quickly, what would you say to someone whose loved one just died? How do you feel about what you just said? Why?

2. What literature or poetry speaks to you? How does it do that?

3. Read a poem about the experience of grief and loss. Reflect on what you experienced.

4. Respond to this statement: "Be creative."

5. Have you ever been to a funeral? What was your experience?

6. Do you participate in rituals? Identify them. What purpose(s) do they serve?

7. Describe or develop a ritual that you might find helpful or meaningful in facilitating the bereavement process following a miscarriage, abortion, or other loss.

The following are some examples of literature that might be helpful in facilitating the bereavement process. Further recommendations and assistance with computer searches can be obtained from your reference librarian.

Hall, D. (1996). Poetry: The Unsayable Said. Port Townsend, WA: Copper Canyon Press.

Levertov, D. (1996). Sands in the Well. New York: New Directions Books.

Lewis, C. S. (1961). A Grief Observed. New York: Bantam Books.

Olds, S. (1992). The Father: Poems. New York: Alfred A. Knopf.

Oliver, M. (1992). New and Selected Poems. Boston: Beacon Press.

Pastan, L. (1978). The Five Stages of Grief: Poems. New York: Norton & Co.

Wolterstorff, N. (1987). Lament for a Son. Grand Rapids, MI: William B. Ferdmans Publishing.

10

◦◦◦

Families and Grief

Thus far our focus has been on grief reactions involving individuals. However, many, if not most, death-related losses occur within the context of a family unit, and it is therefore important to consider the impact the death has on the entire family. Wedemeyer (1986) stated, "Death in a family . . . exposes a basic dynamic tension of family systems: It is a systemwide event and yet is also a personal event for each individual in the family." (p. 338) Viewing grief and loss from this perspective requires the counselor to have some knowledge of families as a system and how family dynamics can affect the grieving process. This chapter is not intended to be a disquisition on family therapy.

GRIEF AND FAMILY SYSTEMS

Nathan Ackerman, in 1938, wrote that the family is a unit itself, having its own psychological and social life. He went on to say that the family is not static, but rather, dynamic. It changes at different times because of internal and external pressures. In viewing the family, Ackerman saw the concept of social roles as important and having several advantages. The first is that it enables one to describe a multiperson system with a plurality of transactions; and, second, roles have the potential to be either complementary or reciprocal. These roles, when clearly defined and agreed upon, allow the family to function in some type of homeostatic balance. The loss of a member of the family group by death (other disruptions or losses may also occur) can result in disequilibrium and disrupting the family's ability to function. Murray Bowen (1978) noted:

> Knowledge of the total family configuration, the functioning position of the dying person in the family, and the overall level of life adaptation are important for anyone who attempts to help a family before, during or after a death. (p. 328)

Many researchers and clinicians agree that the death of a significant family member is the most powerful emotional experience families face (Bowen, 1978; Carey, 1977; Defrain, 1991; Friedman, 1988; Gelcer, 1983; Kell & Rabkin, 1979; McGoldrick & Walsh, 1991; Seaburn, 1990). Some families are able to pull together and share the experience and the pain of the loss. They are able to recover from the loss, assist each other to say good-bye to the deceased, punctuate this completed life cycle in a meaningful way, and begin to plan for the future. The family may assign old roles to new people or develop new ones. They may remember and have a continued connection with the deceased on anniversary dates and at other important moments in the family's life experience.

Other families, for many reasons, are unable to accept the changes necessary to restore homeostasis and move forward with life. These families may have difficulty letting go of the deceased and reorganizing roles. Greaves (1983) saw each change that occurs following the death of a family member as symbolic of the death of the family itself with the primary task being the reestablishment of a new family. Specific factors that have been identified as affecting the grieving process and influencing the degree of family disruption include stage in the family life cycle when the loss occurs, roles played by the deceased; power, affection, and communication patterns, extrafamilial relationships; and sociocultural factors (Goldberg, 1973; Gelcer, 1983; Vess, Moreland, & Schwebel, 1985; Davies, Spinetta, Martinson, McClowry & Kulenkamp, 1986; Lamberti & Detmer, 1993).

Families have several options in responding to the demand for changes caused by the death of a family member. One response is reorganization. The degree of reorganization required would be determined by the number and type of roles that were held by the deceased, as well as the adaptability of the family system. Another response is replacement. This occurs when the deceased was a spouse and the surviving partner decides to remarry; or, when the parents decide to have another child, if the deceased was a child. Either option can be a healthy or unhealthy response depending on a multitude of factors.

The concept of family presented here is based on the belief that the family is a dynamic interactional unit in which all members influence each other. Families, like individuals, have different capacities related to emotional functioning. An important characteristic of families who are able to recover from a death loss is the ability to openly talk about the deceased and feelings related to the loss. Families unable to adequately adjust to loss tend not to tolerate open expression of feelings. They join together in making and/or accepting excuses that allow one or all family members to remain silent. Symptomatic behavior may be seen as a role one or more family members assume that functions to prevent open discussion and keep the family stuck in the grieving process.

An obvious effect of a death loss is the need of the members of the family to renegotiate their relationships with one another and the deceased. This will require agreement to be reached by all members in the family as to who will assume the various responsibilities. In some situations this renegotiation of relationships will be uneventful; however, there are many situations in which it will be extremely painful and even traumatic. This type of difficulty might exist in families where cross-generational alliances or coalitions exist that result in relational conflicts that are often unresolved at the time of the death. The result of this unfinished business is now seen in conflict that surrounds the renegotiating of family relationships. Spark and Browdy (1972) noted that postponed mourning related to one's family of origin impedes experiencing emotional loss and separation within the current family. The following example describes this phenomenon.

A firstborn son had a close relationship with his patriarchal grandfather, who was a very successful businessman. The grandson, like his grandfather, was an extremely high achiever and a source of pride for the elder man. The boy's father, however, was not particularly successful at anything and was a source of disappointment to all the family, including his father.

This cross-generational bonding affected the boy's father's relationship with his son, which was distant. This resulted in the boy receiving most of his paternal support from his grandfather. When the elder man died, these unattended relationship issues compounded and confused the renegotiation of relationships within the family. Such unnegotiated relationship issues, in this example spanning three generations, are prescriptions for anger, resentment, guilt, and unresolved grief. In order to assess the impact of intergenerational conflict, Bowen (1978) suggests taking an extensive family history, which should cover at least two generations as part of the intake process.

Assessing grief within the context of the family system requires consideration be given to three main areas. The first is the family constellation. This includes the makeup and developmental stage of the family. Also of significant importance is the role the deceased and other family members play and the appropriateness of the roles. Since there are many potential roles that are played by family members (e.g., the caregiver, the family head, the value setter, the scapegoat) it is important to identify what and how much of a void has been created in the family system by the death. Bowen (1978) sees the family unit as achieving stasis and calm when each family member is functioning in his or her role and achieving reasonable efficiency. The addition, or, in this case, the loss of a family member and the void created by that role not being filled and functioning results in a loss of homeostasis. If the lost individual filled an important role in the family, it may be imperative that a replacement is found quickly and another family member may be pressed into service so that homeostasis is reestablished.

Characteristics of the family system constitute the second area of assessment. Areas of concern include the degree of flexibility or rigidity in the family, dependence, independence, and individual freedom of each family member, family values and beliefs, leadership style and decision-making process, family resources and support, strengths and weaknesses of the family, and immediate and long-term needs of the family. The quality of emotional relationships within the family unit is extremely important. A family that is well-integrated emotionally will be better able to help each other cope with a death, even the death of a significant family member, with little or no outside help. A family that is not well integrated emotionally may show minimal grief reactions at the time of death; however, there is a large probability that family members will later experience physical, emotional, and/or behavioral symptoms relating to the loss. It is noteworthy for those who work with grieving families to remember that a family's ability to express feelings following a loss does not indicate emotional integration; neither does it increase the level of emotional integration.

The third area to assess is the family's communication styles or patterns. Watzalawick, Beavins, and Jackson in their classic book, *Pragmatics of Human Communication,* state, "It is obvious that communication is a conditio sine qua non of human life and social order." (1967, p. 13) In the family system the rules, norms, and expectations as understood by the members are all dependent on how well or poorly the members communicate. Understanding the family rules regarding the expression of feelings, how these rules are communicated, and the rationale for them is critical in facilitating the mourning process. Davies et al. (1986) found that in less functional families sadness was equated with craziness and solicited comments like, "I've seen enough tears." Another finding was that in functional families, the father was able to express grief openly instead of hiding his feelings or praising his son for not crying at the funeral. As we have seen, death can trigger varied and intense feelings; therefore, having a context in which these feelings can be experienced, identified, and processed is of paramount importance. Families whose rules and communication patterns conspire to suppress the expression of feelings may keep the members from an adequate resolution of their grief.

FAMILY TASKS OF GRIEF

As has been noted, grief occurs on multiple levels: an individual level, a family level, and even a community or societal level. Goldberg (1973) developed a four-task model of family grief that is in many ways similar to that of Worden, except that it focuses on families. Moos (1995), noting the importance of communications in family functioning, added a fifth task (actually, in order, task number 1). In juxtaposing the two models, it becomes obvious that the grief work of families is an extension of individual grief work that is reciprocally interactive with other family members' grief work.

The first task (added by Moos) that faces the family is the need for members to openly acknowledge the death on both a cognitive and emotional level. To accomplish this, family members must talk to one another and share their feelings about the death and its circumstances. Allowing mourning to occur requires acknowledging and accepting that a loss has occurred (Worden's first task). This must be accomplished on an intrapersonal as well as an interpersonal level. As we have seen, this has implications for family communication and interactional patterns. If one family member, for whatever reason, acts to deny the loss, then his or her behavior has implications for the family as seen in the behavior of other members toward that individual and each other.

The second task of family grief is to allow mourning to occur. This parallels Worden's second task of working through the pain of grief and also is interrelated. Working through the pain requires the cooperation of other family members. For example, if open expression of emotion by a family member or members is virtually ignored or subjects eliciting an emotional response are declared taboo, then one or more members may learn to inhibit such emotions and become stuck in the grieving process.

The third task is for the family to relinquish memory of the deceased. What Goldberg is referring to here is relinquishing the idea that the deceased can continue to play an active role in the family. "The person must release himself from attachment to the dead individual." (Goldberg, 1973, p. 400) Worden describes the third task of grief as adjusting to the environment in which the deceased is missing. The family is faced with developing rituals or other mechanisms that allow for inclusion of the memory of the deceased while allowing life to continue and the family to begin to adapt to life without the deceased.

The fourth task is realignment of intrafamily roles. This is seen as a continuation of Worden's third task of grief and beginning the fourth task, which is to emotionally relocate the deceased and move on with life. To accomplish this there must be a redistribution of responsibilities and related roles within the family. This may occur in various ways based on members' ability, age, gender, or whatever criteria the family decides. Each member is faced with some role adjustment, either large or small. Individuals whose response to this realignment is to become helpless can be encouraged to remain helpless by being labeled incompetent or incapable by other family members, who aid them in not developing the skills they need to cope and thereby becoming stuck in the grieving process.

The fifth task of family grief is realignment of extrafamily roles. These roles that are part of or associated with community involvement or extrafamily events must be recast. This, like Worden's fourth task, represents the final task of mourning. Here family members have the opportunity to establish new relationships with old and with new acquaintances.

As with all the theories and models examined thus far, the family grief model is not linear and progression is not step by step but rather is interrelated as families struggle with one or more tasks individually and/or as a group. Members will be at different levels of acceptance and different levels of movement through the process. All of these factors interact, with each member's behavior affecting the other members and contributing to the functioning of the family system.

INTERVENTION STRATEGIES

Problem solving is one basic technique that may help pave the way for enhanced family functioning and grief resolution. As problems are identified and wrestled with, their antecedents and consequences often come to light, as do available options to deal with them. Interventions with families include, but also go beyond, facilitating the tasks of grief.

Families are often ill prepared for the reality of a loss through death, and they lack experience in dealing with the emotional pain that may be involved. Members may struggle with uncertainty and a sense of helplessness. To reduce fear and uncertainty counselors should identify, legitimize, and normalize feelings. It may also be necessary to help families find alternatives to behaviors such as rescuing and/or distancing to cope with unpleasant emotions and/or related fears.

Reframing involves changing the conceptual or emotional viewpoint of family members. The result is a change in the meaning attributed to the behavior of family members without having the family members change the actual behavior (Watzalawick, Weakland & Fisch, 1974). Reframing can create a more positive image of an event or individual. By putting a positive frame on something or someone's behavior, the family can be moved past existing or potential conflicts and on to the process of rebuilding.

Redefining of terms can help to empower families. An example might be crying. Men and sometimes women see withholding of tears as a sign of strength. However, if asked which would be more difficult, showing emotion or appearing stoic, the answer is almost universal; crying. Paradoxically then, real strength may be allowing weakness to show. Losing control is another fear and source of confusion. The experience of intense emotions may be seen or experienced as being out of control. Control is often erroneously seen as having dominion over something. Having sway often comes at a great cost and is not in reality having control. Control is the ability to have or not to have a desired outcome. Control is the ability to tolerate what comes, regardless of what it is. Losing control may in this case be the ultimate way to gain control. Challenging and possibly refining old definitions can make room for new behaviors that promote healthy functioning and facilitate the grieving process.

Facilitating open communication and discussion about the role of mutual support can also be helpful. In addition, each member of the family is encouraged to share with other members what he or she needs from them at this time. Members have the opportunity to validate and respond to the request, which includes negating time, availability, and other factors.

Discussion of family history, including disappointments about career or lifestyle choices, relationship breakdowns, job problems, and previous experience with bereavements may have a positive influence on family functioning and grief resolution. The unfinished business between the deceased and family members must be identified and resolved in a way that allows for reorganization of the family to take place. Understanding the role of the deceased before and after death is necessary before a redistribution of roles and responsibilities can occur.

There is pain associated with a death loss. Suffering is the experience of pain without meaning. To help family members avoid being overwhelmed by their suffering, help them to place it in a context of meaning. The existentialist, Viktor Frankl, founder of Logotherapy, posits that meaning is not invented, but rather, it exists in context and must be found. The following is a true example of a mother who was able to transform suffering into bearable pain through meaning.

The woman was on her way to the market with her young daughter. She stopped at her best friend's house to see if there was anything she could pick up for her. Being in somewhat of a hurry, she parked in the street and, with the motor running, went to her friend's door. Her daughter was somehow able to get out of her car seat and crawl over to the driver's side door and exit the car. As she did, she dislodged the transmission from park, and as she came around the front of the car, it ran over her. Her mother, standing on the front step, witnessed the accident and ran quickly to her daughter, picking her up in her arms. The child was bleeding from her nose and mouth but was able to make eye contact with her mother before she died in her arms. The mother's suffering was enormous, and she was plagued with the picture of her daughter's bloody face as she died in her arms. One of her laments was, "Why did I have to see my child die that way?" The meaning that allowed her to accept her pain and transform it from suffering was to be found in her lament: What safer place is there for a child to die than in her mother's arms? To allow your child to leave this world in such safety does not come without a price, and the price is the painful memory you have of your daughter's face. The mother could not change her fate, but she now had a "why" that allowed her a reason to accept her pain.

DYADIC GRIEF

The couple can be viewed as an interactive grieving system in which partners strive to cope with individual and relational concerns resulting from their loss, usually the death of their child. Following the death of a child, the need for social confirmation and support outside the self is often quite strong and is seen by the overwhelming need to talk to others about the loss. Lifton (1971) noted that people have a strong need for "connection, for meaningful ties to people, ideas and symbols, derived from the past and projected into the future." (p. 248) Couples are in a unique position to help each other in this regard. The marital couple shares a common history and has an established pattern of interaction that may assist in developing an understanding of the loss they have experienced. If the couple are able to develop a shared view within their marriage, they can reduce their ambiguity and uncertainty about the loss, how they are going to cope with that loss, and how they are going to get on with the tasks of life (Gilbert, 1996; Gilbert & Smart, 1992; Patterson & Garwick, 1994). Conversely, couples may also find themselves questioning each other and their marriage as a consequence of the loss. They may find that there is a need to reassess their relationship and their roles as partners, parents, caregivers, and protectors.

Reiss (1981), discussing the family's construction of reality, referred to the family paradigm as the fundamental beliefs, assumptions, and orientations shared by family members. This systemic phenomenon may also be extended to the marital dyad. In experiencing a loss, the couple needs to believe that the loss has a comparable or shared meaning for each person. This appears to be supported by the findings that parents who experience the loss of a child encounter tremendous difficulty accepting that their spouse is grieving in a way that is different from their own (Gilbert, 1996; Gilbert & Smart, 1992; Peppers & Knapp, 1980).

The dyadic system is an interactive system that provides feedback in the form of confirmation and disconfirmation about beliefs and assumptions expressed by each partner concerning the shared relationship and related experiences. In an ideal situation, the dyadic response to the experience of loss is interaction with each other that attempts to confirm the reality of the loss, validates each other's grief reaction, and promotes healing.

Unfortunately, the grief experience following the death of a child is such that it is very difficult and sometimes impossible for couples to provide each other with mutual validation and support (Borg & Lasker, 1988; Frantz, 1984; Rando, 1983, 1984). Parents have said that in addition to losing a child, it seems as if they had lost their spouse for a time (Rando, 1983), or that their spouse was the least helpful person to them in coping with the loss (Frantz, 1984). Individuals grieve differently, and it is not surprising that spouses grieve differently because in many ways they experience different losses. They will not have lost the "same" child; each will have had a different relationship with the child and hence a different experience of loss. Rando (1984) notes that the relationship need not have been a warm, loving one; a conflictual relationship may result in a more complicated grief reaction. This pattern of complication may extend to the couple's relationship after the death, especially if one parent had a conflictual relationship with the child while the other parent's relationship with the child was positive. Regardless of the scenario, each person must struggle with his or her own unique loss while simultaneously coping with changes in his or her spouse and in their relationship. However, it is necessary for the couple to accept and validate each other's loss in order to be available to each other and work through the loss.

Effects on the Marriage

A sequel to the experience of losing a child is that couples may come to view their marriage differently from the view they held prior to the loss. Prior to the loss, they might have seen themselves as sharing common interests, values, and goals. They may have had a working system that allowed them to effectively deal with day-to-day life, including established role behaviors that included validating and supporting one another. This may all change following a loss, as each person now has to consider and deal with his or her unique experience of the loss and his or her spouse's reaction. What was predictable based on previous knowledge, experience, and observations may now be seen as different, contradictory, and unproductive. Struggling with individual reactions and related needs, couples may find themselves overloaded and unable to provide for their spouse. It is at these times that couples may avoid sharing thoughts and feelings. They may avoid each other or even use hurtful comments to create distance, because they feel overwhelmed and unable to provide support to their spouse.

Another scenario involves secrecy or the avoidance of communication. Couples avoid sharing thoughts and feelings because of role expectations regarding appropriate behavior or in attempts to protect one another from obvious pain by not discussing the death. This may also occur if the couple is at very different points in the grieving process. A person who has moved on might not be available to validate his or her partner's experience, due to fears of being pulled back into the grief pit. Whatever the reason, effective communication is the keystone to successful relationships, and keeping thoughts and feelings a secret or not discussing them contributes to feelings of isolation and lack of support and inhibits the grieving process.

Tasks of Dyadic Grief

Many couples will struggle to cope with their loss and its impact on their relationship. They will face tasks of grief similar to those already mentioned. Couples will need to recognize the loss of their child and what that loss has meant for each of them personally. They will need to express the emotions surrounding their loss. Reorganization of the relationship will be necessary, and couples will need to recommit and reinvest in each other.

Acknowledging the loss and sharing feelings and the unique experience of what has been lost requires open and honest communication. Talking about their memories as well as future plans they had made or visualized for themselves and their child contribute to an understanding and acceptance of differences in what each has lost. Allowing open expression of strong emotions serves to validate the loss but may be difficult for some individuals or couples. Having one partner nonjudgmentally and supportively listen can be extremely meaningful. This may have a secondary effect in that seeing their spouse express emotional distress can serve to validate their own. Nonverbal communication such as physical availability, touching, hugging, and/or close physical proximity can carry a great deal of positive information and support. The ability of the couple to share the loss, not necessarily the same experience, but to feel that each is available to the other results in a greater sense of connectedness.

Spending time alone may be necessary at first; however, spending time together without obligations following the loss serves many purposes, not the least of which is reducing isolation and withdrawal. Time spent together may also facilitate a reorganization of the relationship. Having something such as a problem or task to focus on allows the couple to be a couple and to work together. In doing so, roles may be examined and redefined allowing partners to take turns and try out new and possibly more flexible roles. Becoming aware of and accepting differences in one another promotes more tolerance and also allows for the re-exploration of common goals and values. An important shared value will be the importance of the marriage. Once this value is declared by the couple, a reinvestment in the institution and a recommitment to each other should allow a new and different dyadic life to progress.

Gender Differences

Some research findings suggest that styles of grieving tend to be gender related (Damrosch & Perry, 1989; Guntzelman, 1992; Powers, 1993; Rando, 1986). Fathers appear to exhibit steady, time-bound adjustment, whereas most of the mothers reported more chronic distress. Mothers express more sorrow and depression, and fathers indicate that they feel more anger, fear, and loss of control (Defrain, 1991). Mothers have also expressed more feelings of guilt (Peppers & Knapp, 1980). Both fathers and mothers reported deep sorrow and sadness, although mothers were more likely to express negative feelings related to the sorrow than the fathers. Additionally, fathers as a group reported that they preferred not to dwell on feelings, whereas mothers preferred being allowed to express their feelings. Schatz (1986), writing about grief and fathers, notes that for fathers the grieving process is more often internal and may become apparent in indirect ways. Cook and Oltjenbruns (1988) found that men frequently find themselves caught in a "double bind" in that they are taught to contain their emotions "like a man" while also being expected, after a loss, to express their emotions "like a woman." Regardless of how they respond to the loss, they will experience some form of censure for acting inappropriately. Although it is important to avoid stereotyping, it seems helpful to be aware of traditional male social roles and attitudes (e.g., males are always strong, males are self-sufficient, males protect their families) and their potential to impede paternal expressions of grief.

THE OLDER BEREAVED

A large and growing segment of our population is living into their seventies and eighties. With this segment's increase in population comes a large number of older individuals who have experienced bereavement, especially the death of a spouse. It has been mentioned that the acceptance of death as a natural event may lessen the devastating impact following its occurrence; however, this may not hold true for this segment of the population. With advanced age comes the greater probability of multiple losses. Within one's cohort, a number of deaths of friends and extended family is expected. At the same time, the elderly may be experiencing or have experienced losses in multiple areas such as employment (retirement), environment (relocation to retirement settings), previous physical prowess and vigor, and possibly mental functioning. The situation is compounded by the fact that these losses are occurring more frequently and in a shorter amount of time.

Bereavement adjustments are multidimensional in that every aspect of a person's life can potentially be affected by the loss. Older bereaved spouses commonly experience additional difficulties in the areas of loneliness, interdependency and role adjustment, and a personal awareness of death.

Loneliness for the elderly can be both a physical and psychological reality. Many of the bereaved elderly live alone. Lopata (1979) reported that younger widows and widowers were more likely than older ones to move away after the death of a spouse. This can result in a compounding loss of environment and social surroundings that can add to the experience of loneliness. Sometimes relocation is required but not desired. In such cases, the surviving spouse may not be able to continue to afford to live in the home or may be unable to continue to live alone. Likewise, living in the same home one occupied with his or her spouse can intensify feelings of loneliness.

Loneliness is also the result of having been married to and living with the same person for many years. Attachments are numerous, and over the course of years couples normally develop intricate interdependencies. Spouses become highly dependent on each other for certain roles or activities that make adjustment following a loss monumentally difficult.

Elderly men, following the loss of their spouse, may find role adjustment more difficult than their female counterparts. Many elderly men find new roles, particularly relating to homemaking, extremely challenging, whereas many women do not encounter the same difficulty as a result of their self-reliance as homemakers. Elderly women, however, may face challenges in such areas as financial management or physical upkeep of the outside of the home.

Both elderly men and women, having experienced the loss of their contemporaries such as friends, family, or spouse, may have a heightened awareness of their own temporal reality. This acute awareness of one's own personal mortality may complicate already existing difficulties.

In addressing the needs of the bereaved, support groups can be very beneficial. Support groups are particularly advantageous for the elderly in that they provide them with a social support system at a time when theirs is usually diminished. The group further serves to reduce isolation that may frequently occur following the death of a spouse.

QUESTIONS FOR THOUGHT
AND REFLECTION

1. How aware are you of the various roles played by members of your family?

2. What is your role(s) in your family? What role(s) did you have in your family of origin?

3. Most families have rules by which they operate. Can you list yours?

4. Has your family ever experienced a loss of one of its members and had to realign itself? Describe what happened. Was the transition smooth or difficult? Why?

5. Are there family secrets in your family? How does this affect family functioning?

11

Caring for the Caregiver

Most individuals enter the helping profession in order to benefit or to be of service to others. However, there is something unique about the grief experience that precludes our ability to help. Parkes (1972) described the experience as follows:

> Pain is inevitable in such a case and cannot be avoided. It stems from the awareness of both parties that neither can give the other what he wants. The helper cannot bring back the person who's dead, and the bereaved person cannot gratify the helper by seeming helped. (p. 163)

The challenge inherent in this relationship will be a true test of even the finest metal. Aside from the fact that neither party can attain that which is desired, both are confronted with the ultimate reality of death. For the caregiver, this reality if left unexamined may potentially be a major source of stress.

Recall that acceptance and denial as an orientation toward death are neither intrinsically good nor bad. Each must be examined in the context in which it occurs and includes the purpose(s) it serves. This is not only true for the bereaved but also for the caregiver. As caregivers, most of us function somewhere between the extremes of total acceptance and total denial, although the extremes do occur. Denial is probably best understood as a mechanism that allows the individual time to adapt to whatever stressful circumstances are encountered. How one adapts and the mechanisms used can only be assessed when we are able to understand how the stressor is perceived and the goal of the behavior. Whatever adaptive strategy the individual exhibits will be influenced by his or her personal history and also by the other individuals that compromise his or her interpersonal network of relationships, personally and professionally.

In previous chapters we have explored our attitudes toward death and the history associated with those attitudes. Now in order to respond to our own needs as caregivers, it behooves us to explore forthrightly personal concerns we have that influence where on the continuum between acceptance and denial we function.

First, we must acknowledge that not everyone has the ability to work with the terminally ill or grieving people. The need to examine our motivation to work in this area should be clear. Some individuals (professionals as well as others) avoid contact with dying or bereaved people as much as possible. The reasons vary; however, Worden (1991) noted that working with the bereaved touches us personally in at least three ways.

First, it makes us painfully aware of our own losses. This is especially true if the bereaved's loss is similar to a loss the caregiver has experienced. If the caregiver's loss is not adequately resolved, it may serve as an impediment to any helpful interventions. However, if the caregiver has worked through his or her own bereavement and found solace, this personal experience can form the basis for compassion and understanding of the vulnerability that we all ultimately face in loss.

Second, how the bereaved touch us relates to our own anticipation of and fear of loss. Working with the bereaved may heighten our awareness of the inevitability and universality of loss; confronting us with the reality that it can and will happen to us. As an example, consider a caregiver whose concern for his or her children is displayed in overprotective behaviors. Working with an individual who has experienced the death of a child may present special problems for the caregiver, eliciting issues from them that could interfere with the relationship.

The final challenge to caregivers, which we have already explored, has to do with existential anxiety and one's own personal awareness of death. Again, most of us are to some degree anxious about death, but this in and of itself is not a problem. The problem occurs when this is a closet issue that generates blind anxiety and hinders our effectiveness. Sherman (1996) studied nurses and found that individuals who reported higher levels of death anxiety were less willing to work with dying people. It is noteworthy that Sherman also found that the willingness to work with terminally ill individuals can be influenced either positively or negatively by the quality of social support available to them. It is obviously difficult to enter into such an emotional experience as caring for the terminally ill or the bereaved if one feels alone and unsupported emotionally.

Looking at one's own attitudes and experiences with grief and the grieving process will help to identify limitations each of us has with respect to the type of person and grief experience that one is capable of dealing with effectively. In 1977, Worden and Kubler-Ross surveyed 5,000 health professionals on issues of terminal care. One of the issues surveyed had to do with difficulties caregivers encounter working with dying patients. Ninety-two percent of the respondents reported that there were one or more types of dying patients with whom they had special difficulty. This is also true for those who work with the bereaved. Not everyone can or should work with all types of dying or bereaved individuals or families. It is important for caregivers to recognize personal limitations and, when necessary, refer and/or, when appropriate, take time out of the caretaking role.

STRESS AND COPING

Stress can be defined as a personal experience, a perceptual phenomenon that arises from a comparison between the demand on a person and his or her ability to cope (Cox, 1978; Selye, 1974). Vachon (1987) conducted an extensive study of caregivers. She interviewed 600 professional caregivers from hospitals, palliative care facilities, chronic care institutions, and voluntary agencies that worked with dying people. She set her research question in the broad perspective of occupational stress asking what was the basic source of stress and how did they cope with it. What the respondents reported is that they were most stressed by their work environment and occupational roles, not by their direct work with the dying and their families. Vachon noted that it is possible that underlying death anxiety contributed to the stress, but the overall response (evidence) pointed to environmental variables. She concluded that it was within the realm of reason that these individuals were caught up in a role conflict. The conflict was between the technical/professional role they have and the role of humane caregiver. In the work environment, inadequate time exists to fully discharge the requirements of both roles. This time deficiency results in an imbalance between the professional role and the caregiver role and threatens the individual's ability to cope. In attempting to provide the best possible care, it behooves caregivers to be cognizant of these conflicts and also of the fact that they, too, have needs.

Worden (1991) has three recommendations for those who work with the terminally ill, their families, and/or other bereaved. The first is to know your limitations in terms of the number of terminally ill patients and/or other bereaved with whom you intimately work and to whom you become attached at any given time. This recommendation reflects the fact that to work with the dying and/or the bereaved is to work intimately with someone and, to varying depths and degrees, to form attachments to them. To the extent that there is an attachment, there is going to be a loss that the caregiver will need to grieve.

The second recommendation is to avoid burnout. To do this, Worden advocates that the caregiver actively grieve the loss of those with whom the caregiver has worked. He says that he personally finds it helpful to attend the funeral service of a terminally ill person with whom he has been working. Allowing oneself the experience and expression of sadness and other feelings is imperative if burnout is to be avoided.

The third recommendation is that caregivers should know how to reach out for help and know where his or her own personal support comes from. Caregivers are obviously able to help others with their grieving, but may experience difficulty acknowledging when they are in need; or if they are, where to go to get help. Therefore, Worden recommends that grief workers be conscious of where their support comes from, know what their personal limits are, and know how to reach out for help when it is needed. Raphael (1980) also stresses this need for self-awareness and advocates caregivers be involved in some type of continuing support system such as peer support groups, supervision, or case discussion meetings.

ADAPTATION AND GROWTH

Harper (1977) developed a model of the adaptation process that health care professionals progress through as they mature and become more comfortable in working with terminally ill patients who are facing death. The stages in the model represent, according to Harper, the normative sequence of emotional and psychological growth and development that caregivers experience as they mature professionally.

Stage 1. Intellectualization: Knowledge and Anxiety

In the initial stages of work with death and the dying, caregivers tend to view the process intellectually. Their focus is on acquisition of professional information, factual knowledge, and philosophical issues related to death and dying. These activities, while necessary, serve a secondary purpose and are seen as attempts to manage anxiety by intellectually understanding the task at hand and thereby managing the environment. This method of stress and anxiety management may result in the caregiver experiencing difficulty managing interpersonal proximity with the dying patient and his or her family. Working effectively with others requires that one not be too close or too far away. Caregivers at this beginning point are concerned but generally uncomfortable with their role and with death.

Stage 2. Emotional Survival: Trauma

The trauma Harper speaks of in this stage is the shock and surprise that caregivers experience as they are catapulted from a point of relative calm intellectualization into its antithesis that is the emotional upheaval of actual true involvement. Here the reality of a patient's (and possibly the caregiver's own) impending or actual death is confronted. Death is now experienced on an emotional level, and there is a realization that suffering and death are unavoidable. Concomitantly, caregivers are confronted with their own personal impotency and related feelings of helplessness. There may also be growing concern or even pity for patients as caregivers experience feelings of discomfort and cognitive dissonance related to the unfair state that exists between their state of health and that of dying patients. Frustration, guilt, and anxiety are common experiences in this stage.

Stage 3. Depression: Pain, Mourning, and Grieving

This stage represents a crisis in professional growth and development. Those who successfully encounter the tempest will grow, and those who do not will be forced to go (into other fields). This crisis involves the potential for acceptance and, if it occurs, begins the process of accommodation. Acceptance is of death and the reality of death and dying. Caregivers must face and accept that death exists and that despite all their interventions, they cannot make the dying well or the process of dying less difficult. Struggling to accept the loss, caregivers might experience pain, mourning, and grief before moving forward and beginning the process of accommodation.

Stage 4. Emotional Arrival: Moderation, Mitigation, and Accommodation

Caregivers in this stage begin to emerge from the trauma and related emotions experienced in the previous struggles. No longer preoccupied with the unfairness of circumstances or the inevitability and reality of death, caregivers arrive at a point of personal authenticity and an associated sense of freedom. However, this does not mean that caregivers do not experience pain, grief, and mourning when working with the dying. What it does mean is that caregivers are free to experience pain without being incapacitated or overwhelmed by the experience. Emotionally sensitive responses to dying patients by caregivers are now authentically appropriate.

Stage 5. Deep Compassion: Self-Realization, Self-Awareness, and Self-Actualization

If achieved, this stage represents the culmination of the process of growth and development in the caregiver. The ability to relate with deep compassion to the dying patient in full acceptance of the impending death is the hallmark of this stage. Death is understood as the last stage of life as we experience it, and living is also understood at times to be more painful than dying. A caregiver's compassion and concern for the dying patient now translate into activities that are based on a humane as well as professional assessment of the needs of the dying patient and his or her family.

Harper's model provides one view of the process of personal and professional maturity as caregivers and provides a template by which we can prepare for the journey and measure our progress. As with other models we have examined, these stages are not necessarily encountered and/or mastered in sequential order, and not everyone will emerge from the experience at stage five.

WHERE TO GO FROM HERE

Where you go from here and what you should expect to find will be determined on an individual basis; however, there are some resources that should be helpful in the quest. Individuals can gain a quick overview of such topics as training workshops and certification procedures for death educators and counselors from an organization known as the Association for Death Education and Counseling (ADEC). This nonprofit organization was incorporated in 1976 with the purpose of improving the quality of death education and death-related counseling (Leviton, 1993). Scholarly and professional journals are a resource for research and other seminal information, as well as other issues of interest and controversy in the field. A selected list of both professional organizations and scholarly professional journals is included at the end of this chapter.

Students in my classes have come from a variety of fields, including counseling, psychology, nursing, social work, ministry, education, and other disciplines, each desiring to add to his or her competency. With such varied backgrounds come varied expectations, which often makes teaching this class a challenge. What I have discovered, both in my own training and as a teacher of others with varied backgrounds, is that learning in the arena of death, loss, and grief requires an experience that is not only intellectual but also emotional. Journeying with the dying and/or bereaved is a difficult task. The existential-humanist, James Bugental, sees the process of being therapeutic as a searching encounter between a traveler and a guide (Bugental, 1978). The inauthentic guide possesses only an intellectual understanding of the process of death and dying and grief and loss and therefore possesses only an illusion of understanding. In reality, the guide knows neither the hazards nor the rewards of the journey. The authentic guide, however, possesses both an intellectual as well as an emotional understanding of the process, and knows that each journey is new both for the guide as well as the traveler and is aware of both the potential hazards and rewards of the journey. What Bugental is saying is that you cannot guide others in areas where you yourself fear to tread.

The authentic experience is not a tidy one but is rather messy, and it will require deep, in-depth, and intimate discussions, including some that could be severely gut-wrenching. However, if this is a path that you desire to travel and to walk with and guide others, then continue what you have begun. This journey is over; now, reflect on your personal experience and prepare with what you have learned for the next new encounter.

SELECTED NATIONAL ORGANIZATIONS

Center for Crime Victims and Survivors, Inc.
P. O. Box 6201
Clearwater, FL 34618

Center for Loss and Life Transition
3735 Broken Bow Road
Fort Collins, CO 80526

AMEND (Aiding Mothers & Fathers Experiencing
Newborn Death)
4324 Berrywick Terrace
St. Louis, MO 63128

American Association of Suicidology
4201 Connecticut Avenue, NW
Suite 310
Washington, DC 20008

American Hospice Foundation
1130 Connecticut Avenue, NW
Suite 700
Washington, DC 20008

Association for Death Education and Counseling
638 Prospect Avenue
Hartford, CT 06105-4250

The American Academy of Bereavement (a division of
Carondelet Health Care)
2090 North Kolb Road
Suite 100
Tucson, AZ 85715-4149

SELECTED SCHOLARLY
AND PROFESSIONAL JOURNALS

American Journal of Hospice Care
Prime National Publishing
470 Boston Road
Weston, MA 02193

Death Studies
Taylor & Francis, Ltd.
1101 Vermont Avenue, NW
Suite 200
Washington, DC 20005

Illness, Crisis and Loss
The Charles Press
P. O. Box 15715
Philadelphia, PA 19103

Omega, Journal of Death and Dying
Baywood Publishing Company
26 Austin Avenue
Amityville, NY 11701

Suicide and Life-Threatening Behavior
Guilford Press
72 Spring Street
New York, NY 10012

QUESTIONS FOR THOUGHT
AND REFLECTION

1. How do you deal with your own impotency and helplessness?

2. What motivates you to work with the terminally ill or bereaved?

3. Identify the significant losses you have experienced in your life. How have you coped with these, and where are you in the process?

4. How do you deal with stress (personally and professionally)?

5. How difficult is it for you to ask for help?

6. Where does your support (personal and professional) come from?

Epilogue

I t is natural to die. When we were born we began a journey (whether we know it or not) that will ultimately end in death. Everything that is born and lives also dies; it is the natural order of things. This is a very simple concept, but also a very profound one that may challenge us to review and reconsider our views of life and death.

This book attempted to present an introduction to and overview of the phenomenon that is the experience of grief and loss. Working with the bereaved is much like unraveling a braid. The experience of grief and loss is a unique labyrinth of the bereaved individual's personal history, including interpersonal relationships, societal expectations and rules (explicit and implied), and type of and circumstances surrounding the loss. However, facilitating movement through the bereavement process requires one to have some conceptualization of the process; therefore, several models (stage and task) were presented for examination.

In the final analysis, it should be clear that there is no right way to look at death or work with the dying and/or bereaved. I refer back to the caution provided in the preface that admonished readers to critically examine the information presented and its applicability, acknowledging the words of Gordon Allport that each man (or woman) is like all other men, each man is like some other men, and it is also true that each man is like no other man. In the end, both death and dying and the grief experienced by those who survive the loss are very personal and individual experiences. With this in mind, we began; and now we finish. It is my sincere hope that this book has contributed to your learning experience.

References

Ad Hoc Committee of the Harvard Medical School to Examine the Definition of Death (1968). A definition of irreversible coma. *Journal of the American Medical Association, 205*, 337–340.

Ainsworth, M., Blehar, M., Waters, E., & Walls, S. (1978). *Patterns of attachment: A psychological study of strange stimulation.* Hillside, NJ: Erbaum.

Allen, J., Hauser, S., Bell, K., & O'Conner, T. (1994). Longitudinal assessment of autonomy and relatedness in adolescent-family interactions as predictors of adolescent ego development and self-esteem. *Child Development, 65*, 179–194.

Allen, J., Kuperminc, G., & Moore, C. (1997). Developmental approaches to understanding adolescent deviance. In S. Luthar, J. Burack, D. Cicchetti, & J. Weiss (Eds.), *Developmental psychopathology: Perspective on risk and disorder* (pp. 548–567). Cambridge, England: Cambridge University Press.

Aristotle (1962). *The Nicomachean ethics* (Martin Ostwald, Trans.). Indianapolis: Bobbs-Merrill.

Association Quebecoise de Suicidologie (1990). *La prevention de suicide au Quebec: Vers un modele integre de services.* Montreal: AQS.

Baker, J., Sedney, M., & Gross, E. (1992). Psychological tasks for bereaved children. *American Journal of Orthopsychiatry, 62* (1), 105–116.

Barrett, T., & Scott, T. (1990). Suicide bereavement and recovery pattern compared with non-suicide bereavement patterns. *Suicide and Life Threatening Behavior, 20*, 1–15.

Barrett, T., & Scott, T. (1989). Development of the grief experience questionnaire. *Suicide and Life Threatening Behavior, 19*, 201–215.

Bates, J., Maslin, C., & Frankel, K. (1985). Attachment security, mother–child interactions, and temperament as predictors of problem solving ratings at three years. In I. Bertherton & E. Waters (Eds.), *Growing points in attachment theory and research*. Monographs of Society for Research in Child Development, 50 (1-2, Serial No. 209), 167–193.

Beauchamp, T., & Childress, J. (1994). *Principles of biomedical ethics* (4th ed.). New York: Oxford University Press.

Beauchamp, T., & Childress, J. (1989). *Principles of biomedical ethics* (3th ed.). New York: Oxford University Press.

Beauchamp, T., & Childress, J. (1983). *Principles of biomedical ethics* (2th ed.). New York: Oxford University Press.

Beauchamp, T., & Childress, J. (1979). *Principles of biomedical ethics*. New York: Oxford University Press.

Belsky, J., Rovine, M., & Taylor, D. (1984). The Pennsylvania infant and family project III. The origins of individual differences in infant mother attachment: Maternal and infant contributions. *Child Development, 55* (3), 718–728.

Benn, S. (1998). *A theory of freedom*. Cambridge: University Press.

Bersoff, D., & Koeppl, P. (1993). The relationship between ethical principles and moral principles. *Ethics and Behavior, 3* (3/4), 345–357.

Borg, S., & Lasker, J. (1988). *When pregnancy fails: Families coping with miscarriage, stillbirth, and infant death* (2nd ed.). New York: Bantam.

Bowen, M. (1978). *Family therapy in clinical practice*. New York: Aaronson.

Bowlby, J. (1990). *Charles Darwin: A new life*. New York: Norton.

Bowlby, J. (1982). Attachment and loss: Retrospect and prospect. *American Journal of Orthopsychiatry, 52*(4), 664–678.

Bowlby, J. (1980). *Attachment and loss* (Vol. 1, 2nd Ed.). Harmonsworth UK: Penguin.

Bowlby, J. (1980). *Attachment and loss* (Vol. 3). New York: Basic Books.

Bowlby, J. (1980). *Loss, sadness and depression*. New York: Basic Books.

Bowlby, J. (1979). *The making and breaking of affectional bonds*. London: Tavastock.

Bowlby, J. (1977). *The making and breaking of affectional bonds, I, II*. *British Journal of Psychiatry, 130*, 201–210, 421–431.

Bowlby, J. (1973). *Attachment and Loss* (Vol. 2). New York: Basic Books.

Bowlby, J. (1969). *Attachment and Loss* (Vol. 1). New York: Basic Books.

Boyle, J. (1991). Who is entitled to double effect? *Journal of Medicine and Philosophy, 16* (4), 475–494.

Boyle, J. (1980). Toward an understanding of the principle of double effect. *Ethics, 90* (4), 527–538.

Bratman, M. (1987). *Intention, plans and practical reason*. Cambridge, MA.: Harvard University Press.

Braybrooke, D. (1991). No rules without virtues: No virtues without rules. *Social Theory and Practice, 17* (2), 139–156.

Brown, M. (1958). *The dead bird*. Reading, MA: Addison-Wesley.

Buber, M. (1996). *I and Thou* (Trans. Walter Kaufmann original work 1970). New York: Simon & Schuster.

Bugental, J. (1978). *Psychotherapy and process: The fundamentals of an existential-humanistic approach*. New York: McGraw-Hill.

Burt, R. (1979). *The role of law in doctor patient relations*. *New York:* Free Press; Simon & Schuster Adult Publishing Group.

Buscaglia, L. (1982). *The fall of freddie the leaf*. Thorofare, NJ: Slack.

Cain, A. (1972). *Survivor's of suicide*. Springfield, IL. Thomas.

Cain, A., & Fast, I. (1972). The legacy of suicide: Observations on the pathogenic impact of suicide on marital partners. In A. C. Cain (Ed.), *Survivors of suicide* (pp. 145–155). Springfield, IL: Charles C. Thomas.

Calhoun, L., & Allen, B. (1993). The suicide of a child: Social perception of stepparents. *Omega: Journal of Death and Dying, 26* (4), 301–307.

Calhoun, L., Selby, J., & Abernathy, C. (1988). Suicidal death: Social reactions to bereaved survivors. *Journal of Psychology, 116* (2), 255–261.

Calhoun, L., Selby, J., & Abernathy, C. (1984). Suicidal death: Social reactions to bereaved survivors. *Journal of Psychology, 116* (2), 255–261.

Calhoun, L., Selby, J., & Selby, L. (1982). The psychological aftermath of suicide: An analysis of current evidence. *Clinical Psychology Review, 2,* 409–420.

Calhoun, L., Selby, J., & Steelman, J. (1984). A collation of funeral directors impressions of suicide deaths. *Omega: Journal of Death and Dying, 19* (4), 365–373.

Campbell, J., Swank, P., & Vincent, K. (1991). The role of hardiness in the resolution of grief. *Omega: Journal of Death and Dying, 23* (1), 53–65.

Carey, A. (1977). Helping the family and the child cope with death. *International Journal of Family Counseling, 5* (1), 58–63.

Carter, B., & Brooks, A. (1990). Suicide postvention: Crisis or opportunity. *School Counselor, 37* (5), 378–390.

Cassidy, J., & Berlin, L. (1994). The insecure/ambivalent pattern of attachment: Theory and Research. *Child Development, 65,* 971–991.

Chaplin, J. P. (1985). *Dictionary of psychology.* New York: Bantam Doubleday Dell.

Childress, J. (1990). The place of autonomy in bioethics. *The Hastings Center Report, 20* (1), 12–17.

Clardy, A. (1984). *Dusty was my friend: Coming to terms with loss.* Human Sciences.

Clayton, P., Desmaris, L., & Winokur, G. (1968). A study of normal bereavement. *American Journal of Psychiatry, 125* (2), 168–174.

Conway, P. (1988). Losses and grief in old age. *Social Casework, 69* (9), 541–549.

Cook, A., & Oltjenbruns, K. (1998). The bereaved family. In A. S. Cook & K. A. Oltjenbruns (Eds.), *Dying and grieving: Life span and family perspective* (pp. 91–115). Fort Worth, TX: Harcourt Brace.

Corr, C. (1995). Entering into adolescent understandings of death. In Earl Grollman (Ed.) *Bereaved children and teens: A support guide for parents and professionals,* pp. 21–35. Boston: Beacon Press.

Cox, T. (1978). *Stress.* Baltimore: University Press.

Crittenden, P. (1988). Relationships at Risk. In J. Beisky & T. Nezworski (Eds.), *Clinical implications of attachment* (pp. 136–174). Hillsdale, NJ: Erlbaum.

Crockenberg, S. (1981). Infant irritability, mother's response, and social support influences on security of infant–mother attachments. *Child Development, 52,* 857–869.

Cruzan v. Director, Missouri Department of Health, 110 S. Ct. 2841 (1990).

Damrosch, S., & Perry, I. (1989). Self-reported adjustment, chronic sorrow, and coping of parents of children with Down Syndrome. *Nursing Research, 38* (1), 25–30.

Darwin, C. (1981). *The decent of man, and selection in relationship to sex* (Vol. 1). Princeton, NJ: Princeton University Press (Original work published 1871).

Davies, B., Spinetta, J., Martinson, I., McClowry, S., & Kulenkamp, E. (1986). Manifestations of levels of functioning in grieving families. *Journal of Family Issues, 7,* 297–313.

Defrain, J. (1991). Learning about grief from normal families: SIDS, stillbirth, and miscarriage. *Journal of Marriage and Family Therapy, 17,* 215–232.

Doka, K. (1995). Children mourning, mourning children. Washington DC, US: Hospice Foundation of America.

Doka, K. (1995). Coping with life threatening illness: A task model. *Omega: Journal of Death and Dying, 32* (2), 111–112.

Doyle, P. (1980). Grief counseling and sudden death. Springfield, IL: Charles C. Thomas.

Dworkin, G. (1976). Autonomy and behavior control. *The Hastings Center Report, 6* (1), 23–28.

Edelstein, L. (1943). The Hippocratic Oath: Text, Translation and Interpretation. Baltimore: Johns Hopkins University Press.

Engel, G. (1964). Grief and grieving. *American Journal of Nursing, 64*, 93–98.

Engel, G. L. (1961). Is grief a disease? *Psychosomatic Medicine, 23* (1), 18–22.

Farnsworth, J., Pett, M. A., & Lund, D. A. (1989). Predictors of loss management and well-being in later life, widowhood and divorce. *Journal of Family Issues, 1* (1), 102–121.

Feiel, H. (1971). The meaning of death in American Society: Implication for education. In B. Green & D. Irish (Eds.), *Death Education: Preparing for Life.* Cambridge MA: Schenkman.

Finnis, J. (1991). *Moral absolutes: Tradition, revision, and truth.* Washington, DC: Catholic University of America Press.

Fox, S. (1988). *Good grief: Helping groups of children when a friend dies.* The New England Association for the Education of Young Children.

Frankena, W. (1973). The ethics of love conceived as an ethic of virtue. *The Journal of Religious Ethics, 3* (1), 21–31.

Frantz, T. (1984). Helping parents whose child has died. In T. T. Frantz (Ed.), *Death and grief in the family* (pp. 11–26). Rockville, MD: Aspen Systems.

Freeman, S. (1999). The principle of double effect and virtue ethics: A search for complementarity in end-of-life decision making. *Illness, Crisis & Loss, 7* (4), 333–345.

Freeman, S. (1991). Group facilitation of the grieving process with those bereaved by suicide. *Journal of Counseling Development, 69* (4), 328–331.

Freeman, S., & Ward, S. (1998). Counseling the Bereaved: What Counselors Should Know. *Journal of Mental Health Counseling, 20* (3), 216–226.

Friedman, E. (1988). Systems and ceremonies: A family view of the rites of passages. In B. Carter & M. McGoldrick (Eds.), *The family life cycle: A framework for family therapy* (pp. 459–460). New York: Gardner Press.

Freud, S. (1917). Mourning and melancholia. In standard edition of the complete psychological works of Sigmund Freud (Vol. 14). London: Hogarth Press, 1957.

Fulton, R., & Fulton, J. (1971). A psychosocial aspect of terminal illness: Anticipatory grief. *Omega, Journal of Death and Dying, 2*, 91–99.

Futterman, E., Hoffman, I., & Sabshin, M. (1972). Parental anticipatory mourning. In B. Schoenberg, A. Carr, D. Peretz, & A. Kutscher (Eds.), Psychosocial aspects of terminal care. New York: Columbia University Press.

Gamino, L., Sewell, K., & Easterling, L. (1998). Scott and White grief study: An imperical test of predictors of intensified mourning. *Death Studies, 22* (4), 333–355.

Garcia, J. (1993). The new critique of anti-consequential moral theory. *Philosophical Studies, 71* (1), 1–32.

Gelcer, E. (1983). Mourning is a family affair. *Family Process, 22*, 501–516.

Gilbert, K. (1996). We've had the same loss, why don't we have the same grief? Loss and differential grief in families. *Death Studies, 20*, 269–283.

Gilbert, K., & Smart, L. (1992). *Coping with infant or fetal loss: The couples healing process*. New York: Brunner/Mazel.

Ginsberg, H., & Opper, S. (1987). Piaget's theory of intellectual development. Englewood Cliffs, NJ: Prentice-Hall.

Glick, I., Weiss, R. S., & Parkes, C. M. (1974). *The first year of bereavement*. New York: John Wiley & Sons.

Goldberg, S. (1973). Family tasks and reaction to the crisis of death. *Social Casework, 54,* 219–228.

Gorer, G. (1965). *Death, grief, and mourning*. New York: Doubleday.

Gray, R. E. (1987). Adolescent response to the death of a parent. *Journal of Youth and Adolescence, 16* (6), 511–525.

Greaves, C. (1983). Death in the family: A multifamily therapy approach. *International Journal of Family Psychiatry, 4* (3), 247–261.

Green, J. S. (1972). The days of the dead in Oaxaca, Mexico: An historical inquire. *Omega: Journal of Death and Dying, 3* (3), 245–262.

Grossmann, K., Grossmann, K. E., Spangler, G., Suess, G., & Unzner, L. (1985). Maternal sensitivity and newborns' orientation responses as related to quality of attachment in northern Germany. In I. Bretherton & E. Waters (Eds.), *Growing points of attachment theory and research.* Monograph of the Society for Research in Child Development, 50(1-2 Serial No. 209), 233–257.

Guntzelman, J. (1992). Grief and the early intervention practitioner. Keynote address, *When a child dies:* Third Annual Conference on the Training Consortium for Early Intervention Services. Baltimore, MD.

Hall, D. (1996). *Poetry: The unsayable said.* Port Townsend, WA: Copper Canyon Press.

Harper, D. (1977). *Death: The coping mechanism of the health professional.* Greenville, SC: Southeastern University Press.

Hauerwas, S. (1985). *Character and the Christian life*. Notre Dame: Notre Dame University Press.

Haworth, L. (1986). *Autonomy: An essay in philosophical psychology and ethics.* New Haven, Conn: Yale University Press.

Hazen, B. (1985). *Why did Grampa die? A book about death.* New York: Golden.

Heidegger, M. (1962). *Being and time.* New York: Harper & Row, pp. 210–241.

Horowitz, M. (1998). Diagnostic criteria for complicated grief disorder: Dr. Horowitz replies. *American Journal of Psychiatry, 155,* 1306.

Horowitz, M., Wilmer, N., Marmar, C., & Krupnick, J. (1980). Pathological grief and the activation of latent self-images. *American Journal of Psychiatry, 137,* 1157–1162.

Inhelder, B., & Piaget, J. (1952). The growth of logical thinking from childhood to adolescence. New York: International Universities Press.

In *re Quinlan,* 70 N. J. 10, 355 A.2d 647 (1976).

Irish, D., Lindquist, K., & Nelsen, V. (Eds.) (1993). *Ethnic variations in dying, death and grief: Diversity in universality,* Washington DC: Taylor & Francis.

Isabella, R., & Belsky, J. (1990). Interactional synchrony and the origins of mother–child attachment: A replication study. *Child Development,* 62, 373–384.

Isabella, R., Belsky, J. & von Eye, A. (1989). Origins of infant mother attachment: An examination of interactional synchrony during the infants first year. *Developmental Psychology, 25* (1), 12–21.

James, W. (1890). *The principles of psychology* (Vol. 1, p. 293). New York: Henry Holt.

Kaffman, M., Elizur, E., & Gluckson, L. (1987). Bereavement reactions in children: Therapeutic implications. *Israel Journal of Psychiatry and Related Sciences, 24* (1–2), 65–76.

Kantrowitz, M. (1973). *When Violet died.* New York: Parents' Magazine Press.

Kastenbaum, R. (2001). *Death, society, and the human experience.* Rockleigh, NJ: Allyn & Bacon.

Kastenbaum, R. (1977). *Death, society, and the human experience.* St. Louis: Mosby.

Kavanaugh, R. (1974). *Facing death.* Baltimore: Penguin Books.

Keenan, J. (1992). Virtue ethics: Making a case as it comes of age. *Thought, 67* (265), 115–127.

Kell, R., & Rabkin, L. (1979). The effects of sibling death on the surviving child: A family perspective. *Family Process, 8,* 471–477.

Klass, D. (1999). Developing a cross-cultural model of grief: The state of the field. *Omega: Journal of Death and Dying, 39* (3), 153–178.

Klass, D. (1988). *Parental grief: Solace and resolution.* New York: Springer.

Klass, D., Silverman, P., & Nickman, S. (1996). *Continuing bonds: New understandings of grief.* Washington DC: Taylor & Francis.

Koop, C., & Grant, E. (1986). The small beginnings of euthanasia: Examining the erosion in legal prohibitions against mercy killing, *2* (3), 585–634.

Kubler-Ross, E. (1969). *On death and dying.* New York: MacMillan.

Lamberi, J., & Detmer, C. (1993). Model of family grief assessment and treatment. *Death Studies, 17,* 55–67.

Lasker, J. N., & Toedter, L. J. (1991). Acute versus chronic grief: The case of pregnancy loss. *American Journal of Orthopsychiatry, 61* (4), 510–522.

Lazare, A. (1979). Unresolved Grief. In A. Lazare (Ed.), *Outpatient psychiatry: Diagnosis and treatment* (pp. 498–512). Baltimore: Williams & Wilkins.

Leliaert, R. M. (1989). Spiritual side of "good grief": What happened to Holy Saturday? *Death Studies, 13,* 103–117.

Lenhardt, A. (1997). Disenfranchised grief/hidden sorrow: Implications for school counselors. *School Counselor, 44,* 264–270.

Levertov, D. (1996). *Sands in the well.* New York: New Directions Books.

Levine, S. (1984). *Who dies: An investigation into conscious living and conscious dying.* New York: Anchor/Doubleday.

Leviton, D. (1993). Association for Death Education and Counseling, In R. Kastenbaum and B. Kastenbaum (Eds.), *Encyclopedia of death.* New York: Avon.

Lewis, C. S. (1961). *A grief observed.* New York: Bantam Books.

Lewis, M., & Feiring, C. (1989). Infant, mother, and mother–infant interaction behavior and subsequent attachment. *Child Development, 60,* 831–837.

Lifton, R. (1973). The sense of immortality: On death and the continuity of life. *American Journal of Psychoanalysis, 101,* 141–148.

Lifton, R. (1971). *History and human survival.* New York: Random House.

Lifton, R. (1968). *Death in life: Survivors of Hiroshima.* New York: Random House.

Lindemann, E. (1944). Symptomology and management of acute grief. *American Journal of Psychiatry, 101,* 141–148.

Lindemann, E., & Greer, I. (1953). A study of grief: Emotional responses to suicide. *Pastoral Psychology, 4* (39), 9–13.

Lopata, H. (1979). *Women as widows.* New York: Elsevier.

Lorenz, K. (1963). *On aggression.* New York: Bantam.

Lund, D. A., Caserta, M. S., & Dimond, M. F. (1986). Gender differences through two years of bereavement among the elderly. *The Gerontologist, 26* (3), 314–320.

MacIntyre, A. (1981). *After virtue: A study in moral theory.* Notre Dame: University of Notre Dame Press.

Maher, M. F., & Smith, D. (1993). I could have died laughing. *Journal of Humanistic Education and Development, 31* (3), 123–129.

Main, M. (1990). Cross-cultural studies of attachment organization: Recent studies, changing methodologies and the concept of conditional strategies. *Human Development, 33* (1), 48–61.

Main, M. (1981). Avoidance in the service of attachment: A working paper. In K. Immelmann, G. Barlow, M. Main & L. Petrinovich (Eds.), *Behavioral development: The Bielefeld Interdisciplinary Project* (pp. 651–693). New York: Cambridge University Press.

Main, M., & Hess, E. (1990). Parents' unresolved traumatic experiences are related to infant disorganized attachment status: Is frightened and or frightening parental behavior the linking mechanism? In M. T. Greenberg, D. Cicchetti & E. M. Cummings (Eds.), *Attachment in the preschool years: Theory, research and intervention* (pp. 161–182) Chicago: University of Chicago Press.

Main, M., & Solomon, J. (1986). Discovery of an insecure-disorganized/disoriented attachment pattern: Procedures, findings, and implications for the classification of behavior. In T. B. Brazelton & M. Yogman (Eds.), *Affect development in infancy* (pp. 95–124). Norwood, NJ: Ablex.

Marrone, R. (1997). *Death, mourning and caring.* Pacific Grove: Brooks/Cole/ Wadsworth.

McCormack, J. (1981). The principle of the double effect. In J. McCormack (Ed.), *How brave a new world: Dilemmas in bioethics* (pp. 413–429). Washington D.C.: Georgetown University Press.

McGoldrick, M., Almeida, R., Hines, P., Garcia-Preto, Y., Rosen, E., & Lee, E. (1991). Mourning in different cultures. In F. Walsh & M. McGoldrick (Eds.) *Living beyond loss: Death in the family* (pp. 176–206) New York: W. W. Norton.

McGoldrick, M., & Walsh, F. (1991). A time to mourn: Death and the family life cycle. In F. Walsh & M. McGoldrick (Eds.), *Living beyond loss* (pp. 30–48). New York: W. W. Norton.

Meara, N., Schmidt, L., & Day, J. (1996). Principles and virtues: A foundation for ethics decisions, policies and character. *The Counseling Psychologist, 24* (1), 4–77.

Montaigne, M. (1992). *The Complete Essays.* New York: Viking Penguin.

Moore, M., & Freeman, S. (1995). Survivors of suicide: Implications for group as a post-vention. *Journal for Specialists in Group Work, 20* (1), 40–47.

Moos, N. (1995). An integrated model of grief. *Death Studies, 19,* 337–354.

Nagy, M. (1948). The child's theories concerning death. *Journal of Genetic Psychology, 73,* 3–27.

Nees, D., & Pfeffer, C. (1990). Sequelae of bereavement resulting from suicide. *American Journal of Psychiatry, 147,* 279–285.

Neimeyer, R. (1998). Death anxiety research: The state of the art. *Omega: Journal of Death and Dying, 36* (2) 97–120.

Neimeyer, R. (1998). *The lessons of loss: A guide to coping.* New York: McGraw-Hill.

Neuberger, N. (1962). Cited in J. Frank, "Nuclear Death—The Challenge of Ethical Religion," *The Ethical Platform* (29 April, 1962).

Oakley, J. (1996). Varieties of virtue ethics. *Ratio, 9* (2), 128–152.

Olds, S. (1992). *The father: Poems.* New York: Alfred A. Knopf.

Oliver, M. (1992). *New and selected poems.* Boston: Beacon Press.

Osterweis, M., Solomon, F., & Green, M. (Eds.) (1984). Bereavement: Reactions consequences and care. Report by the Committee for the study of Health Consequences of the Stress of Bereavement, Institute of Medicine, National Academy of Sciences. Washington, DC: National Academy Press.

Parkes, C. (2000). Comments on Dennis Klass's article "Developing a cross-cultural model of grief." *Omega: Journal of Death and Dying, 41* (4), 323–326.

Parkes, C. (1990). Risk factors in bereavement: Implications for the prevention and treatment of pathologic grief. *Psychiatric Annals, 20* (6), 308–313.

Parkes, C. (1970). The first year of bereavement: A longitudinal study of the reaction of London widows to the death of their husbands. *Psychiatry: Journal for the Study of Interpersonal Processes, 33* (4), 444–467.

Parkes, C. (1970). Seeking and finding a lost object: Evidence for recent studies to bereavement. *Social Science and Medicine, 4* (2), 187–201.

Parkes, C. (1964). Recent bereavement as a cause of mental illness. *British Journal of Psychiatry, 110* (465), 198–204.

Parkes, C., & Brown, R. (1972). Health after bereavement: A controlled study of young Boston widows and widowers. *Psychosomatic Medicine, 34* (5), 449–461.

Parkes, C., & Weiss, R. (1983). *Recovery from bereavement.* New York: Basic Books.

Pastan, L. (1978). *The five stages of grief: Poems.* New York: Norton & Co.

Patterson, J., & Garwick, A. (1994). Levels of meaning in family stress theory. *Family Process, 33,* 287–304.

Pattison, E. (1978). The living-dying process in C.A. Garfield (Ed.). *Psychosocial Care of the Dying Patient.* New York: McGraw-Hill.

Pellegrino, E. (1985). The virtuous physician and the ethics of medicine. In E. Shelp & D. Thomasma (Eds.), *Virtue and Medicine: Explorations in the Character of Medicine* (pp. 237–256). Dordrecht, Netherlands: D. Reidel.

Peppers, L., & Knapp, R. (1980). *Motherhood and mourning: Perinatal death.* New York: Praeger.

Piaget, J. (1960). *The Child's Conception of the World.* Patterson, NJ: Littlefield Adams.

Piaget, J. (1973). *The Child and Reality: Problems for Genetic Psychology.* New York: Grossman.

Plimpton, E., & Rosenblum, L. (1987). Maternal loss in nonhuman primates: Implications for human development. In J. Bloom-Feshbach & S. Bollm-Feshbach (Eds.) *The psychology of separation and Loss* (pp. 63–86), San Francisco: Jossey-Bass.

Powers, L. (1993). Disability and grief: From tragedy to challenge. In G. H. S. Singer & L. E. Powers (Eds.). *Families, disability, and empowerment: Active coping skills and strategies for family interventions* (pp. 119–150). Baltimore: Paul H. Brookes Publishing Co.

Prigerson, H., Bierhals, A., Kasi, S., Reynolds, C., et al. (1996). Complicated grief as a disorder distinct from bereavement related depression and anxiety: A replication study. *American Journal of Psychiatry, 153* (11), 1484–1486.

Punzo, V. (1996). After Kohlberg: Virtue ethics and the recovery of the moral self. *Philosophical Psychology, 9* (1), 7–23.

Pynoos, R. S., & Nader, K. (1990). Children's exposure to violence and traumatic death. *Psychiatric Annals 20* (6), 334–344.

Rando, T. (1996). Complications in mourning traumatic loss. In K. Doka (Ed.), *Living with grief after a sudden loss* (pp. 139–160). Washington, DC: Hospice Foundation of America.

Rando, T. (1986). *Parental loss of a child.* Champaign, IL: Research Press Co.

Rando, T. (1984). *Grief, dying and death. Clinical interventions for caregivers.* Champaign, IL: Research Press.

Rando, T. A. (1993). The increasing prevalence of complicated mourning: The onslaught is just beginning. *Omega: Journal of Death and Dying, 26* (1), 43–59.

Rando, T. A. (1987). The unrecognized impact of sudden death in terminal illness and in positively progressing convalescence. *Israel Journal of Psychiatry and Related Sciences, 24* (1–2), 125–135.

Rando, T. A. (1983). An investigation of grief and adaptation in parents whose children have died from cancer. *Journal of Pediatric Psychology, 8* (1), 3–20.

Range, L., & Goggin, W. (1990). Reactions to suicide: Does age of the victim make a difference? *Death Studies, 14* (3), 269–275.

Raphael, B. (1983). *The anatomy of bereavement.* New York: Basic Books.

Raphael, B. (1980). A psychiatric model for bereavement counseling. In B. Mark Schoenberg (Ed.) *Bereavement Counseling: A multidisciplinary handbook.* Westport, Conn.: Greenwood Press.

Raphael, B. (1977). Preventive intervention with the recently bereaved. *Archives of General Psychiatry, 34,* 1450–1454.

Raphael, B., & Middleton, W. (1990). What is pathologic grief? *Psychiatric Annals, 20* (6), 304–307.

Raphael, B., & Middleton, W. (1987). Current state of research in the field of bereavement. *Israel Journal of Psychiatry and Related Sciences, 24* (1–2), 5–32.

Raphael, B., & Nunn, K. (1988). Counseling the bereaved. *Journal of Social Issues, 44* (3), 191–206.

Raz, J. (1986). *The morality of freedom.* Oxford: Clarendon Press.

Reed, M., & Greenwald, J. (1991). Survivor–victim status, attachment and sudden death bereavement. *Suicide and life threatening behavior,* 21, 385–401.

Reiss, D. (1981). *The families construction of reality.* Cambridge, MA: Harvard University Press.

Reite, M., & Boccia, M. (1994). Physiological aspects of adult attachment. In M. Sperling & W. Berman (Eds.), *Attachment in adults* (pp. 98–127), New York: Guildford Press.

Rubin, S., & Schechter (1997). Exploring the social construct of bereavement: Perceptions of adjustment and recovery in bereaved men. *American Journal of Othopsychiatry, 67,* 279–289.

Rudestam, K. (1977). Physical and psychological response to suicide in the family. *Journal of Consulting and Clinical Psychology, 45* (2), 162–170.

Ruskay, S. (1996). Saying hello again: A new approach to bereavement counseling. *Hospice Journal,* 11, 5–14.

Rynearson, E. (1988). The homicide of a child. In F. M. Ochberg (Ed.), Post-traumatic therapy and victims of violence (pp. 213–224). Philadelphia, PA: Brunner/Mazel.

Rynearson, E. K. (1990a). Pathologic grief: The queen's croquet ground. *Psychiatric Annals, 21* (6), 295–303.

Rynearson, E. K. (1990b). Personal reflections: Is grief pathologic? *Psychiatric Annals, 20* (6), 294.

Rynearson, E. K. (1987). Psychotherapy of pathologic grief. *Psychiatric Clinics of North America, 14* (3), 487–499.

Sable, P. (1991). Attachment, loss of spouse, and grief in elderly adults. *Omega: Journal of Death and Dying, 23* (2), 129–142.

Sanders, C. (1986). Accidental death of a child. In T. A. Rando (Ed.), *Parental Loss of a Child* (pp. 181–190). Champaign, IL: Research Press.

Sanders, C. (1989). *Grief: The mourning after.* New York: Wiley.

Sanders, C. M. (1979–1980). A comparison of adult bereavement in the death of a spouse, child and parent. *Omega: Journal of Death and Dying, 10* (4), 303–322.

Scharlach, A. E. (1941). Factors associated with filial grief following the death of an elderly parent. *American Journal of Orthopsychiatry, 61* (2), 307–313.

Schatz, W. (1986). Grief of fathers. In T. A. Rando (Ed.), *Parental loss of a child.* Champaign, IL: Research Press.

Schenidman, E. (1969). On the nature of suicide. San Francisco: Jossey-Bass.

Schneider, J. (1984). *Stress, loss, and grief: Understanding their origins and growth potential*. Baltimore: University Park Press.

Seaburn, D. (1990). The ties that bind: Loyalty and widowhood. In E. M. Stern (Ed.), *Psychotherapy and the widowed patient* (pp. 139–146). New York: Hawthorne Press.

Seay, B., Hansen, E., & Harlow, H. (1962). Mother infant separation in monkeys. *Journal of Child Psychology and Psychiatry, 3,* 123–132.

Selye, H. (1974). *Stress without distress.* New York: McGraw-Hill.

Sherman, D. (1996). Nurses' willingness to care for AIDS patients. *Image, Journal of Nursing Scholarship, 28,* 205–214.

Shuchter, S. (1986). *Dimensions of grief: Adjusting to the death of a spouse.* San Francisco: Jossey-Bass.

Shuchter, S. R., & Zisook, S. (1990). Hovering over the bereaved. *Psychiatric Annals, 20* (6), 327–333.

Siggins, L. (1966). Mourning: A critical survey of the literature. *International Journal of Psycho-Analysis, 47,* 14.

Silverman, E., Range, L., & Overholser, J. (1994). Bereavement from suicide as compared to other forms of bereavement. *Omega: Journal of Death and Dying, 30* (1), 41–51.

Silverman, P., Nickman, S., & Worden, J. (1992). Detachment revisited: The child's reconstruction of a dead parent. *American Journal of Orthopsychiatry, 64* (4), 494–503.

Simos, B. (1979). *A time to grieve.* New York: Family Services Association.

Smith, P., & Pederson, D. (1988). Maternal sensitivity and patterns of infant–mother attachment. *Child Development, 59,* 1097–1101.

Smith, P., Range, L. M., & Ulmer, A. (1992). Belief in afterlife as a buffer in suicidal and other bereavement. *Omega: Journal of Death and Dying, 24* (3), 217–225.

Solomon, M. (1982). The bereaved and the stigma of suicide. *Omega: Journal of Death and Dying, 13* (4), 377–387.

Spark, G. and Browdy, E., (1972). The aged are family members. In C. Sager & H. Kaplan (Eds.), *Progress in group and family therapy.* New York: Brunner/Mazel.

Speece, M., & Brent, S. (1996). The development of children's understanding of death. In C. A. Corr & D. M. Corr (Eds.), *Handbook of childhood death and bereavement.* New York: Springer Publishing Co.

Spohn, S. (1992). Notes on moral theology. *Theological Studies, 53* (1), 60–74.

Stillion, J., & McDowell, E. (1996). Suicide across the life span: Premature exit. Philadelphia. PA: Taylor Francis.

Stroebe, M. (1993). Coping with bereavement: A review of the grief work hypothesis. *Omega: Journal of Death and Dying, 26* (1), 19–42.

Stroufe, L. A., & Waters, E. (1977). Attachment as an organizational construct. *Child Development, 48,* 1184–1199.

Sudnow, D. (1967). Passing on: The social organization of dying. Englewood Cliffs, NJ: Prentice-Hall.

Teehan, J. (1995). Character, integrity and Dewey's virtue ethics. *Translations of the Charles S. Peirce Society, 31* (4), 841–863.

Tedeschi, R., & Calhoun, L. (1993). Using the support group to respond to the isolation of bereavement. *Journal of Mental Health Counseling, 15* (1), 47–54.

Thomas, L. (1996). Virtue ethics and the arc of universality: Reflections on Punzo's reading of Kant and virtue ethics. *Philosophical Psychology, 9* (1), 25–31.

Thomas, L. (1974). *The lives of a cell: Notes of a biology watcher.* New York: Viking Press.

Tobacyk, J. J., & Mitchell, T. P. (1987). The out-of-body experience and personality adjustment. *The Journal of Nervous and Mental Disease, 175* (6), 367–370.

Tolstoy (1960). *The death of Ivan Ilych and other stories.* New York: Signet Classics.

Tolstoy (1931). *War and Peace.* New York: Modern Library.

Ulmer, A., Range, L. M., & Smith, P. (1991). Purpose in life: A moderator of recovery from bereavement. *Omega: Journal of Death and Dying, 23* (4), 279–289.

Vachon, M. (1987). *Occupational stress in the care of critically ill, the dying, and the bereaved.* Washington DC, US: Hemisphere Publishing Corp.

van der Hart, O., & Goossens, F. A. (1987). Leave-taking rituals in mourning therapy. *Israel Journal of Psychiatry, and Related Sciences, 24* (1–2), 87–98.

van der Wal, J. (1990). The aftermath of suicide: A review of empirical literature. *Omega: Journal of Death and Dying, 20* (2), 149–171.

van Gennep, A. (1960). *The rites of passage.* Chicago: University of Chicago Press (Orig. pub. 1908).

Veatch, R. (1985). Against virtue: A deontological critique of virtue theory and medical ethics. In E. Shelp (Ed.) *Virtue and medicine: Explorations in the character of medicine,* 329–346. Dordrecht, Netherlands: D Reildel.

Vess, J., Moreland, J., & Schwebel, A. (1985). A follow-up study of role functioning and the psychological environment of families of cancer patients. *Journal of Psychological Oncology, 3* (2), 1–14.

Volkan, V. (1973). More on "linking objects." Paper presented at the Symposium on Bereavement. Columbia Presbyterian, Medical Center, New York City. November, 1973.

Volkan, V. (1972). The linking objects of pathological mourners. *Archives of General Psychiatry, 27,* 215–221.

Watzalawick, P., Beavins, J., & Jackson, D. (1967). *Pragmatics of human communication.* New York: Norton.

Watzalawick , P., Weakland, J., & Fisch, R. (1974). *Change: Principles of problem formation and problem resolution.* New York: Norton.

Westberg, G. (1962). Good-grief. Philadelphia: Fortress Press.

Wolfelt, A. (1988). Death and grief: A guide for the clergy. Muncie, IN: Accelerated Development.

Wolfelt, A. (1983). *Helping children cope with grief.* Muncie, IN: Accelerated Development.

Wolterstorff, N. (1987). *Lament for a son.* Grand Rapids, MI: William B. Ferdmans Publishing.

Worden, J. W. (1991). *Grief counseling and grief therapy.* New York: Springer.

Worden, W. (1996). *Children and grief: When a parent dies.* New York: The Guilford Press.

Wortman, C. B., & Silver, R. C. (1989). The myths of coping with loss. *Journal of Consulting and Clinical Psychology, 57* (3), 349–357.

Yalom, I. (1995). *The theory and practice of group psychotherapy.* New York: Basic Books.

Zisook, S. & DeVaul, R. (1985). Unresolved grief. *American Journal of Psychoanalysis, 45,* 370–379.

Zisook, S., Shuchter, S. R., & Lyons, L. E. (1987). Predictors of psychological reactions during the early stages of widowhood. *Psychiatric Clinics of North America, 10* (3), 355–368.

Index

TO THE OWNER OF THIS BOOK:

I hope that you have found *Grief and Loss: Understanding the Journey* useful. So that this book can be improved in a future edition, would you take the time to complete this sheet and return it? Thank you.

School and address: _____

_____

Department: _____

Instructor's name: _____

1. What I like most about this book is:_____

_____

_____

2. What I like least about this book is: _____

_____

_____

3. My general reaction to this book is: _____

_____

_____

4. The name of the course in which I used this book is: _____

_____

5. Were all of the chapters of the book assigned for you to read? _____

   If not, which ones weren't?_____

6. In the space below, or on a separate sheet of paper, please write specific suggestions for improving this book and anything else you'd care to share about your experience in using this book.

_____

_____

TAPE HERE.

DO NOT STAPLE.

TAPE HERE.

DO NOT STAPLE.

FOLD HERE

NO POSTAGE
NECESSARY
IF MAILED
IN THE
UNITED STATE

BUSINESS REPLY MAIL
FIRST-CLASS MAIL   PERMIT NO. 102   MONTEREY CA

POSTAGE WILL BE PAID BY ADDRESSEE

Attn: Lisa Gebo

BrooksCole/Thomson Learning
60 Garden Ct Ste 205
Monterey CA 93940-9967

FOLD HERE

OPTIONAL:

Your name: _____ Date: _____

May we quote you, either in promotion for *Grief and Loss: Understanding
the Journey,* or in future publishing ventures?

Yes: _____   No: _____

Sincerely yours,

Stephen J. Freeman